CHERYL FERGISON

Behind the Scenes

CHERYL FERGISON

Behind the Scenes

m
B

MIRROR BOOKS

MIRROR BOOKS

Written with Lydia Veljanovski

1

First published in hardback in Great Britain and Ireland
in 2025 by Mirror Books, a Reach PLC business.

www.mirrorbooks.co.uk
@TheMirrorBooks

ISBN: 9781917439251
eBook ISBN: 9781917439268

Photographic acknowledgements:
Alamy, MirrorPix, Joshua Brandwood, Chris Brudenell

Every effort has been made to trace copyright. Any
oversights will be rectified in future editions.

Editing and Production: Christine Costello
Cover Design: Chris Collins

Printed and bound by CPI Group (UK) Ltd,
Croydon, CR0 4YY.

For my beautiful son Alex

Foreword

by Steve McFadden

They say you can choose your friends not your family, but, every now and then, someone comes along who blurs that line completely. That's Cheryl. She's not just a mate, she is my sister in all but blood. I call her 'sis', she calls me 'big bruv', and if I'd ever had a sister growing up, I'd have wanted her to be just like Cheryl.

She's also godmother to my daughter Frankie and not a birthday or Christmas goes by without Cheryl giving her gifts – whether she can afford them or not. That's just who she is. Generous to her core, full of love and completely adored by everyone who gets to know her.

From the moment I met Cheryl, we just clicked. Being around her was like being in school at the back of the classroom mucking about behind the teacher's back. We were like a pair of naughty kids, laughing and winding each other up. But underneath all that mischief was something deeper: this effortless honesty between us. I could say anything to her and she could say anything to me. There was no judgement or filter, just total openness and that wicked, brilliant humour of hers.

She's the kind of person who, in a room full of chaos, will

pop up like a cheeky little meerkat, bright-eyed, full of energy, always hunting for the funny side. In a world where people seem constantly offended or looking to be divisive, Cheryl's a proper breath of fresh air. She's not interested in negativity, she wants to lift people up, make them laugh, and leave them feeling better than when she found them.

And let's not forget, she is a brilliant actress. Cheryl has got real range; she can make you laugh one minute and have you in tears the next. She belongs on a stage, in a film, on telly, anywhere people can see what she's capable of. I've seen her magic up close. She even performed at my mum's 70th birthday – on the top of a Dutch barge, no less – strumming a guitar and belting out Beatles songs the whole way down the Thames. Heads were definitely turning.

But despite all her talent, life hasn't always gone easy on her. She's had her share of knocks – actually far more than most – but she's never let anything hold her back or keep her down for long. She is a soldier and she soldiers on. She finds the gold in the grit, even when life's thrown her a curveball.

I remember her saying to me, after she was diagnosed with cancer, that she understood why some people say it's the best thing that ever happened to them. Not because it is, of course, but because it forces you to stop, take stock, and start living every day like it truly matters. And that is what Cheryl does. She lives with heart and purpose.

When Cheryl tells a story, people listen. She is engaging and holds court like no one else. I'm a very, very proud big brother.

With love,
Steve McFadden

Foreword

by David Walliams

Early on in Cheryl's career she auditioned for a small role in Little Britain. Matt and I were instantly struck by Cheryl's enormous comic talent.

The part was 'Big Fat Lesbian'. The humour wasn't subtle! As soon as we began working with her, Matt and I knew we had found a kindred spirit. She made us belly laugh ever time we shot the scene, even the way she walked into the room in character was hilarious.

That was 20 years ago, and I remember thinking then that Cheryl deserved to be a huge star.

Soon after she starred in Eastenders, and I was delighted to see the nation falling in love with Cheryl, as Matt and I had a few years before.

Whenever I write something for TV I think, 'is there a role for Cheryl?' Not only is she hilarious, she is wonderful company. Kind, generous, inventive, smart and fun. Exactly the kind of person you want to see first thing in the morning when you walk into the make-up trailer at dawn. She always makes me smile.

I am very lucky to count Cheryl as a friend, and she always

asks after my son and mum, the two most precious people in my life. She will have a special place in my heart forever.

Cheryl is a hilarious performer and a born storyteller. This is the funniest and most moving book I have read in years. Her story is full of humour, heartbreak and drama. I am so glad she is finally sharing it with us all.

With love,
David Walliams

Author's Note

You have probably bought this book because you know me for playing Heather Trott on *EastEnders*. 'Our Hev' – you know, the big girl with the big headbands and even bigger heart.

Heather was a hopeless romantic, always looking for love but never quite finding it. She was a kind and loyal friend, a cheese lover and a George Michael superfan. Millions followed through her life's highs and lows. You cried when she cried and laughed with her too, but what you never knew was what was happening behind the scenes.

I, Cheryl Fergison, had a life off-screen filled with just as much drama as any soap opera script. My late and great pal Barbara Windsor once told me, "Cheryl, darling, never show the public when you are down. People out there don't need to know what's happening inside, just greet them with a smile and make them happy."

Of course, Barbara was right, you don't want to tell fans about your struggles when they come up for a selfie in the local Asda. But I do feel it's finally time to be honest with you all.

My story is one that many of you might be able to relate to. Just because I'm 'off the telly' doesn't mean life has been all red carpets and fat wallets. Truth is, there have been times when I couldn't rub two coins together, let alone afford a rug under my feet.

There is so much you don't know. But if it was Cheryl, not Heather, who was a character on *EastEnders* then I would have had far more of those theme tune *Duff, Duff* moments. Here is the real story.

Prologue

March 2018

Sitting on a bench in a car park in Dartford just beside the shopping centre, people trudge past, bags in hand, but my eyes are fixed on the red and white face of the 1980s clock tower. Time seems to slow until a voice pulls me back.

"Heather! Heather!"

A woman in a bright red mac beelines towards me, a little sausage dog trotting at her heels. "I miss you on Enders," she beams, plonking herself down next to me. "I was so sad when you died."

For the next few minutes, we chat. About Albert Square, about whether I've stayed mates with Shirley and Phil, about drinking in the Queen Vic. "Do you still love George Michael and sing karaoke?" she asks.

I smile, answering her questions, then tell her about the show I'm in at the Orchard Theatre, just next to the shopping centre. *Menopause the Musical.*

"That's great, Heather," she says. Then, after a beat: "Do you think you could ever forgive Ben Mitchell for killing you?" I laugh and the woman then asks for a selfie, hoisting her little dog into the shot. *Click.*

"I'll get this framed," she says. "Me, Pepperami and Heather Trott. What a day!" And with a wave, she heads across the car park and through the shopping centre doors.

It's a strange thing, being back here and getting recognised for a role I once played – just a stone's throw from a theatre with my name above the door. Because what that stranger doesn't, and couldn't, know is that I have sat on this bench many many times before.

Before *EastEnders*. Before Heather Trott. Before fame. Actually, long before anyone gave me a second glance, let alone asked for my photo.

It was this exact bench that was my respite during the darkest days of my life. It was here where I came when I was homeless and living in a nearby women's refuge with my son Alex, who was just a toddler. We had run away because I didn't feel safe with my ex-husband. I was broken and trapped without a penny to my name. The neon lights of showbiz were a far-off dream.

For months back in 2003, coming to the car park was a daily ritual – one we only missed if it was too rainy or windy. I would load up the pram with nappies, some juice or a snack and wheel my son through the town centre to our spot. Alex would be bawling – he was a difficult child, which I later learned was due to his ADHD and autism – and we had no money to buy anything so we'd just sit here for hours, staring up at the clock tower.

Every half-hour, the clock would chime and these little mechanical figurines of Hansel and Gretel would appear from a tiny red door beneath the clock face. There were two scenes: first, the little blond children knocking on the door of the gingerbread house, all icing sugar and painted pretzels. Then the platform would turn to show Gretel pushing the wicked witch inside the oven as Hansel looks on from inside a cage. Alex absolutely loved it and it stopped him from crying, but for me it was just another way to mark the time passing.

Another half-hour gone. We would often sit there for three hours at a time. That's six chimes, six lots of gleeful giggles from Alex and six micro-breaks from misery for me. Sometimes Alex would fall asleep and I would push the pram to-and-fro, terrified and alone with my own thoughts, 'What was I going to do?'

I'd blink away the tears. They would do no good and I wouldn't want Alex to see me upset.

Only at night, once he had fallen asleep, would I allow myself to cry. Lying on the top bunk in our tiny room filled with black bin bags of stuff from the life we escaped, I'd sob into the pillow so as not to wake him.

I felt like a failure. I couldn't provide for my son, I'd let him down. This tiny human with his cheeky grin and thick lashes was counting on me but life was spinning out of control.

Suddenly, the clock starts to chime, bringing me back to the present and away from those painful memories. Looking up at the little red door, it remains shut. No Hansel and Gretel, no mechanical magic. Time has passed and things have changed. I have changed too.

I get up from the bench, straighten my coat and make my way to the theatre for rehearsals.

Chapter One

It was a sunny August afternoon in Isleworth, West London, when Avril Folly's stomach began to cramp and the 17-year-old doubled over in agony. She wasn't sure what to do. Her parents wouldn't be home for hours and the pain was only getting worse. 'I need to get help', she thought, clutching her belly.

Hobbling outside, she banged on the neighbour's door, tears spilling down her cheeks. She barely managed to point at her stomach before she was helped into the car. Appendicitis, they reckoned and off to A&E she went.

Hours later, her parents burst through the doors of West Middlesex Hospital, breathless and frantic. "We're here to see Avril Folly. She's had her appendix out," they announced.

What a shock it must have been when they found their teenage daughter, who had spent nine months carefully concealing her pregnancy, sitting up in bed, cradling a red-faced baby in her arms. You see… *Duff. Duff. Duff. Duff.*

Talk about a dramatic entrance. I was born on 27 August 1965 and while my birth certificate said Cheryl Oldfield, my family has always joked that I was born an appendicitis.

Growing up, I never thought much of the story, but now that I'm a mum myself, I can't understand how a 17-year-old managed to hide a pregnancy for nine whole months. She wore baggy clothes, ate bigger portions and passed it off as weight gain but deep down, she must have been terrified. I know I would have been and, looking back, if anyone deserved a Soap Award, it was my mum for pulling that off.

Like Avril, I have never had my appendix removed, but that isn't the only thing we had in common. Mum looked just like me, she was a bigger lady with an open smiley face and thick brown hair. She was funny like me too. But Mum didn't want to be with my real dad so he wasn't in my life as a youngster. Maybe this was because he smelled like raw mince. Only joking, but he did work at Smithfields Market, handling meat all day, which I find funny because I have been a vegetarian since I was 14.

When I was born, everyone rallied round. Family members rushed to buy baby clothes and bring things we might need and aside from my surprise birth, we were a pretty normal working-class family. Money was tight, but the family was always about and I was often found playing with my cousins outside.

I was a big round child with my hair cropped short. To be honest, I looked a lot like a little boy, but I was happy. We took family holidays with my Nanny Beatrice, who worked as a cleaner, and my granddad Charlie, who was a bricklayer, to places like Bognor Regis, staying on caravan sites or spending time on the beach.

Mum would sometimes go on dates, dragging me along in the back of the car. One man, don't ask me his name because it's all a blur, seemed like a big deal and we even moved in with him. His house wasn't on an estate, it had a garden with an actual lawn and a conservatory. To me, it felt like a mansion, like we were living the high life.

However, a few months in, they had a blazing row. I heard her storming upstairs and when I peeked into the room, she was in the wardrobe, chucking out armfuls of women's clothes and chopping them up with scissors.

"You will never wear these again!" she screamed, slicing through a silk blouse. "How dare you!" She stuffed the shredded clothes into a black bin liner, stormed down the stairs and yelled, "Come on, Cheryl. We're leaving."

I didn't ask questions. I just grabbed my coat, followed her out to the car and we sped off like we were escaping a crime scene. Mum never did tell me the full story of what happened with the man and I never asked. But perhaps she couldn't bear the idea that her boyfriend might have nicer dresses than her.

Life really changed for the first time when I was seven and Mum met my step-dad John. I liked him. He was tall and kind with movie star looks and sandy blond hair. He was a coach driver and I would get 50 pence for cleaning out his bus when he brought it home which was all good fun.

I'd never read books or had books at home at my nan's house so my step-dad was the first person to introduce me to reading and to the stars. He would let me look up through telescopes at the starry night sky and it wasn't long before we moved out to Richmond to stay with his parents.

I was frightened of sleeping at my step-nan and granddad's house because there was a black box under the bed which I thought must be a coffin. I used to lie in bed wide-eyed with fear, ears pricked for any sounds coming from the undead monster beneath. It could come up and eat me at any moment, I reasoned.

After a few days, I summoned the courage to kneel down and look under the bed. I tentatively pulled out the box and opened it to find an acoustic guitar and that was that. Like the Bride of Frankenstein, I fell in love with the monster and here began a life-long passion for music. I would play John's guitar as much as I could, even though the strings made my fingers bleed.

One afternoon, before Mum and John got married and he adopted me in 1973, they took me to a funfair on Richmond Green. The rides were spinning, the music blaring from tinny speakers and people were shrieking with glee into the summer sky. The whole place fizzed with energy and I had a fistful of candy floss sticking to my fingers when we spotted the rifle range.

"Go on, have a go," John said, handing me a few coins. I squared up like an action hero, gripped the rifle, aimed... bullseye!

"Not bad," grinned a tall, thin man next to me, who was also firing shots. "You are like a little Annie Oakley!"

Mum and John suddenly started whispering and nudging each other, eyes wide and pointing at the man. "Oh my God. Oh my God," they whispered between them.

I had no idea what their problem was and was far too focused on the target to care. It wasn't until we walked away that Mum, practically exploding with glee, told me, "Do you know who that was? That was Richard Beckinsale!"

Yes, the famous actor who had just started starring in prison comedy *Porridge* alongside Ronnie Barker, had been shooting next to me. He was young, handsome, effortlessly cool and completely oblivious to the fact that my parents were combusting in his presence. Mum and John dined out on that story for weeks and that was the first time I realised that some people were famous and this could make other people happy.

But aside from being a celebrity hotspot, life in Richmond wasn't all breezy. My mum was headstrong and I don't think she liked living with her mother-in-law so arguments would often break out. I wasn't their real grandchild either, so I guess it was too much under one roof. It was no surprise when, not long after we had moved in, Mum, John and I packed up and left.

The only problem was we didn't actually have anywhere to go. The council hadn't sorted a house yet, so social services placed us in what they called "emergency housing", which turned out to be a disused hospital. It was eerie. The corridors echoed when you walked and the place smelt of disinfectant and old plaster. We slept in what used to be a hospital ward, with those old metal-framed beds and peeling paint on the walls. But the strangest thing? The bathroom. We had to bathe in what used to be the hospital morgue. Mum and John tried to make the best of it, but even as a kid, I knew it was odd.

From death, quite literally, came a kind of rebirth, when we were eventually offered a new home and a new life in Peter-borough. A three-storey house on a friendly council estate. It was a real community, the type where everyone knew every-one's business – just like in Walford – and it was here that my character and the plot line of my life began to take shape.

"Everyone be quiet," Mum hissed. "Get behind the sofa."

My siblings and I hit the floor, we knew the drill. Another knock at the door. Don't move a muscle. A minute passes, then another. The coast is clear. He's gone. Mum exhales, then strolls to the record player and drops the needle onto Cliff Richard, letting his dulcet tones smooth over the silence.

This would happen often, hiding from the Provident man when he came knocking for the money my parents owed. Provident lent cash to struggling families at sky-high interest rates and their collectors came round like clockwork, flicking through their little books, tallying up what you owed. Sometimes Mum would send me to the door to perform what must have been my first acting role. My line?

"I am really sorry my parents are not here. Can you come another day?"

Mum and John were always short of cash, stuck in a cycle of spending it and trying to make more. Money just seemed to slip through their fingers like sand. It wasn't long before they had more mouths to feed too. My half brother Glen arrived when I was eight and two years later my half-sister Helen was born. Although we ate well, often too well given my large frame, my parents were under pressure which led to big fights as we sat down at the dinner table.

"We need more coming in," Mum would say through clenched teeth.

"I've told you, they won't give me any more bloody overtime, woman!" John would snap, slamming his fist onto the table so hard the cutlery jumped.

Back and forth they went like Pat and Peggy in the Queen Vic, until John would inevitably lob his bowl of spaghetti bolognese at the wall. I'd sit stunned as the thick red sauce oozed down the purple wallpaper and onto the floor. Mum would storm out, my siblings would sob. It may sound dramatic, because it was. We had to re-paper the walls at least three times because of it.

When they weren't fighting about money, Mum and John were down the bingo hall trying to win some. If they were lucky, we'd be treated to a Chinese takeaway or a KFC which was the height of luxury and always an ice cream (or two) when the van passed by – no wonder I wasn't thin.

If they lost, things weren't quite as cheerful and off I went on my bike to avoid the arguing. I didn't much enjoy them going to bingo as it meant I had to babysit, which I did far more than I should have. But I understood it even then; bingo wasn't just how they gambled, it was their escape hatch. For a few hours, they weren't skint or stressed or arguing over the electricity bill, they were hopeful, laughing with their mates and dreaming about what they'd do if they won big. It was their chance to feel lucky.

My mum wasn't idle though, she tried as many money-making schemes as Del Boy Trotter. She cleaned houses, looked after the elderly and would do anything to bring in a bit of extra cash. I remember her throwing Tupperware parties for the neighbours, selling Avon makeup and even hosting Ann Summers events.

I'd set out the sausage rolls and cheap wine while the "sexy undies" lady would show up with a suitcase full of hilarious outfits. Watching my mum's mate Gwen, who lived across the street, trying to squeeze into a saucy nurse's outfit was a sight to see. She wasn't exactly a twiglet and as she struggled to zip it up, the whole room erupted in fits of giggles. I was too young to realise those outfits were for them to wear for their middle-aged husbands, which was probably a blessing as I knew all their husbands! Still, it was all a lot of fun. Our house was constantly filled with giggles, which made up for a lot of things.

Then there were the Christmas crackers. Mum would sit at the table making them all year round and I'd help, stuffing paper crowns and corny jokes inside like some kind of festive elf in Santa's grotto. I had other roles too.

"Go on," she'd whisper as we entered the shop. "Keep her talking."

So I'd do my part, standing at the counter, all animated, chatting to the shopkeeper about school, the latest book I was reading, or whatever new instrument I was trying to master. I'd lay it on thick, my performance so captivating that she never noticed Mum down by the deep freezer, quietly swapping labels on chickens, legs of lamb and joints of beef, getting the bigger cut for the smaller price. I was the little Artful Dodger to her Fagin and we put on a good show.

Chapter Two

While I tell my son Alex, who is now 26, that I love him every day, my mum wasn't one for emotions. I knew she loved me, but I don't know if this is a generational thing, or if she was just a bit hardened to life, but she would never cuddle or hug me. It was always me bouncing around trying to make her laugh and pulling her into an embrace. But there was one thing that always lit her up: watching me perform.

Music was my passion. I played a number of instruments by the time I was a teenager, the saxophone, the drums in the school steel band, but it was my acoustic guitar that was my first real love. After practising on John's, I painstakingly chose one out of a catalogue, that was about £140 and my parents paid it off weekly. Again, looking back this is probably one of many examples of them living beyond their means, only adding to the debt, but I still have it now, pride of place in my living room.

But back in Peterborough, an 11-year-old me filled the house with the sounds of strumming and singing. I practiced every chance I got and my family couldn't help but notice. It didn't take long before Mum, ever the entrepreneur, started setting up gigs for me to earn cash.

Over the top of a small hill near our home, there was a row of bungalows filled with elderly people and they became my first audience. Mum would place chairs on the grass, put on a spread of tea and biscuits and charge them five pence each to watch me sing. My setlist was pure gold – 'Streets of London' by Ralph McTell, 'Leaving on a Jet Plane' by John Denver – songs that got the oldies tapping their slippers. It may not have been the O2 Arena, but I felt like a star.

The thrill of performing wasn't just about the music; it was the applause and the praise. "Oh, that girl can really sing, can't she?" or "That's lovely guitar playing," they'd say to Mum and those words stuck to me like gold stars. The approval was addictive and later, when I was a teenager and I started busking in the town centre, it also became about the money. I was the first kid busker in Peterborough and one busy day I earned £150, which is an absolute fortune in today's money. It showed my worth. I loved performing because I was able to show that I was worth something.

At 14, I set my heart on a saxophone. Now, I didn't know how to play one, but that wasn't the point. So I started saving every single penny I made from my Saturday job at the local shop. My parents didn't even know how much money I had been making and saving under their noses, but the saxophone I wanted cost £390. I skipped school one day to travel to London and buy it. When I walked through the door and plonked it on the kitchen table, Mum was fuming.

"Where the bloody hell have you been? You've missed school! I've had them on the phone!" Then she clocked the case and narrowed her eyes. "What's that?"

I took a breath. "I've been to London," I said, trying to sound casual. "I bought a saxophone."

She went ballistic. "What? You what?! You got on a train

on your own? Are you mad?! And how much was it?" she snapped. "That could've paid a couple of bills off Cheryl, we really needed that money!"

I couldn't feel too guilty though, because everytime I looked at my saxophone I felt a burst of joy. But while playing music was my first love, a close second soon came along. I was 11 years old when I fell in love – proper, all-consuming, heart-thumping, stomach-flipping love. My parents told me it was just a phase, that it was just puppy love, but what did they know? I thought about him all the time and imagined our lives together.

In my mind, I was already close with his family and would borrow clothing from his sister Marie. I also got on great with his brothers Virl, Tom, Alan, Wayne, Merrill, Jay and Jimmy. I had come to the decision that I would probably one day move to Utah and become a Mormon, whatever that was. It all sounded very exotic.

Yes, later, Heather Trott, the character I played on *East-Enders*, would be famously obsessed with George Michael, but in my teens, my heart belonged to one man and one man only: Donny Osmond. I adored everything about him from his impish good looks to his dazzling smile to his funky outfits and velvety singing voice. To me the teen idol was complete perfection.

"Mum, what's a Mormon?" I asked, one day as I passed her another paper joke to stuff into a shiny Christmas cracker.

"It's a weird American thing where men have lots of wives," she replied, not even looking up.

Brilliant, I thought. If Donny Osmond could have lots of wives, then surely my chances had just gone up significantly?

I was definitely in there. I started mentally designing my purple wedding dress – purple, of course, being Donny's favourite colour. I was completely obsessed. Every spare moment was spent singing his songs into my battered purple hairbrush, belting out the lyrics as if I were performing to huge crowds at Madison Square Garden.

My bedroom became a shrine to Donny, his grinning face gazing down at me from posters plastered all across the walls. His eyes twinkled, as if to say, "Cheryl, one day, it'll be you and me together."

I had a secret too, one that would've had my parents in stitches if they had ever found out. I used to practice kissing on my Donny posters, full-on, eyes-closed, romantic snogs. The problem was, I was so dedicated to this act that I'd wear out the posters in the area around his mouth and I had to regularly swap them out so my parents didn't twig that I was smooching paper.

Luckily, I had a solid supply. There was no shortage of Donnys to pucker up to because I was a proud card-carrying member of the Donny Osmond Fan Club, which meant I collected all sorts of memorabilia from the LPs to posters and badges and my prized possession; a Donny Osmond lampshade. Now that's what I call romantic mood lighting.

And because purple was Donny's favourite colour, it became mine too. We couldn't afford all the Donny-themed merchandise, but I wore purple socks every chance I got. If I couldn't yet move to America to be with him, at least I could represent him on my feet.

In those days, you were either Team Donny Osmond, Team Jacksons, or Team David Essex. And I was staunchly and passionately Team Donny. I got into full-blown debates at school about why he was better than the rest and sometimes they got a little bit heated. It would have blown my tiny mind to know that, years later, I'd actually meet Donny, David and some of the Jacksons.

But back then, it was all just a dream and a fantasy love. I loved Donny Osmond so much and I felt that he understood me. He was my rock, so it makes sense that it was in his music that I found comfort the day my girlhood came to an end.

It was the 6 June 1977, and the whole country was caught up in the excitement of Queen Elizabeth II's Silver Jubilee. Streets were draped in red, white and blue, with bunting strung from lampposts and windows, fluttering in the warm summer breeze. The air buzzed with excitement and on our estate, we did things properly. Long trestle tables groaned under the weight of sausage rolls, trifle and every variation of a sandwich known to mankind. Kids dashed about with sticky fingers and faces, adults cracked open cans of beer and a record player blasted 'Dancing Queen' by ABBA from someone's front step.

I was in my element, holding court with the other kids, putting on my best Queen's English and leading a very off-key rendition of 'God Save the Queen'. In between dramatic bows, I stuffed myself with cheese and pineapple sticks, egg mayo vol-au-vents and a rainbow of cakes from the heaving party table.

Across the table, my mum was in full celebratory mode, looking every bit the part in a dress covered in paper love hearts and a Union Jack bowler hat. She was laughing with John and some neighbours, when suddenly she called over to me.

BEHIND THE SCENES

"Love, I'm out of fags! Can you pop to the shop?"

I wiped my hands on my shorts and nodded, grabbing the sweaty handful of coins she thrust at me. Even at 11, I was already well-known at the corner shop and back then, no one batted an eyelid at a kid buying a pack of Lambert and Butler.

I hopped on my bike, pedalling down the road, the party's laughter and music still ringing in my ears. The sun was starting to dip, casting long shadows and I remember feeling carefree, the wind whipping through my hair.

It was on the way back that it happened. When I was passing some large bushes, a man stepped out of nowhere and shoved me off my bike into the tangled undergrowth. Before I could scream, he was on me, his large rough hands grabbing at my chest, his body rubbing against mine, his breath hot and sour. As he assaulted me, he was laughing. That's what I remember most – the sound of his cruel callous cackle. I can't tell you what he looked like, only that he was much older and much bigger. I don't know if he was drunk, but that laugh is still burned into my brain.

Then, as suddenly as he appeared, he was gone. I don't know how long I lay there, stunned with heart pounding – it felt like an hour, but it was probably only a few minutes. I didn't understand what had just happened or why he wanted to grab my body. I knew that it was wrong – completely, unquestionably wrong – but I didn't have the language or understanding to explain why. I didn't know anything about sexual things or trauma. No one had told me what to look out for. No one had explained that people could do something like that. I hadn't even had the "birds and the bees" talk yet.

Eventually, I sat up, brushing dirt from my arms, wincing at the scratches. It might sound strange but my bike was my first concern. It was my pride and joy, so I picked it up, checked it over. Then, with shaking hands, I got back on and rode home.

When I got back to the celebrations, everything had changed. I sat down, trying to be invisible. The joy of the afternoon, the laughter and the fun, had all been left behind in that bush. I couldn't smile and couldn't touch the food in front of me. It all felt so wrong and I felt wrong too.

"What's the matter, Cheryl?" my mum asked, finally noticing her daughter was as deflated as a popped balloon. "You haven't touched your Eton Mess?"

Staring down at the soggy pudding, crushing bits of meringue with my fork I simply mumbled, "I... I'm fine."

"No, you're not," she said firmly, her eyes narrowing. "Let's talk."

Before I could protest, she took me by the arm and practically frog-marched me into the house, shutting the door with a sharp click. The walls felt closer than usual, the air heavier and there was suddenly a tightness in my chest. I didn't know where to start, but once the first word tumbled out, I couldn't stop. "Mum, um... This man pushed me off my bike into a bush and he was grabbing at my chest..." It was like something bursting inside me, words and sobs, all spilling onto the living room carpet like a knocked-over cup of tea.

My mum's face drained of colour. "What? What did you say?" she whispered, rushing outside and calling for John. Telling him was harder than I expected. I'd always told John everything, he was my funny, warm step-dad who read to me at bedtime and let me look at the stars through his telescope. But now, he seemed so manly and serious, like a stranger. I felt embarrassed but he listened without interrupting then, as my words dried up he exhaled slowly, like he'd been holding his breath the entire time. "We have to ring the police."

The policeman arrived not long after. He was tall and broad, his uniform crisp, his notebook at the ready but he didn't offer any kindness, no reassuring smile, no gentle encouragement. I told my story for the third time that day, my voice quieter now and he scribbled notes on his little flip pad, nodding occasionally, but his expression didn't change. I'm not sure if he believed me. I'm not sure what I'm supposed to feel. Relief? Fear? Shame? I felt all of them at once and it was too much.

Then, just as he turned to leave, he looked at my parents and, in a tone so casual he could have been asking about parking, says, "Well, a lot worse things are going to happen to her in the future."

Mum and John froze, looked at him, then at me in disbelief. I didn't understand what he meant, but something about the way he said it made my stomach twist. Even now, as an adult, I know how wrong that comment was to say in front of a traumatised child. But back then, I just shuddered, suddenly terrified of what might lie ahead.

I don't remember much of what happened after that. I know the adults talked in low, serious tones, but I went straight up to my room and shut the door, drowning out their voices by sticking on a record.

Then I got into bed, pulled the duvet over my head and let Donny's voice fill the room, soft and familiar, like a hug.

Tears slid down my cheeks, soaking into my pillow. I sang along, my voice cracking. Later on, Mum came up to check on me and sat on the edge of my bed. We didn't speak, she just stayed with me for a while and that was enough. But after that night, we never spoke of it again. I knew something had changed, but I pushed it to the back of my mind.

Chapter Three

Mum and John had gone out to bingo and while my siblings were downstairs playing, I slipped into the bathroom and locked the door. Standing in front of the mirror, I examined my 12-year-old body, grabbing a handful of my belly and twisting it this way and that, as if I might suddenly sculpt it into something I liked. Nope, still me. I pinched at my sides, watching the way the flesh puckered under my fingers. Why am I so big? I had always been fat, as long as I could remember.

Even as a small child, I had a funny relationship with my body. I remember going down the slide at the park and getting wedged halfway. The other kids lined up behind me, impatient, while I wriggled and tried to free myself like Winnie the Pooh in Rabbit's front door. Eventually, I managed to shuffle my way down.

Then there was the crocheted woolley swimming costume. My lovely Nanny, bless her, actually crocheted me a swimsuit which clearly was not water-resistant. I was so excited to wear it, until I got in the water. The second it was submerged, it turned into a saggy, waterlogged net, dragging down in all the wrong places. I emerged from the pool looking like a trawler had fished me out of the deep.

I had always been bigger than the other kids, but I didn't

dislike my body then. That changed after the man in the bushes. He took something from me that I didn't understand, something invisible but heavy. After that day, my body didn't feel like mine anymore – it felt like a problem, something to be ashamed of. I thought of it differently because I couldn't understand why it could be used for something other than running around in the playground, dancing or getting me from A to B. My budding breasts, which had arrived too soon, became a burden, a target. By the time I was nine, I was already wearing bras and at school I was teased mercilessly. "Fatty!" they'd chant. "When you walk, the whole earth shakes!"

I had taken my step-dad's surname when he and Mum got married, so I was no longer Cheryl Oldfield, I was Cheryl Campbell. Of course, kids, with their infinite creativity when it comes to cruelty, found an angle. In the seventies, Campbell's Soup sold tins of meatballs, so naturally, I became Meaty, or Meatball.

Looking back, I can see exactly how my weight struggles began. Food was love in our house, but it was also law. You finished what was on your plate, whether you were hungry or not. "Cheryl, eat it all up," Mum would say and that was that. Complaining wasn't an option. The phrase was always the same: "There are children starving in Africa." And so, I'd sit there, shoveling down every last bite, swallowing past fullness and doing what I was told.

When I decided I wanted to be a vegetarian aged 14, things got trickier. My mum didn't understand it one bit. "Don't be so ridiculous," she'd huff. "What do you think you're going to eat, then?"

So, instead of making meat-free alternatives, she just piled my plate high with potatoes and whatever else was lying around. I'd end up eating double portions of everything to compensate. To her credit, Mum did think she was helping. She'd protect me fiercely from the bullies. I'd come home, upset after being called fat and she'd be furious on my behalf.

"Don't take no notice of them," she'd say, marching around the kitchen like a general preparing for battle. "They're stupid. They don't know anything."

But she never really looked at how she was feeding me. She never clocked that the massive portion sizes weren't exactly setting me up for success.

Food was how we bonded, too. Even as an adult, the two of us would sit together, polishing off an entire packet of chocolate digestives without a second thought. We weren't just eating, we were sharing and this was our thing. But as a result, somewhere along the way, food stopped being just fuel. It became a comfort, a reward and a coping mechanism. A way of filling up something inside me that had nothing to do with hunger.

Even at the height of my fame, when I was on *EastEnders*, I would binge eat in secret and my weight ballooned to a size 26. If I wasn't driving home Linda Henry – who played Shirley, my character's best friend – I'd stop at the garage in Borehamwood, load up on food and eat the whole way to my house. Nearly two hours of biscuits, cakes, crisps. Anything to fill the void.

But in the playground, no one cared about the reason I was fat, they just saw that I was and that was enough. My clothes didn't help either, they were never on trend. I would be sent to school in any old thing that my mum could afford, usually adult clothes cut and cropped to fit my shorter and wider frame. Like many kids that stand out in some way, I quickly learned to deflect any teasing with humour. Beat the bullies to the joke and make them laugh with me, not at me – it's a defence mechanism and what I have done for a lot of my life. These days, when trolls attack my appearance online, I find myself using that same tactic. The social media comments section and the playground are not really such different beasts when it comes to name-calling.

But even I couldn't laugh everything off and there was one girl who made my life hell. At school, there was what I would describe as the 'Haves' and 'Have-nots.' I was firmly in the second category. If it was raining, I would have to go to school without an umbrella and I would have muddy socks and wet shoes. I'd smell all damp and just have to sit in the class steaming myself off.

But this girl, let's call her Sophie, would always have an umbrella. Her socks would be white and she would smell lovely. She was a good-looking girl too with blonde hair and bright skin – all the boys liked her and the girls wanted to be her. She had everything, but she still found the time to bully me.

Sophie was a master of cruelty. Mentally, she'd push me and push me, whispering jabs about my weight, passing notes across desks filled with nasty little cartoons or hurling stationery at the back of my head when the teacher wasn't looking. She'd giggle with her friends, glancing over to see if I was crumbling yet. Day in, day out, she chipped away at me. And I just took it and took it and took it. Until one day, I didn't.

BEHIND THE SCENES

I was sitting on a wall in the playground, minding my own business, when she strutted over, her little gang of disciples trailing behind her. "Oh look, it's the big fat cow," she sneered. "You're going to break that wall, fatty, if you keep sitting on it." I felt my cheeks flush red and I jumped down. She smirked, "Oh look, the cow is going to stampede me!"

Something in me snapped. Before I even knew what I was doing, my fist connected with her face. It was like a scene from a film; time slowed down and for a second, nobody moved, then blood started trickling from just below her right eye. The silver ring Mum had bought me a few weeks earlier had sliced her skin.

Silence. Then chaos. Teachers descended, Sophie wailed, her friends gasped like I'd just committed murder and I was dragged to the headteacher's office, where I sat staring at my hands, still shaking, as the reality of what I'd done sank in.

What followed was a blur of apologies. To Sophie, to the school, to my parents, but no sorry could undo what had happened. Mum and John were furious and I was excluded from school for a few days. Honestly, that didn't bother me, I wanted to hide anyway, so I locked myself in my room, cranked up the Donny Osmond and replayed the moment over and over in my head. I was shocked by my own strength. I was scared of what I was capable of.

But I did learn something that day. People can be horrible to you, but you don't have to be horrible back. I couldn't control what others said or did, but I could control how I responded.

School got a bit easier after that – my outburst might have got me in a lot of trouble but it also meant the bullies largely backed off. I poured all my energies into my music and found myself on a freezing, muddy November morning in 1980, standing in the middle of Ferry Meadows, in Nene Park, Peterborough, clutching a pair of drumsticks so tightly my fingers were numb. Around me, my school steel band shivered in unison, our breath misting in the air as a telly crew fussed about with cameras and clipboards.

TV host Keith Chegwin, full of energy despite the cold, bounced around in a puffer jacket and I was filled with excitement. The school steel band I play bass drum in are going live on Noel Edmonds' *Swap Shop*.

If you grew up in the 70s or 80s, you'll know *Multi-Coloured Swap Shop* was the holy grail of Saturday morning telly. For anyone else, imagine a chaotic, glorious mix of celebrity guests, live phone-ins and the legendary "Swaporama" where kids bartered their old belongings for something new, or at least, new to them.

I could barely believe we were actually there, but before I knew it, the cameras started rolling. Mr Wilkinson, our music teacher, gave the nod and we launched into 'Yellow Bird', a Caribbean folk classic. You'd think I'd be nervous, playing live on national TV, but I was in my element, hammering away at my steel drum like I was the headline act at Notting Hill Carnival.

Then came my big moment. Keith Chegwin, grinning ear to ear, bounded over with his microphone to interview a 15-year-old me. I still have the photo: me, beaming in my Liverpool FC scarf, standing next to him with the exact same haircut he had, that sort of looked like someone had plonked a pudding bowl on our heads and gone at us with blunt scissors.

"What have you brought to swap?" he asked, mic in hand.

"A Jackie magazine annual," I said, hopefully. "And I want to swap it for KerPlunk."

No-one did swap with me that day, but lots of the kids at school wanted to trade places when they saw me on TV.

The funny thing is, by then, I actually loved school. When I was younger, the bullying had made it miserable, but as I grew into my confidence, the jibes stopped. They could barely get me to go home half the time and I had brilliant teachers who saw something in me before I even saw it in myself.

Mr Wilkinson, with his neatly trimmed mustache and sharp suits, basically gave me free rein in the instrument cupboard. "Go on, have a go," he'd say, as I clattered around with guitars, drums and anything else that made a decent racket.

Then there were my drama teachers, Mr Merritt and Ms McGuinness, who lit a fire in me I didn't even know was there – I cannot overstate how much they changed my life. That's the thing, if you find someone who believes in you, it can make all the difference.

Before long, Meatball (yours truly) was cast as Nancy in the school production of *Oliver!* – standing centre stage, belting out 'As Long As He Needs Me' like my life depended on it. I was never the Queen of the Cool Crowd, but by Year 11, I'd found my tribe. I had a solid gang of mates and my best friend was Sharon Spaulding. Her family were Jamaican and their house was always filled with music, proper wall-to-wall sound. They even had a piano and Sharon and I would sit side by side, trying to write songs and bash out little tunes.

By then, I had a clear vision of what I wanted next: drama

school. No plan B, no hesitation. I knew exactly where I was headed and my parents were horrified... "Why don't you want to be something normal?" they said. "Be a nurse."

But let's be real, years of babysitting my younger siblings had already taught me I was not built for dealing with vomit, poo, or anything like that. That career path was a hard no. Instead, I had my heart set on Rose Bruford College in South East London. When the prospectus arrived, I must've read it a hundred times, staring at those happy students, all laughing on the lawn. "That's gonna be me," I told myself.

And then, in 1983, I got an audition. This was it. Mr Merritt and Ms McGuiness thought I could do it and helped me choose my audition pieces and I practised until I was blue in the face. I was ready, I was going to be an actor, nothing could stop me. Except, of course, reality.

I took the train down to Bexley, South London, audition fee paid and backpack full of scripts, plans and dreams. And then? A great, big, resounding no.

When the rejection letter arrived I retreated to my room red-faced and convinced I'd never make it, but after some gentle encouragement from my teachers, I decided I wasn't going to give up that easily. So, I stayed on at school in sixth form and tried again the following year. Another audition and another no. I tore the rejection letter up and threw it in the bin.

By the third time, I was less hopeful, sitting on the train down to London. I arrived in the waiting room subdued, watching the other kids, fresh first-timers buzzing with excitement. As the budding actors did their vocal exercises and bounced about the room trying to be cast as star of the show, I caught the eye of one boy sitting alone, poring over his lines.

BEHIND THE SCENES

"Hi, I'm Graeme," he said, putting out an elegant hand for me to shake. "Come here often?" he added with a smirk.

"Actually, I do," I laughed. "It's my third year auditioning. They should have a loyalty card system."

And just like that, we became pals. He was shy at first with a kind smile and a wicked sense of humour. I didn't yet know it, but Graeme would soon become one of the first gay male loves of my life. I have always loved the LGBTQ+ community and Graeme was my gateway into this gorgeous, glittering world. It was an instant friendship, we were inseparable all that day and after the audition, we celebrated our efforts with a trip to a Wimpy burger joint, where we split a portion of fries like a pair of starving artists.

A few weeks later, a letter landed on my doormat from the college. It was a yes and I shrieked with delight. The first person I told? Graeme. My hands shook as I typed the numbers into the house phone. "Hello, is Graeme there? It's Cheryl. I got in! Did you?"

"Yes, babe. I did," he says. "This is going to be amazing!"

My life was about to change. I could feel it in the air.

Chapter Four

Sunlight bounced off banners, whistles pierced the air and rainbow flags rippled above the thousands-strong crowd of people packed into Trafalgar Square.

It was London Pride, 1986, the city alive with joy and protest, like the whole of London has turned out in support of the LGBT+ community.

At 20 years old, dressed in my green combat trousers and scuffed black boots, I stood shoulder to shoulder with Graeme in the throng, holding our handmade sign that read "Gays are revolting! Gay revolution!" The atmosphere was electric, so many people standing together, out and proud, waving banners and flags. Above the sea of faces, signs that read "Body Positive", "Black Lesbians", and "Stop violence against lesbian and gay men…"

As we marched across the River Thames towards Kennington Park, we chanted, "We're here! We're queer!" shoulder to shoulder. It was exhilarating – I'm not gay, but I knew there and then, these were my people and Graeme too was grinning from ear to ear.

At that time, so much of gay culture was still underground. We were in the midst of the AIDS epidemic and people were scared. Yet in this crowd, everyone is holding their heads high. It made me proud to see my best friend beaming with such defiance and joy and it felt like we were all part of something truly historic, because we were.

During my time at Rose Bruford College I became very political, spending many weekends at protests and evenings at feminist discussion groups. It was a very political course and I spent half my time outside of South Africa House or in Trafalgar Square trying to free Nelson Mandela, instead of doing college work. So much so, that when he was finally freed in 1990 I couldn't help feeling a small sense of personal achievement. I am only joking, but I was always at some protest or another, supporting women's rights, gay rights, worker's rights and rights of all humans really. It felt empowering to raise my voice and feel like it mattered, even in a small way.

It was a highly sensitive environment at college. People could take offence quite easily. We were all young, passionate and figuring things out and the politics of language, identity and allyship were front and centre. I prided myself on being an ally and an activist, someone who stood up for what was right. But even I got it wrong one day.

We were in rehearsals, just mucking about in between scenes and I turned to Graeme and said, "Shut up, you f**got." It was something we said to each other in private, in our own friendship bubble, which was mostly queer. It had been reclaimed, used playfully, affectionately, but this wasn't home and the moment the word left my mouth, the air changed. The room fell completely silent.

"You can't say that, Cheryl!" someone snapped from across the room.

My face flushed crimson, I could feel it rising from my chest all the way to my ears. Graeme and the director, who was also gay, tried to stick up for me, saying he wasn't offended but everyone else was disgusted and I was mortified. My heart was pounding and I felt like a traitor to everything I believed in. I just grabbed my things and left. I got on a train home and didn't come back that night, even though I was meant to, I just wanted to hide. Later, Graeme rang me. "Come back to rehearsals, Cheryl. It's okay," he said gently. But I couldn't, I was too ashamed.

Eventually of course, I returned, and that day aside, I really did have an absolute riot at drama college. By my second year, I was living in a flat with Graeme and my friend Sayan, who was a musical director and as beautiful as she was cool. We spent most nights drinking at the local student pub until we got barred for being too rowdy and had to resort to drinking cans from a corner shop in a portacabin at the college. Sayan, Graeme and my house were always full of music, fun, creativity and a lot of parties filled with amazing friends like Christine, who was older and a brilliant actor who always supported me. They ended up being lifelong friends. Someone was always strumming a guitar, singing or blasting out something on the keyboard at 1am, with fairy lights blinking from every surface.

While I was at college I also joined a band called Lucy The Cat, where I played the saxophone. We had a mix of original songs and covers and for a bunch of young people trying to make it big, we actually weren't half bad. We played the odd gig around London and one night, we landed a spot at The Mean Fiddler in Camden; a venue that, in our eyes, was practically Wembley.

That night felt like a big deal, but what made it even more special was that my mum had actually come to watch. Now, Mum wasn't exactly one for big gestures of support. She wasn't the type to yell "That's my daughter!" from the crowd or wave a homemade banner, but she had turned up and that, to me, meant the world. I wanted to do something to mark the occasion, to show her I appreciated her being there.

So, in a moment of what I thought was absolute genius, I turned to David, our lead singer and said, "I want to dedicate the next song to my mum."

David frowned. "Are you sure?"

"Yeah, why?" I asked.

He gave me a funny look but shrugged. "Alright then."

So I grabbed the mic and, feeling like the ultimate rock star, I announced, "This next one's for my mum!" The crowd cheered, the band struck up the intro and then, at full volume, we launched into: "Roxannneee! You don't have to turn on the red light!"

Mum's face dropped and I could see her standing rigidly and shaking her head. After the gig, she stormed over and grabbed me by the arm. "Why in God's name would you dedicate that song to me? Do you even know what it's about?" she hissed.

"Erm... yeah?" I said weakly. I absolutely did not. "It's about a tart, Cheryl! A tart!"

I felt my face burn hotter than the stage lights. "Oh. I just knew you liked The Police. I didn't realise..."

She shook her head and laughed. "You're such a bloody idiot!"

Life wasn't just about being on stage and playing music

though, I was studying theatre and education, not the traditional drama course, so alongside acting, I also learned to teach in schools and prisons. We performed in the local community, creating our own productions and helping underprivileged kids come out of their shell which I absolutely loved. It wasn't just about performing; it was about using theatre to connect with people, to tell real stories in unexpected places.

One day, a group of us, including Graeme, were asked to take our play to a drama festival in Utrecht, Holland. Excitement was at an all-time high as it was our first international trip as performers and it was all we could talk about for weeks. All the students stayed in the same hostel and on the first day, we planned to explore the town before going to one of the festival performances in the evening.

Now, drama students have a reputation for being a bit... experimental. And let's just say, many of my classmates enjoyed their fair share of the 'wacky baccy' but weed was never my thing. In all honesty, drugs scared me. What if I took something and ended up running naked through the streets, convinced I was a dragon? I liked to be in control and the idea of losing my grip on reality wasn't appealing.

But we were in Holland, and in Holland it was legal. My friends were adamant that I should experience it at least once so we wandered into a coffee shop and I was immediately hit by the thick, herbal scent of cannabis. I'd never been anywhere like this before, it was a bright and colourful oasis, filled with artsy types gesticulating as they put the world to rights.

Some of my friends were already smoking joints, but behind

the counter there were rows of delicious-looking baked goods that gleamed temptingly.

"Go on, Cheryl, just try one. You'll love it. They are space cakes, filled with weed," Graeme pleaded, holding a large brownie aloft like it was a BAFTA Award. He was giggling, the joint already doing its job spectacularly.

"I don't know... What if something goes wrong?" I protested, eyeing the snack like it was a ticking time bomb.

"Nothing will go wrong," he assured me. "It's just a bit of fun and it's in a brownie babe, you love brownies." He had a point, I did like brownies. Feeling a spark of rebelliousness, I took a deep breath and chomped down on the gooey brownie. Then I waited.

Thirty minutes passed. Then an hour. Absolutely nothing. No giggles, no floating sensation, no sudden urge to discuss the meaning of life.

"What am I supposed to feel? It's not working," I huffed, disappointed. There was only one logical conclusion, I was clearly immune to weed. Some people were naturally resistant to drugs, right? Maybe I had a superpower, maybe I was just built differently. There was only one way to test the theory. I bought another one and scoffed that down too. Feeling very pleased with myself, I strutted into the theatre with my friends, ready to watch the play. Our group of slightly drunk and increasingly high drama students were already causing a scene. One of our mates had smuggled in a big bag of Grolsch beer and every few minutes, you'd hear the distinct clink of a bottle being cracked open. The shushing from other audience members grew louder, but I still felt totally, completely normal.

And then… *BAM*, it hit me like a freight train. "Graeme! Graeme!" I whispered urgently, my voice thick with panic. "I've lost my tongue. I can't find my tongue!"

Graeme, mid-swig of beer, choked. "What?"

"I can't find my tongue! Help me!" I hissed.

Then, according to eyewitnesses (because I personally have no memory of this next part), I dropped down onto all fours and started crawling along the row, shoving past my friends' feet. To the horror and confusion of the audience, I then scrambled down the aisle, frantically pleading, "Has anyone seen my tongue? I can't find it!"

The performance continued on stage, but the real show was happening in the stalls, starring me, Cheryl, The Girl Who Misplaced Her Own Tongue. An usher, understandably concerned about the madwoman disrupting their performance, swiftly grabbed me by the arm and escorted our entire group out of the theatre.

The next morning, I woke up in the hostel to the sound of sniggering. My friends sat around my bed, already armed with a new catchphrase. "Have you lost your tongue, Cheryl?"

Thankfully, by the next day when we had to perform our own show, the drugs were well out of my system. Otherwise, I imagine I would have been thrown out of drama school before my career even began.

Chapter Five

"You're going to have to change your name," my tutor told me one afternoon, matter-of-factly.

"What? But that's my name!" I protested but she wasn't having any of it. Turns out, there was already an actress called Cheryl Campbell and she was a good one too. She starred opposite Bob Hoskins in *Pennies from Heaven* and even popped up in *Chariots of Fire*. Fair enough. I got the message.

So, about a year after leaving drama school, having slogged it out in community theatre, I finally got my first 'proper' acting gig, which meant I could register for the Actors' Equity Association (AEA) and get an Equity Card. In those days, you couldn't really work unless you had the Equity card and were part of the union; all the decent jobs were union jobs and you'd be laughed out of the audition room without that little piece of plastic. It was the golden ticket and I was determined to earn mine.

For this, I had to change my name, so I thought I may as well make it something meaningful. And what better way than to honour my step-dad? I decided to take his middle name. From now on, I'd be Cheryl Fergison.

Feeling chuffed with my decision, I headed home to tell him and my mum, who were now living in South East London, card in hand.

"That's nice, love," said John, nodding in approval, before suddenly pausing, his brow furrowing. "But... Fergison? My name is Ferguson, with a U."

Oh well, it was too late. But it didn't matter, Cheryl Fergison was ready to take on the acting world. The job? Working at the Way We Were Museum on Wigan Pier doing historical reenactments. Okay, it wasn't going to win me an Oscar, but I was 23 and the money was good and it meant I could join the union, so I was thrilled. It also felt like the start of something real – proper costume, real scripts, a schedule! The museum put me in touch with people to organise a houseshare and one of them was a man called Pete Whitfield. He collected me from the station platform, carrying my bags to our new digs. He had kind, sparkling eyes and a cheeky sense of humour and we instantly clicked.

The job was not a disappointment either, in fact, it was actually really great fun. There were five actors working at any one time and we would rotate different scenes and roles which brought the history of Wigan to life. I would play an Edwardian woman who went to join the Suffragettes, in a wide straw hat and long skirt, waxing lyrical about Votes for Women to passing visitors. I also used to perform in the mock Victorian schoolroom, playing 'All Things Bright and Beautiful' on the piano, pumping the old bellows with my feet. Sometimes, schoolchildren would join in and sing and I'd feel like a proper schoolmistress.

But the happiest times were when Pete and I had scenes together. We played a married couple during the Victorian period, as the Industrial Revolution powered ahead. Pete was Harry, a happy-go-lucky miner and I acted the role of Sarah, his long-suffering but ever-loving wife. We lived together in a small cottage and visitors would cram in to watch the scenes we wrote ourselves. We'd bicker about money and the risks of Harry's work, sometimes we would act out the aftermath of Harry having had an accident down the mine. There was no sick pay back then, so that was tough.

We'd even take imaginary holidays to Blackpool and for that scene we had two fake donkeys as props. "I want to go on the donkey, Harry, do let me!" I'd wail.

"No, you can't go on t'donkey," Pete would reply in a thick Wigan accent. "You'd break the donkey's back."

The audience would roar with laughter at the slapstick silliness of me trying to mount the animal, as my husband pulled me back. Sometimes the crowd laughed so hard we'd have to pause the scene to let them recover. It was like live theatre, every day – with the bonus of period costumes.

Pete and I put on a great performance as husband and wife, probably because we were spending a lot of time together. We'd head into work before 9am and when we finished at 5pm, all of us actors would head to The Bee's Knees pub. Sometimes, after that, we'd go to a local club, play pool and dance until two in the morning. It was the best kind of chaos – laughter, music, friendships that felt like family. We spent a lot of time boozing and surviving on pasties or chips at the end of the night, but we were young and having fun.

It was obvious that Pete and I had a connection. We just clicked instantly. A few weeks into the job, the two of us were in the cottage again, acting as Harry and Sarah and talking about what we'd do on our upcoming trip to Blackpool. He said, "I'm going to get you a stick of Blackpool rock, love."

And then he leaned in and kissed me, right on the lips, in front of the audience – like it was the most natural thing in the world.

He'd never done that before and I was completely taken aback. We often ad-libbed and improvised the scenes, but this wasn't Harry kissing Sarah, I knew it was Pete kissing Cheryl. From that moment on, we were a couple and totally inseparable.

Pete was one of a kind. He was just like an old-fashioned gentleman, from the clothes he wore to his interests and manners. Although I met him when he was in his early 20s, he was always an old man inside. He wore old man clothes, things such as flat caps, waistcoats and cord trousers and he walked with his hands in his pockets, like a 1950s film star who'd wandered off the set of *Brief Encounter*. Pete loved old things like Laurel and Hardy and we went to see Norman Wisdom do stand-up several times. He would spend every penny he had either going to see plays or feeding his autograph collection. He collected the signatures of stars, from theatre legends to film icons and could tell you stories about every one.

It was lovely being with Pete. We had the same passion and shared vision for life. We supported each other in everything and we were in love. It was like having a best friend and lover in one and being with him was like wearing the most comfortable pair of slippers. That's the way it felt: very cosy and warm. We were both actors, in and out of work, so we understood each other and we had so much fun together. He made every day feel like a little adventure.

After over a year of happy, cosy Wigan life, we made a

decision, we'd give London and acting a proper go. We packed up our bits and bobs and moved into the same flat I'd once shared with Graeme. He moved out, Pete moved in and just like that, a new chapter began. Together.

It turned out to be one of the best decisions we ever made, because not long after, in 1990, I landed my very first job in the West End. I was 24 years old and could hardly believe my luck. It was an Alan Ayckbourn play called *Man of The Moment* at the Globe Theatre on Shaftesbury Avenue, starring acclaimed actors Michael Gambon – yes, Dumbledore in the Harry Potter series – and Peter Bowles of *To The Manor Born* fame.

Okay, I was only in the ensemble and an understudy for a lead actress, but I had a two-week run at the part when the lead was off sick. Most of my time was spent backstage in our dressing room or sitting on the rooftop terrace with the other cast members, chatting, people-watching and generally enjoying the thrill of it all. We had a lot of time to kill when not on stage, but I never got bored.

You couldn't be bored in Soho in the early '90s, because it made for spectacular people-watching. It was so alive and full of action and we had a front-row seat to all types of drama. There was a carnival of characters on every corner from buskers, drag queens and preachers to tourists and punks.

I even became quite friendly with the local sex workers, watching their red lights flicker on in the windows across the street. They would tell us their tricks of the trade and I couldn't help but respect their hustle. There was one particular scam where they'd get Yale keys cut and say to foreign punters, "Give me £50 up front. This is the key to the door around the corner, it's a yellow door and I'll be there in five minutes. You take the key and let yourself in; we can't be seen together because of the police."

We'd watch from the window as the men tried the door to no avail, then wandered round in circles, looking baffled and broken, until they gave up. It was like street theatre – both a tragedy and a farce in one.

My mum was super proud that her daughter was in a West End play and would come backstage to hang out with the stars. While I was happy that she wanted to come and visit me, there was some questionable behaviour that took place. She would arrive in her smartest clobber, swapping her South London twang for a faux-posh accent as if she were the one on the playbill. She'd fawn over the other actors, practically curtsying when she met Peter Bowles which, I have to admit, was a sight to see. She transformed into a real life version of Hyacinth Bucket from *Keeping Up Appearances* – all airs and graces – leaving me both amused and surprised.

Mum would make the actors cups of tea and say lovely things about the show, but her brashness sometimes made me want the floor to open up and swallow me whole. She clearly liked being in that atmosphere, but she never really looked comfortable in it. She was a bit of a loose cannon and once, she turned to Peter Bowles and said, "Oh, I didn't realise you had that much hair. It looks much thinner on the telly."

I wanted to melt. Still, I suppose I embarrass my son these days, so it's all part of the cycle, it's a mother's right.

Pete – my Pete, not Peter Bowles – worked on the stage door at the same theatre. For most men, this might have been hard, watching their girlfriend go in every day to do the job

they dreamed of doing, but not him. He was always supportive, unwaveringly kind and never showed a hint of jealousy.

When that play wrapped, Pete came to watch and support
me when I joined the Royal Shakespeare Company and
performed in various productions before I returned to the
Globe to act in a play called *Blue Angel* in 1992.

One afternoon, after a matinee performance, I was chatting
with *Outnumbered* actress Claire Skinner, who was also in
the show, when I dashed downstairs to grab some food. "I'll
get the sandwiches!" I yelled as I sprinted off down the stairs
and straight into none other than Al Pacino, the *Scarface*
legend himself. I nearly knocked him over. He fixed me with
that legendary stare, the one that could slice through steel,
and then he grinned. "Great show, great show!" he said in
that unmistakable New Yorker growl.

And what did I do? I froze. This was my one chance to be
effortlessly cool and say something witty, maybe even clever.
Instead, I spluttered, "Err… thanks, Al." Thanks, Al?! Like
we were old mates? I walked away dazed, clutching a limp
cheese sandwich and dying inside. What an idiot. I replayed
the encounter in my head for days, each time cringing harder
than the last.

Years later, Linda Henry, Paul O'Grady and I went to 'An
Evening With Al Pacino' at a theatre in London where he
spoke about his career. Afterwards, we met him backstage
and even Linda, usually holding court and chatting with
everyone, was tongue-tied. She was actually visibly shaking,
but I got it, the man was electrifying.

I also got close to another screen legend during that time too,
although not in the way I expected. I appeared on *'Allo 'Allo*

in the early 1990s and played a character called Desiree who was part of the fictional Communist Resistance in occupied France and being larger than most actresses, I wasn't exactly dressed in designer clobber.

The costume department gave me a pair of thick, itchy woollen trousers, horrible things. I cursed them throughout the scene; they chafed, they scratched and I couldn't wait to get them off, but when I went to hang them up at the end of the day, I noticed a label stitched into the waistline. It read: "Ronnie Barker."

Apparently, the comedy king had worn them while filming *Open All Hours*. Suddenly, those trousers felt different... special, almost sacred. I like to think a bit of his comic genius rubbed off on me that day – even if it was just on my bum. But this was far from my only brush with the rich and famous, even in those early days of my career.

I had passed my driving test when I was living up in Wigan, probably the proudest moment of my life at the time, but when I finally got round to sorting the insurance back in London, the price nearly knocked me sideways. It was absolutely extortionate. I mean, I knew I wasn't exactly Lewis Hamilton, but come on.

In between acting jobs, I was working in community theatre – going into schools, community centres, old people's homes, even doing restorative justice programmes, helping people put together plays. It was rewarding, but it wasn't giving me Hollywood star wages. I was living off instant noodles, dodgy boilers and getting paid in post-performance biscuits.

So I called up the insurance company to see if there'd been

some mistake. "Why is this so expensive?" I asked, expecting some clerical error.

"Well, Miss, it's because of your profession," the grumpy woman on the other end said of the line, all businesslike. "Because of my job?" I stuttered.

"Yes, you're an actor," she said. "What's that got to do with anything?" I continued. "Well," she said. "Actors work unsociable hours and also there's the risk of you driving famous people around in your car."

I nearly choked on my cup of tea. Driving famous people around? I don't even know any famous people! The most well-known person I'd had in my car was my Pete and I doubt anyone in London recognised either of us from Wigan's Way We Were museum. We were more likely to crash the car from laughing too hard than ferrying celebs about town.

Flash forward a few months and wouldn't you know it, I found myself in a play called *What Now, Little Man?* in Greenwich alongside none other than Anita Dobson – *East-Enders* royalty, Angie Watts herself. We clicked straight away: two council estate girls with the same sense of humour, full of chat and passion.

Back then, Anita was dating Brian May, the guitar legend from Queen, who she is now married to. One day there was much excitement backstage, as Brian was coming to watch the show. After the performance, he came backstage and met us all. He was very down to earth and friendly and had absolutely none of the so-called rockstar ego. I called Brian and Anita the "The Two Hairdos" because, much like me and Keith Chegwin on *Swap Shop* in 1980, they both had matching barnets. Theirs were the height of fashion, with long cascading curls and a fringe. Between the two of them, they looked like they were in a L'Oréal ad for glam rock locks.

Anita turned to me and said, "Brian likes Chinese food. Is there anywhere good in Greenwich?"

"Course there is!" I said, ready to be her personal takeaway directory.

"Would you mind walking down with him just to show him where it is?" she said. And she didn't have to ask me twice.

So, there I was, strolling through the streets of Greenwich with an actual rockstar, chatting about prawn crackers and crispy duck like it was the most normal thing in the world. When we got back, Anita asked if I could drive them to their car and that's how I ended up, hands clenched tight on the wheel, driving at a snail's pace, ferrying Brian May through South London in my battered old motor. The very thing that had made my insurance go through the roof had actually come true. I was driving one of the stars of Queen, the biggest and coolest band of all time. That insurance woman was a bloody prophet.

But that wasn't the only time during my theatre career that I would come face-to-face with Queen. In 1995, when I was 29, I did a play called *Cyrano de Bergerac*, the 1897 classic about a gifted poet too self-conscious about his big nose to confess his love for his cousin Roxane. My character was Lise, the baker's wife and the lead was played by Robert Lindsay, the Olivier Award-winning actor who also played the dad in *My Family*.

In one scene, Bob had this grand monologue while I, in the background, was rolling dough and making bread. One day in rehearsal, he turned to me and said, "Cheryl, I have a funny idea. While I'm doing my speech, just out of the corner of my eye, I'll be watching you. And you can knead the dough, shape it like a baguette, hold it like a penis, wiggle it about, then slap it on the table. Big comic phallus. What do you reckon?"

Of course it was a genius idea, like most things that Bob said and the audience clearly thought so too as during that scene they always roared with laughter. One night, he suggested I take it further and make some balls out of dough to add to the phallic penis. All well and good, except for one tiny problem: Queen Elizabeth II and Prince Philip were in the royal box that night.

"Listen, Bob, I'm worried," I said before curtain-up.

"Why?" he asked.

"I know it's funny, but I cannot be making dick dough and smacking it on the table in front of Her Majesty the Queen. I just can't," I wailed. "I could be tried for treason!"

"Cheryl, it'll be fine," he assured me. "Do it. Not just for the Queen, but for the audience." And so, I did it. I pretended to fondle a huge phallus and testicles in front of the Head of State. And the audience laughed even harder that night, maybe because of the balls, or maybe because they knew the Queen was watching.

Later on, after the show had finished, I found myself sweating in a line-up, waiting to have my moment with the Queen. I curtseyed and she smiled. She then whispered something to me, which I know it's not protocol to repeat, but suffice to say: one was definitely amused!

Chapter Six

Life was starting to take shape and I was very happy. I'd performed in front of royalty, met Brian May and was working a lot. Pete was carving out his career too and making a name for himself, even starring in a pantomime with Zsa Zsa Gabor in Los Angeles. We were still very much in love and one day he whisked me off to Stratford-upon-Avon for a romantic weekend to go and see a play.

We wandered around the cobbled streets, popping in and out of quirky little shops, holding hands like teenagers. In a tucked-away secondhand bookshop, Pete bought me a beautiful old edition of Shakespeare's sonnets with gilded pages and faded corners. Then we stumbled across an antiques stall, where he picked out a delicate little marcasite ring and slipped it onto my finger with a smile.

I was properly made up and we sat on the banks of the River Avon reading poetry to one another, the water glinting in the early evening light. It felt like something out of a film. I was really romantic at heart and Pete was the dream man for me.

When we got back home, we put the sonnet book on the shelf, pride of place, right next to all the knick-knacks we'd collected – a mix of old theatre programmes, novelty figurines and postcards from places we couldn't afford to stay in. I wore the ring every day. It wasn't THE Ring – no proposals, no big questions – but it meant something. It was a quiet little promise, a moment in time and I cherished it.

But when I took stock of all the things we had, there was something missing. I was 32 years old and like so many women in their early 30s, I felt that tug in my chest, not indigestion, but that ache for a baby. Someone to sing lullabies to and love endlessly.

I started to feel… well, broody and I thought Pete would make the best dad, I just knew it. We often visited his nieces and nephews and he was wonderful with them, doing silly voices and attentively listening to their stories. He was so caring that it only strengthened my belief that he was the one.

Then, one afternoon, in 1997, after meeting him for lunch in Soho, Pete handed me a large duffle bag as he was heading back to work at a nearby theatre. "Can you take this back for me? Just some laundry," he said casually.

"Of course," I replied, hopping on the bus.

I was at home, stuffing Pete's smelly clothes into the washing machine, when I found it. Right at the bottom of the bag was a shiny pornographic magazine.

I frowned. Why would he need that when he had me? Yes, the sex had lessened in recent years, but I thought that was normal; relationships wax and wane, right? We'd been together for seven years. I flipped through the pages, confused and then it hit me.

The photos were all of men.

I felt genuinely sick, my stomach churning and I stared at the glossy pages as if somehow the images might change, as if I had misunderstood what I was looking at. How could Pete, the future father of my children, be looking at gay porn?

"I found the fucking magazine!" I screamed once Pete arrived home and the colour drained from his face. I then lost my shit and I mean really lost my shit. I was so confused and hurt, I didn't understand how he could do this to me. Yes, all of it was about me. I ranted and raved and hurled hurtful abuse, desperate for an explanation that might make it all make sense.

At first, he pleaded with me to stay. Then, once I had calmed down, his beautiful face crumpled. "I do love you, Cheryl. You know I love you. I love you so much, you are my soulmate and I am yours. It's just… I have started to realise I am attracted to men. I promise you, I have never been with a man, I have never cheated on you, or anything like that. I love you."

It was really sad, probably the saddest conversation I have ever had. I remember him saying, "I hate myself. I hate myself for being this." And I hated him too, I am ashamed to say, and I told him as much. It felt like my heart had been ripped out of my body and trampled on the floor. The relationship was over.

For the next year, I was full of rage and I blamed every gay man for my heartbreak. I even blamed Graeme, who was living in Manchester by this time and refused to take his calls. I wrote him a letter explaining how hurt I was, how unfair it was, how cruel it was for this to happen to me. Me, me, me, me. I didn't care that Pete, who I loved, was also hurting.

I pride myself on being an LGBT+ ally. My son is gay, my best mates are gay, I perform at Prides and I feel completely at home in the community, but for months I couldn't see past my own pain. I was angry in a way I had never known. I let bitterness consume me and blamed the gay community for something that wasn't anybody's fault. I couldn't cope and wasn't ready to.

Then one day, about eight months later, everything changed. I bumped into Pete with his new partner and I could see that he was truly happy. It was like a fog lifting. The anger, the hurt, the resentment, it all loosened its grip on me in that moment because how could I be angry at someone I loved for being who they truly are? We started to rebuild as mates. Graeme, bless him, took me back as his friend, despite how I had pushed him away and thank God he did, because I don't know what I'd do without him.

Before Pete died in 2013, after a stellar career starring in films such as *Wide Eyed and Legless* with Julie Walters and *Wind In The Willows* with the Monty Python team, we even got to share the stage again.

We were in *Cinderella* together in 2012 – me as the Fairy Godmother, him as one of the Ugly Sisters in full drag – the irony wasn't lost on either of us. I think, in a way, our love was stronger than Cinderella and Prince Charming's, because real love, the kind that lasts beyond pain, isn't about fairytales. It's about seeing each other, accepting each other and never letting go. And I never have.

* * *

In the aftermath of my split with Pete, I'd more or less sworn off relationships. I wasn't looking for love, not even lust – men were simply a no-go area. I was doing what all the women's magazines and well-meaning mates tell you to do: "Focus on yourself, Cheryl. Reconnect with you." So that's what I tried to do, going to auditions, writing poetry, learning new songs on my guitar. I was even going for long walks, trying to clear my head and convince myself I was one of those strong, independent women who recharge with fresh air and a decent pair of trainers instead of emotional chaos and cake. But the truth is, I was still heartbroken, just trying to patch myself up one to-do list at a time.

Around that time, I popped to the doctor for a check-up. Nothing major, just a general MOT. But while I was there, I mentioned that I'd been getting a bit of pain down below, not all the time, but enough to make me think, Hmm… that's not right, is it?

He gave me that look, you know the one. And before I could finish explaining, he was already trotting out the old classic. "Well, you really need to lose some weight," he said, as if it was a revolutionary diagnosis.

Why do doctors always do that? Honestly, if I'd gone in with a stubbed toe, I'm sure he'd have blamed it on my BMI. "Sprained wrist? Have you considered SlimFast?" I wanted to say, 'I'm fully aware I'm not a size eight, thanks, but maybe try treating the actual symptoms instead of just my dress size.'

Anyway, he did agree to run some tests, probably just to shut me up. A few weeks went by and then I got the call. "We'd like you to come in for a follow-up appointment." That phrase always makes your stomach lurch a bit, doesn't it? I sat in the chair, trying to look calm while fiddling with the strap on my handbag. The doctor came in, shuffled some papers and then hit me with it. "You have polycystic ovaries," he said. I blinked. "Right… and what does that mean?"

He didn't pause. Didn't soften the blow. Just looked straight at me and said, "It means you'll find it very difficult to have children." He had all the bedside manner of a fed up parking warden on a double shift. I felt like someone had pulled the floor out from under me. I nodded dumbly, trying to take it in, but inside I was spiralling. I didn't have anyone I wanted to have kids with at that exact point in my life, but the idea of not being able to? That stung. It felt like someone had quietly closed a door behind me and bolted it, without asking.

I left the surgery in a daze, blinking into the daylight like I'd just been walloped with a frying pan, and what did I do next? I headed straight to the supermarket and wandered the aisles in a zombified state, grabbing crisps, chocolate, doughnuts, anything with sugar, salt and absolutely no nutritional value. I just needed comfort. Something I could control. I got home, put on my comfiest joggers, curled up on the sofa, stuffing my face. Every mouthful was a mix of sadness and rebellion.

Take that, useless body, I thought. You can't tell me what to do, but I'll tell you what I will do: eat my weight in jam doughnuts and still be here tomorrow.

Chapter Seven

A few months later, it was a normal Friday night and I was plonked on the sofa, watching *This Life*. If you've never seen it, it was this brilliant '90s TV series about a group of law graduates navigating life and love in London, but I wasn't watching for the drama, I was watching for Ferdy.

Ferdy, played by Ramon Tikaram, was dark and brooding, with a long thick ponytail. He played Warren's boyfriend in the show and as their romance played out on screen, I remember thinking, 'God, he's gorgeous. I love him'. Yes, yes, I know falling for a man who is into men, heard that one before Cheryl. But he was just so handsome. He didn't even have to say much; he just had to smoulder into the camera and I was gone.

Then, another thought popped into my head, 'I'm going to go out tonight and find myself a Ferdy.'

So, I grabbed the phone, called a mate and a skip, a jump and a tube ride later, I was walking into a bar in London. And just like an unrealistic romantic comedy – there he was, my real-life Ferdy.

He was muscular, mysterious, with long dark hair – and even better than that, he was staring right at me. "Hi," he said, swirling a whiskey glass in his hand. "I'm Jay."

We got to chatting and he tells me he is from Afghanistan.

"Where is that?" I ask. Geography was never my best subject and he explains, telling me in very broken English that he is a refugee, having just fled the Taliban. He had been trying to get to America, because he had family there, but somehow through some twist of fate he was here next to me.

Time seeps into the early hours and we stayed glued to the spot, chatting about our lives. He struggled to articulate lots of things due to the language barrier, but I felt I understood him and we arranged to meet again. Then again, and again.

Before I knew it, we were in a relationship. Jay was a Muslim, but he didn't need me to cover up my body or anything like that. He wasn't a strict one, as he drank alcohol, but he did pray every day. I'm not religious, so I assumed all hell would break loose when he told his parents, who had fled to Holland, that he was with me, but it didn't.

Jay was also 10 years younger than me, so he was only in his early twenties. Given his refugee status there were, of course, some elephants in the room. One evening, while I was washing dishes, I summoned up the courage to ask him. "Are you going out with me because I am British or something? Is it a passport you want? What do you want?"

He looked stunned. "No, no I love you. That is the reason," he insisted.

Just as well, because only six months into our relationship, I discovered I was pregnant. I bawled in the bathroom. It was a miracle, a total miracle. I had been told by a doctor that I couldn't have a child naturally due to my polycystic ovaries – and now this.

Jay was equally pleased and we moved in together in South London, into a little flat in Woolwich with thin walls and dodgy central heating. It wasn't glamorous, but it was ours. My acting dreams were put on the back burner when I met Jay and I trained to be a Crown Court Usher, a job I worked in throughout my pregnancy – it was a means to an end and nothing more.

One evening, after seeing a friend, I met Jay following his shift doing Pizza Hut deliveries by the North Woolwich Tunnel. He smelled like pepperoni and petrol. As we were walking along, he turned to look at me and my growing bump and said, "Well, we might as well get married then."

It wasn't a question, more of a statement. But I agreed. Looking back, it was hardly romantic. There was no engagement ring, no bended knee or big proclamations of love, but at least we were going to be a family.

And then my world changed forever. On 28 June 1999 Jay and I were slouched on the sofa, half-dozing and half-watching some rerun of a show we'd seen a hundred times, when suddenly I felt it. A sharp pang, low and sudden.

"Ooh," I said, clutching my belly. Then came another and then another and just like that, I knew I was in labour. The thing was, I was 33 and had a planned C-section booked in. My baby boy was already measuring very large inside the womb which had caused me to become diabetic. He was too big to deliver naturally, the doctors had said, so everything had been scheduled: calm, clinical, under control. But babies, as it turns out, don't give a toss about plans, he had his own ideas.

Unlike my mum – who gave birth after concealing her pregnancy – I did have someone with me who knew what was going on, but still, I envied her. She got driven to the hospital. Me? My waters broke but I had to take the Number 177 bus. Yep, the bus.

BEHIND THE SCENES

Jay didn't drive and we were skint at the time. The idea of splashing out on a taxi apparently didn't occur to either of us, or maybe we were just in shock. Jay followed behind on his motorbike, weaving through traffic behind and popping up at traffic lights to wave madly at me through the scratched-up plastic windows like he was in some low-budget rom-com. "I'll see you there!" he shouted, as if I was off for a pedicure and not in active labour.

By the time we got to the hospital, the contractions were coming thick and fast, like tidal waves of agony rolling through me with no mercy. I could barely walk and a nurse took one look at me and shouted for a wheelchair. I was whisked onto the ward and the pain was like nothing I'd ever felt. Deep, bone-crushing, soul-splitting pain that swallowed me whole. They gave me an epidural and, for a while, it seemed to work, but then... it wore off.

And when it did, I was screaming and begging. "I can't do this! He's not coming out!" I sobbed. "Just get a hammer and hit me over the head! I want to die, I don't want to do this anymore!"

The midwives were trying to stay calm, but the tension in the room had shifted. I could see it on their faces, real panic, the kind they try to hide but can't quite manage. The baby's heart rate was dropping fast.

Suddenly it was all systems go. People were shouting and rushing around. I heard someone say "emergency C-section" and before I could take another breath, I was being wheeled down the corridor under glaring lights. That's the last thing I remember.

I woke up in the hospital room, alone. No doctors, no

nurses, no Jay and no baby. Just silence. I turned my head and saw an empty cot beside me with a photo of a small baby placed next to it, which was captioned "Baby Campbell" – I wasn't yet married and this was my legal name.

Panic jolted through me. Where was he? I felt sick, I couldn't breathe, then I heard a strange, guttural cry. It was loud and wild and full of pain. It took me a few seconds to realise this sound was coming from me.

"Where is my baby? Is my baby dead?!" I screamed. My voice was hoarse and hysterical. A nurse burst in and tried to calm me down.

"He's in intensive care," she said. "But he's okay. He's going to be okay."

There had been complications. The cord had been wrapped around his neck. Jay came in a few minutes later, eyes wide, exhausted but smiling. "He's beautiful," he said. "And he is huge, he weighs ten pounds."

Two days later, when I could finally sit up, they wheeled me into the neonatal unit to see him. He had lots of wires going into him, he was yellow because of jaundice, he had a thick head of hair and two teeth, but he was completely beautiful.

The incubator made this strange humming sound, like a small engine. The air smelled of antiseptic and plastic tubing. I sat by his side, listening to the rhythmic beeping of the monitors, terrified of what might happen if one of those sounds changed. It was a world of numbers and charts and silent prayers.

I couldn't hold him at first. He had been starved of oxygen during birth, so they put him on all these drips and were monitoring his blood, his sugar levels and all that. There were too many wires, tubes, beeping machines and I could only put my hand through the little incubator door after scrubbing up like I was entering a clean room at NASA.

I spent lots of my time pumping to try and give him milk, but nothing was coming out. I felt useless, because I felt like I couldn't be a mum as much as I wanted to. There was this baby that I was told I couldn't have right there in front of me, I couldn't hold him or feed him. It was like someone saying I'd won the lottery, but they weren't going to give me the cheque.

For that first week, I was there every day, two or three times a day, trying to express milk, or sitting next to him. All I could do was talk to him and sing to him. I just hoped he would hear me and know that I was his mum. I sang anything I could think of from Donny Osmond to Cliff Richard and music in the charts at the time, anything with love in it.

After a fortnight I could finally hold him, cradling and kissing him even though I was still in a wheelchair. And after four weeks of sleepless nights and worries, I was finally able to take him home. We chose the name Alex, largely because it was the only British name that Jay knew how to spell as he wasn't very good at writing in English at that time. "We can call him after Alexander the Great," he said proudly.

And great our son truly was. Jay and I were both completely in love with Alex. We were besotted, really, just smitten with this beautiful big baby we'd somehow made. Jay was a hands-on dad. His son was his pride and joy in those early days and he really did muck in with everything; nappies, night feeds, winding, walking up and down the hallway at 3am. But if I'm honest, I was grateful for that help because I wasn't in a good place physically. The birth had been very traumatic and it had really taken it out of me. My body felt wrecked and to make matters worse, I started bleeding and didn't stop. It wasn't your usual post-birth bleeding either, this was something else.

For the best part of a year, I bled constantly. I couldn't leave the house without enormous blood clots suddenly falling out of me. I'm not exaggerating, I had to wear actual baby nappies because normal sanitary pads just couldn't cope, they'd leak within minutes. I was changing them every 20 to 30 minutes, just to keep going. If I had to nip down to the baby clinic to get Alex weighed, I'd have to pack three or four nappies just for myself to change.

Even just walking from one room to the next left me breathless and faint and I felt trapped in my own body, like it wasn't mine anymore. I lost my appetite, then found it again in comfort food. The fatigue was bone-deep, not just tiredness, but this fog of exhaustion that sat on my chest and wouldn't let up.

It was horrendously degrading and there were days I didn't recognise myself in the mirror; pale, puffy, barely functioning. I couldn't work, I could hardly go out. I was physically drained, emotionally fragile and silently wondering if I'd ever feel like me again.

One day, my friend Naomi dragged me out to B&Q for some air and a bit of normality. We weren't even two minutes into the shopping trip when I had to rush to the toilet again. I came out, defeated, clutching yet another nappy and she looked at me and said, "Cheryl, this really isn't normal. You need to get this sorted."

She was right, of course. I went to the doctor, finally pushed for answers and, after a long conversation, I was fitted with a Mirena coil which changed everything. The bleeding gradually eased, my energy started to come back and slowly, so slowly, I began to get back to me.

People don't talk enough about the aftermath of birth. They talk about the miracle of it, the joy, the surge of love and that sweet baby smell. And yes, it is a miracle, but it can take a lot of grit to recover from and that suffering is too often done in silence.

So if you're reading this and you're in the thick of it, if you're bleeding, aching, crying in the middle of the night, wondering if you're doing any of it right, I see you. I've been you. And I want you to know: you're doing better than you think and you're not alone.

Chapter Eight

"He's gone! He's gone!" I screamed. "Quick, stop the car!" It was the middle of the night on Blackheath roundabout and Jay leapt into the back seat to help our tiny baby.

He lay Alex's limp body on a mat and started giving him baby CPR, while I looked on in horror. "Please be okay, baby. Please be okay baby," I said over and over. After what felt like hours, but was probably less than a minute, Alex's tiny frame splutters, his eyes flicker and pink starts to return to his face.

And just like that… the colour seeps back into my world too.

Jay scoops him up, rocking him gently as tears stream down both our faces. Neither of us speak for a while – we were too shaken, too stunned. It's not the sort of thing you can ever prepare for. One moment you're singing lullabies, the next you're begging the universe to give your baby another breath.

It wasn't just a one-off though, this unfortunately happened very often when Alex was a baby. He had febrile convulsions; terrifying fits brought on by sudden spikes in temperature. One minute he'd be fine, the next he'd go rigid, stop breathing, or collapse without warning. Every single time, it felt like I was watching my baby die and those were, without question, the scariest moments of my life.

BEHIND THE SCENES

As any new mum knows it is a joy to get your baby to go to sleep, but when Alex was in the cot I didn't shut my eyes much. I was constantly worried that he would stop breathing, so I was wracked with worry and the sleep deprivation and anxiety meant I was constantly on edge.

It's the reason I am completely sober and haven't touched a drop of alcohol since I became pregnant with Alex. Not because I had any kind of issue with drinking, not at all, but because I'm utterly terrified of not being in control, of not being able to act if something goes wrong.

Just the thought of a sip of wine makes me feel unsafe, like I am dulling my instincts, numbing my reactions – I needed to be on red alert 24/7. It was exhausting, but it became second nature.

Even now, decades later, that feeling hasn't left me. A few years back, I was holidaying in Majorca with Steve McFadden, who plays Phil Mitchell on *EastEnders* and he turned to me and said, "It's alright Cheryl, you can have a glass of wine. Your son is miles away and he is safe." But the answer is still the same. I feel I need to have my wits about me just in case of the worst.

That may sound dramatic to some, but once you've stared down the barrel of that kind of fear, you don't ever want to be caught off guard again. I made a promise to myself and to Alex, to be there. Every second. Fully present.

That fear never fully leaves you, does it? I am sure anyone out there who has had a sick child, or knows someone that has, will agree it changes you as a person in ways that you can't even describe.

Despite our constant fears about Alex, Jay and I finally tied the knot when he was about six months old. We didn't have much money, but we wanted to make things official for our son, and Jay was very traditional.

Every girl dreams of her wedding day, don't they? A vision in white, a dashing groom, a string quartet playing softly in the background while your guests dab away happy tears with monogrammed tissues. A cake so beautiful you don't want to cut into it and someone wafting past with flutes of champagne on a silver tray.

Yeah... that wasn't mine. Jay and I married in May 2000 at Woolwich Registry Office and in front of a few friends and family members I became Cheryl Saddiqi. It wasn't exactly a fairytale wedding. In fact, I didn't enjoy the day one bit. We then had a terrible reception under the fluorescent lights of our local community centre, which had all the charm of a dentist's waiting room.

Jay turned up with a massive black eye because he'd been mugged two nights earlier while working a shift on his Pizza Hut delivery bike. So in all our wedding photos, he looks like he's just gone 12 rounds with Mike Tyson. He also looked very young and very scared. Me? I was wearing this off-white twinset that made me look like I was chairing a Women's Institute meeting. Cream, short-sleeved, slightly shapeless. With my short hair and tired eyes, I looked about 50 and I had just had Alex so I wasn't feeling very attractive.

If it weren't for my lovely friend Naomi who catered the wedding and my friend Christine from college who went above and beyond with flowers and some second-hand decorations, we would've had nothing but a few folding chairs and a stack of paper plates. They did their best to bring a bit of sparkle to a very drab setting and bless Christine, she did a good job with what she had.

Some of Jay's Afghan relatives came along and they seemed to have a good time because they were dancing all night. At least someone had fun because Alex, my beautiful baby boy, screamed through the entire thing. He cried, he howled, he wailed like a banshee and no-one could settle him. He wasn't poorly, he was just... done. We all spent most of the reception taking turns to wheel him around the hall in his pushchair, trying desperately to soothe him like a set of knackered zoo-keepers. It was like a relay – "Your turn. I've done five laps already."

There was no first dance. No romantic toast. No magical moment. We didn't even go on a honeymoon.

One great sadness was that my mum wasn't there at my wedding. She'd been by my side throughout my pregnancy, but we had a falling out just before Alex was born and weren't on speaking terms. You know those arguments that start small but somehow snowball into something ridiculous? It was one of those. Pride got in the way and before we knew it, weeks turned into months. I kept telling myself, "I'll call her tomorrow", but Mum and I were both as stubborn as each other.

A few months later, in the evening, the doorbell rang and I remember thinking, Who on earth is that at this hour? I wasn't in the mood for visitors and assumed it was probably a nosy neighbour or someone trying to flog dodgy double glazing, but when it buzzed again, something in my gut told me to go to the door.

It was my half-siblings Helen and Glen, standing there on

the doorstep, their faces ghostly pale. My stomach flipped before they even spoke. "We... we've got something to tell you about Mum," Glen stammered.

I knew, instantly. I felt the blood drain from my face and time seemed to slow down.

"She passed away this evening," Helen said gently. "We've come straight from the hospital."

Their voices became a distant hum, like I was underwater. Everything around me blurred. My eyes drifted to the stereo across the room where the display was flashing the words: Goodbye. Goodbye.

It always did that when it was switched off, just part of the system rebooting, but this time, it felt different. It felt personal. After Helen and Glen left, I walked over to the stereo, intending to turn it on. That's when I noticed, it wasn't even plugged in.

My eyes welled up, Mum had always believed in the afterlife and so did I. We'd made a pact, if one of us passed first, we'd send a message, some kind of sign, and there it was, a final goodbye, right in front of me.

I was broken, wracked with guilt – she had never even met Alex. She died at just 52 from heart complications, right before her triple bypass surgery. That evening, she'd been out with Helen who later told me that she had said, "I'm going to get in contact with Cheryl. I need to make things right."

She was going to pick up the phone. She was going to reach out, but she never got the chance. I should have got there first and that thought will haunt me for the rest of my life. I know she's still with me, though, I can sense she is around. She would have been beside herself when I got the call for

EastEnders, because she loved that show. When I first joined the cast in 2007, I swear I could feel her on set with me. I'd sit in Albert Square on Arthur's bench and talk to her.

"Mum, I've done it. I'm here. Pam St Clement is just like you, she even looks like you, she's my adoptive mum now." I'd sit there, chin up to the sky, half-laughing, half-crying, imagining what she'd say. "Oh, my girl, you always were a show-off."

And I'd whisper back, "I miss you so much, Mum. I hope I've made you proud."

Chapter Nine

After my mum's death, being in London didn't feel the same and I needed a change, So, in 2001, we moved up to Salford, to a council estate, for a fresh start in a city neither of us really knew.

Jay set up a small security firm while I handled the admin, balancing spreadsheets in between nappy changes and nursery runs. Alex was enrolled in a daycare a couple of days a week and, funnily enough, he was with the twins who played Bethany Platt in *Coronation Street*. Due to child labour laws, roles involving kids are often played by twins. One day, I got a call from the nursery. "Mrs Saddiqi? Alex has pulled one of the girls' hair." Well, I suppose my son had a knack for terrorising soap stars.

He was a difficult child – loud, full of boundless energy and oh, how he could scream. Proper, ear-splitting, soul-rattling screams. There were times I thought I'd lose my mind. But he was also my bright, funny and curious little boy and I loved him beyond words. I would do anything for him.

My marriage however was not what I had hoped it would be. With Jay, it felt like everything we did was what he wanted to do; I was isolated and seeing my friends less and less. If I wanted to go see someone he would ask, "Who are you going to see?" and also, why was I going? I always found that last one a bizarre question because I wanted to see my friends because it was time for me to enjoy and have fun.

But he didn't like it. He'd say, "What? So you expect me to look after Alex on my own?" I'd try to explain that I had Alex all day and he had freedom because he was going to work and seeing friends, but I was just stuck at home. That I didn't have any time to myself and I felt like I had lost me and I didn't know who I was anymore. But he'd just go, "You sound stupid, Cheryl. Stop talking rubbish." It did not seem that we were a team.

I thought, is this love where you do all these things for somebody, but they don't really do anything for you in return? I didn't have much to compare the relationship to, apart from Pete. That had been so different, he had been romantic, thoughtful and kind – Pete had tried to make me happy. He had brought me flowers just because, made me laugh until I wheezed and listened, really listened, when I needed to talk. But then I thought, well, Pete was gay, so maybe that wasn't real true love. Now I know that it was, but back then I was lost and very alone, even though Alex was by my side.

The same year we moved to Salford, the world changed. Two passenger jets, hijacked by Al-Qaeda, crashed into the Twin Towers in New York. A tragedy that sent shockwaves across the globe, but for us, it also changed things closer to home. My name was Cheryl Saddiqi and people on the estate knew that Jay was Afghan. There had always been a certain edge, a fizzling of hostility just beneath the surface, but after 9/11, it boiled over.

One afternoon, I was out walking with Alex, pushing him in his stroller, just trying to enjoy the crisp air. As we crossed the road, a young woman's voice rang out. "Oi! You dirty Afghan lover!" I wheeled Alex up onto the curb, slowing to a stop, my mind scrambling. Surely, she didn't mean me? But then she was there, up close, her face twisted with hate. And before I could react, she spat, the glob of saliva landing on the pram. On my baby's pram. "That's for 9/11," she hissed, before marching off, head high, as if she'd just done her civic duty.

I didn't say a word. I couldn't. I just stood there, frozen in shock. My husband had fled Afghanistan as a refugee, he was not a terrorist sympathiser, he was a victim. He hadn't been safe in his own country and now, it seemed, he wasn't safe here either – and neither was our son.

Alex started to cry and the sound snapped me back. I leaned down, kissed his cheek and turned the pram around, walking as fast as my shaking legs could carry me back home. The moment I got through the door, I grabbed a cloth and scoured the pram, scrubbing and scrubbing as if I could wipe away the racism, as if I could cleanse the world for my son.

That evening, I waited for Jay to come home, my anger simmering, my stomach still knotted. When he finally walked through the door, I told him what had happened and he sighed, shaking his head, then pulled me into a hug. "I'm sorry, Cheryl," he murmured against my hair and then, just like that, he was gone again, heading out for another job.

He'd started doing that a lot lately; popping home for a quick meal before disappearing into the night. He'd sit down, shovel in his dinner with barely a word, then mutter something about work or a friend needing help before grabbing his keys and vanishing. He'd been a hands-on dad at first, changing nappies, doing the late-night feeds, but more and more, I felt like I was raising Alex alone. Bath time, bedtime, the tantrums, the cuddles – it was all me – and while I didn't mind being there for my son, it hurt that Jay no longer seemed interested in being part of that world. There was a distance between us now. That aching hollow loneliness was settling in.

Things took another turn for the worse one ordinary morning when Jay and I were getting ready to go shopping. I was wrestling Alex into his car seat, which felt like trying to get an octopus into a jam jar. "Come on, love, work with me here," I huffed, finally clicking the buckle into place. He giggled, his little legs kicking against the seat like it was the funniest thing in the world.

I climbed into the passenger seat, frazzled but ready. I pulled the seatbelt across my body and then it hit me. A scent. Light, sweet, floral and powdery, but definitely not mine.

"Jay, why can I smell women's perfume on the seatbelt?" I said, sniffing it again like a bloodhound. He barely looked at me.

"I don't know what you're talking about."

"The seatbelt. It smells like some woman's perfume," I said, staring at him now. "And it doesn't smell like mine."

He snapped his head round, a flicker of annoyance flashing in his eyes. "You're imagining things, Cheryl."

"I'm not. It's strong. I can smell it right here." I held the strap up to my nose again, as if that might prove my point.

Jay let out an exaggerated sigh, drumming his fingers on the steering wheel. "It's probably one of the lads from work. Their aftershave or something. You're being paranoid."

"Oh, come off it. Since when do the boys at your security firm smell like a duty-free perfume counter?"

He turned away, staring out of the windscreen. "Are we going shopping or what?"

There it was, defensiveness wrapped in deflection. He was a little too quick to dismiss and a little too sharp with the tone. To this day, every time I get into a car and pull on a seatbelt, I sniff it. It's instinctive, a reflex I can't shake. The scent of betrayal, it's lodged somewhere deep in my memory, impossible to scrub away. I began to suspect that my husband was cheating on me, but I tried to convince myself I was wrong.

"I am crazy. I am not being cheated on. Anyway, with all the weight I have put on since childbirth, I should be grateful to have a husband like Jay. Who else could ever want me?"

These were the things Jay tried to make me believe whenever I confronted him. He would explode in anger, twisting my doubts against me, making me feel small, making me feel like the problem. But deep down, I knew, I felt it in my gut.

One day a phone bill came through the post, with a list of calls to a number I didn't recognise. My hands trembled as I punched the digits into the keypad and when the phone dial tone rang, a woman answered.

"Hello?" I hung up. I did this a few times, each time pressing *141 in front of the number so she couldn't trace the call. I just couldn't believe it. I didn't want to.

I confronted Jay again. "I know you're cheating on me. How could you do this?"

His whole body stiffened and his eyes turned black with rage. He called me crazy. He called me disgusting. He called me every name under the sun, ripping apart my looks and size and then, before I could react, I was against the door, then falling to the floor as he walked right past me and out into the night.

That was the moment I knew I should leave him, but how could I? I didn't have a single penny and he was Alex's dad after all and maybe he'd bumped into me? Maybe it was my fault. Maybe I was wrong about the cheating? Maybe I am worthless. Dark thoughts swam around my mind.

But I knew how it had made me feel. We didn't talk about it, I never confronted him. Instead we just continued as normal. Him making excuses to shirk his responsibilities and me left sitting alone with Alex. Alone and miserable.

But the phone was beckoning me and I decided to ring the number again. "Hello?" she said. I hung up. I rang again, "Hello?! Who is this?" said a man's voice. It was Jay's. I put the phone down, his words still ringing in my ears. My blood ran cold.

"Graeme, will you come with me," I asked, a few days later, after some solid detective work on my part. I knew where Jay and this other woman were meeting, in a disused car showroom that his firm were doing security for. "I want to confront them." We got in the car, with Alex in the back and Graeme drove to the location. When we arrived, I took a deep breath and walked up to ring the buzzer. "Jay, I know you're in there. You need to come out and talk to me." A long pause. Then, "I can't come out. Go home."

"No, Jay," I said, my voice steady now. "You need to come out. It's important. Alex is here and so is Graeme. We've driven all this way." Silence. Then, finally, the door buzzed open.

I stepped inside and was met with a sight that made my

stomach turn. A dingy, makeshift love nest. A mattress on the floor. The place littered with little touches of them. A space they had claimed, built, lived in while I sat at home believing his lies.

And there, perched on the dirty bed she shared with my husband, was a skinny blonde woman, sipping a bright blue WKD like it was the most natural thing in the world. Jay stood next to her, caught in the headlights, but still silent, still unwilling to give me anything. Not an apology, not an explanation, not even an ounce of shame.

The woman explained that Jay had already separated from me and that we were getting a divorce, so he had obviously been lying to her too. "He told me you were long gone," she added, only half apologetic.

All the belittling, the control, the bullying and the gaslighting. The physical assault. He'd made me feel it was all my fault, that I was disgusting and worthless. And now, the final truth. Something inside me snapped. That night, I packed up the car, chucking all my possessions into black bin liners, strapped Alex into his seat and drove to London, leaving my marriage, and Jay, behind.

Chapter Ten

London had been so exciting when I was younger, so full of
promise, adventure and the kind of chaos that felt exhilarating.
I had moved there to 'be somebody' and now, here I was,
arriving back a failure. Everything felt overwhelming as I
drove into the capital, with the car boot crammed full of my
life and little Alex wailing beside me.

We moved in with my friend Naomi for a few days and she
was an angel – properly took us in, fed us, gave us space to
breathe. But Naomi had her own life and a husband and kids
to take care of. There was another problem too. Jay knew
where Naomi lived and he was threatening to take Alex away
from me and I couldn't deal with that. He was my boy and I
wanted to protect him. I needed a proper way out.

So, I made a decision. I packed up what little I had and
went to a women's refuge in Dartford. It was behind a main
road and tucked away from view, but the unsuspecting town
house was a safe haven for at least eight women and their
kids, at any one time.

Inside, Alex and I were given our own small room with a
bunk bed. The walls were bare, the furniture basic, but as I
plonked myself down on the bed I felt something I hadn't in
a long while: safe. The refuge staff were wonderful, they were
trained counsellors, so you could just go and talk to them

and it didn't feel like a session. They would just sit with a cup of tea and ask how you were and if there's anything you need.

Alex, thankfully, was only four and young enough not to fully understand what was happening. He played with the other kids, shrieking with laughter in the garden, which was full of donated toys from tricycles to dolls to swingsets and games. He was happy in those moments and I clung to them like a lifeline. But then, out of nowhere, he'd stop. He'd look up at me, wide-eyed and ask, "Where is Dada?" And just like that, my heart would break all over again.

Some nights, I'd wake up to the sound of women sobbing in the corridor. New arrivals, clutching their children, wearing the fear they had escaped from like an invisible cloak.

Some women stayed for weeks, others for months. Everyone had a different story and while some were too afraid to tell theirs, others shared them in hushed voices over tea and biscuits, their words carrying the weight of unspeakable things. Although I was grateful to be there, some of these conversations made me feel like I was a fraud. I'd look around and think, Oh God, that woman's much worse off than me. Look at her black eyes. Look at her bruises. Look at her broken wrist. Her kids saw that. They lived through it. That's terrifying. I remember whispering to one of the counsellors, "I feel like I shouldn't be here. Like I've taken someone else's space."

She gave me a look. You know the one; half sympathy, half 'don't be so bloody daft.' Then she said, "Cheryl, abuse isn't just about bruises. It's about control. It's about fear. It's about how someone can be made to feel worthless just with words. That's just as damaging."

Still, the days stretched on, long and empty. I didn't know

what to do with myself. Some afternoons, Alex and I would sit in the car park, watching that old clock on the nearby building, just to pass the time. Every hour, Hansel and Gretel would pop out from a tiny door below the clock face and Alex would giggle, his little hands clapping in delight. Anything to make Alex laugh – it kept me going.

But that handsome funny little boy was very hard work, bouncing from tantrum to affection in seconds. He'd scream, throw things, make his tiny presence very known. Then, just as suddenly, he'd stop, lift his little arms to me, demanding to be picked up, as if none of it had happened.

Alex was my world, the one thing I knew I'd done right and every night, as I lay there in that tiny room, staring up at the ceiling, I'd make a promise to him in my head: "I don't know how yet, but I'm going to make this better. I'm going to build us a life. I don't want to let you down."

It wasn't quite so simple, however. Jay had been trying to contact me constantly since Alex and I left and after months of living in the refuge, I finally gave in. Even with everything we had been through, guilt was creeping in. Was it fair to keep Alex from his dad? Even if Jay and I weren't together, I still wanted them to have a relationship. I thought about my own mum and the pain of not having let her into Alex's life. So, when he rang for what must have been the thousandth time, I answered.

By that point, about four months into refuge life, I was growing more confident. I was still waiting for housing, but the heartbreak had dulled. "Hello, Cheryl. It's me, Jay. Please don't hang up. Just let me see my son. Please," he begged. I paused. Then, finally, I said, "Okay."

We started with supervised visits in one of those small, sterile rooms where everyone pretends it's normal, even though it's anything but, and Jay seemed different, he was softer, kinder. Alex was over the moon to see him and I couldn't take that happiness away from him.

Eventually, we moved to a meeting in a park in Dartford. Watching Alex run around, laughing with his dad, made my heart ache and the thought crept in unbidden that maybe, just maybe, Jay had changed. Then, after eight months in the refuge, I got a council house, a fresh start and a clean slate. Three weeks later, Jay moved back in.

Anyone would be screaming, "CHERYL, NO! DON'T DO IT!" And, believe me, hindsight is a smug little so-and-so, but at the time, I wanted to believe him. I needed to. He was saying all the right things too.

He told me he loved me, that he'd be there for Alex and he banged on about how sorry he was. I bought it because the alternative was admitting that some people never change and, well, I thought I needed the help. It was 2003 and Alex was nearly at school age and raising him all by myself was a lot.

Jay got a job at a shopping mall and Alex and I would meet him for lunch. It was… fine. Not perfect, but not awful either and we'd sit in the food court, munching on chips or a slice of pizza, trying to make it feel like a little family outing.

This time around I felt – and, in retrospect, justified it to myself – that Jay and I being together wasn't really about us, I just wanted Alex to have a dad. We acted like a family again, cooking dinner, sitting on the sofa and watching telly like we were just a normal couple. I wasn't happy, not really, but I told myself I was fine and, some days, pretending was easier than facing the truth.

There wasn't really any love or romance, but I wanted what was best for my boy and I felt that having his father in his life was it. Suck it up, Cheryl, I thought, life isn't all romance, rainbows and butterflies. It's about nappies and bills and keeping the peace. Perhaps true love wasn't something that was meant for me.

Chapter Eleven

Slowly, quietly, I started edging back into acting. I didn't even have an agent at the time, so when Alex was off at nursery or school and I had a quiet moment in our second flat, I started writing to agents, explaining my situation. That I was a mum, that I couldn't tour, that I couldn't be away for long stretches, but I was available, I was ready and I wanted to work.

Then along came Howard Cooke – my agent for many years until recently. He believed in me and took a chance on me, which I am so grateful for. Soon, I was back on telly. I did a stint on *Casualty* – a big deal at the time – and I was thrilled. Then in 2004 came *Little Britain*, where I worked with Matt Lucas and David Walliams. David played Linda, "the big fat lesbian", as my character Joanna Harding oh-so-delicately called him. They gave me a short, scruffy wig and ten fake piercings. I looked like I'd crawled out of Camden Market's lost property box.

During the scene, David kept corpsing. Every time I opened my mouth, he'd burst out laughing. "Stop it, Cheryl. Stop it!" he kept saying.

"I'm not doing anything!" I said back, which only made Matt start laughing too.

At the end of the day, David asked me to go for a walk which was a bit odd, actually. He was quiet, thoughtful and we just strolled along, me wondering if he was going to tell me off for making him laugh, then he turned to me. "Did you enjoy filming today?"

"Yeah, it was fun," I said, a bit cautious.

"Well," he said, "Matt and I – well, we only usually laugh at each other. Not at guest performers. Not unless they're long-term cast."

I froze. "Okay…?"

He smiled. "I just wanted to say, you made us laugh. A lot. You were very funny. I wish we had more roles for you, but everything's already been cast."

I was floored. I'd always known I could get a laugh just from pulling a face, but hearing that from them was something else. Maybe it had helped wearing Ronnie Barker's old trousers after all?

Around that time, I also did an episode of *Doctor Who*, just one, but it was still another big deal. I played Mrs Lloyd, a woman during the Blitz of London, who was ushering people into air raid shelters, and looking after her family. Not long after, I was performing in *Mother Courage*, a Bertolt Brecht play at The Scoop which is the famous outdoor amphitheatre near the River Thames and Tower Bridge in London, when a man showed up at the dressing room door with a life-sized Dalek, just so I could sign it. He hadn't even seen the play, he'd just travelled across the country for my autograph, after seeing me briefly in the cast.

Honestly, I wish I'd been paid in memorabilia for that job rather than money, it would've saved me a fortune. Why? Because Alex, he didn't care when I was on *EastEnders*, not one bit, in fact, he found it all a bit embarrassing, but *Doctor*

Who? That was a different story. Suddenly, I was cool and every bit of money I made went on *Doctor Who* stuff. Cards, books, toys, DVDs and posters. He had the lot.

Then, in 2005, I was cast in *EastEnders*. *Duff, duff, duff, duff...* Or not. Here's something many people won't remember, except the die-hard fans. Two years before I played Heather Trott, I was in a single episode as 'Meg'. I looked nothing like Heather. My hair was slicked back, I had a prison uniform on and I put on this gruff, almost Phil Mitchell-like voice. My scene was in a prison cell. Big Mo, played by Laila Morse, came to visit me and at one point, I mentioned some 'lairy cow' kicking off inside. That 'lairy cow' was in fact Kat Slater, Jesse Wallace's character. She was making her big return to *EastEnders* and no one knew.

Still, I was thrilled just to be in the show – Graeme and I had been obsessed with *EastEnders*. Obviously we loved *Corrie*, but I remember watching the first episode in our flat when we were at drama college. It was so exciting, starting with a bang with a pensioner being murdered in his flat. Funnily enough, the way I got the role came down to a connection I'd made nearly a decade earlier. Back in 1996, when I was in a play with the lovely Anita Dobson, there was a woman named Julia who was friends with the director and would bring us cups of tea and sit in on rehearsals. One day, she left, saying she'd landed a new job at the BBC.

Years later, I found out that Julia had joined *EastEnders* as their casting director and she was the one who suggested me for that first prison role. I remember turning up and being pointed towards a Portakabin, there wasn't much fanfare or red carpet for the small roles! I met Leila and Jesse and it was surreal, standing on a set I'd watched on TV for years. I hadn't done that much telly at that point, some bits and pieces here and there, but this felt huge.

After filming, I caught up with Julia to thank her very much for the role. "You're welcome," she said. "You did great. You never know. If the character comes up again I will give you a call." I didn't hold my breath though, that's the nature of acting; you take the job, do your best and move on.

For the next couple of years, that's exactly what I did. I focused on being a mum and, finally, after months of persistence, nagging the school, chasing doctors, pushing for answers, I finally got Alex properly assessed. The diagnosis came: ADHD and Autism. Just like that, so many things suddenly made sense.

The big meltdowns, the screaming and shouting over things that seemed tiny to everyone else, the way he'd destroy something one minute then curl up in tears the next; it wasn't naughtiness or bad behaviour. He just didn't have the tools to cope with the world in the way it was being handed to him.

It explained why he couldn't eat certain coloured foods, or why he hated when anything on his plate touched. God forbid beans dared to invade the mashed potato territory. It also explained the way he'd line up all his toys in perfect rows, with such meticulous attention it would make a librarian weep.

At first, a doctor prescribed Concerta, a slow-release form of Ritalin which is a stimulant to help manage the symptoms of ADHD. And while it did help him focus, I quickly realised it was dimming the brightness in my little boy. He was quieter, more compliant during the day but the sparkle in his eye faded until the medication wore off. I didn't want a "manageable" child if it meant losing who he really was.

I made the decision to take him off the medication and lean into a more holistic approach. We focused on understanding him, not changing him. We learned what worked and we talked it through in a way that made sense to him.

I also leaned into his passions, especially Lego. He could sit for hours, completely absorbed. Slowly, we built a toolkit of strategies that helped him navigate the world on his terms. Understanding how his mind worked meant I could support him properly and this was the biggest win of all.

Acting-wise, I kept trucking along – bits in *Bad Girls, The IT Crowd* – but hands down, one of my absolute favourite jobs (if not my favourite day ever) was when I was cast in *The Life and Times of Vivienne Vyle*, alongside my comedy idol, Jennifer Saunders.

Now, don't get too excited, My role was "Fan with Baby" which was hardly a difficult part to get to grips with considering I was already a mum and a die-hard Jennifer Saunders fan. It was a one-day shoot and I spent most of it in a car with her I was too shy to talk to her. I only had one line, but honestly I barely remember delivering it. I was too busy internally combusting over the fact that I was sitting next to Jennifer flipping Saunders. It felt like I'd somehow wandered onto the set of *Ab Fab*, which Graeme and I used to quote obsessively.

It wasn't a big acting job. It wasn't going to make me a household name. But, to this day, it remains one of my all-time favourites, just because I got to work with one of my faves. Even if my career wasn't soaring, I was still doing what I loved; earning a living, telling stories and feeling lucky every step of the way.

Then it came… the big one.

The sun blazed down as I walked through the gates of Elstree Studios, my heart pounding in time with my footsteps. This was it, the audition. I signed my name in the book at reception, the pen scratching against the paper and headed into the waiting room.

Where was everyone? I was expecting a sea of women who looked just like me – 20-odd big girls of varying ages, all clinging to their scripts like life rafts, silently sizing each other up in quiet competition. That's how these things usually go, but no, this time the room was empty. My stomach twisted, had I got the wrong time? Was I late? I looked at my watch, 4pm, that's what they said, wasn't it?

Trying to steady myself, I pulled out the script. Heather Trott. Who is she? A small part, I assume. I'd been practicing for weeks, but still, I have no idea how big the role is. I flicked through the pages again, mouthing the lines to myself when a man pops his head around the door.

"Cheryl… Cheryl Fergison? Can you come this way please." I followed him into the auditioning room.

"We've got this new character and we'd like to see how you read for it," says a casting director, pen poised. Showtime.

Nerves fizzled under my skin and the air was cool, the studio lights buzzing faintly. I can barely remember what happened next; just flashes. A read-through with another actor, a camera rolling, the feeling of slipping into someone else's skin, the lines I had rehearsed over and over tumbling out and my voice filling the space. Who was the other actor?

I couldn't tell you. What was the scene? Not a clue. It's funny, the way adrenaline makes everything blur.

At one point, I caught a glance at the casting director's face, watching me intently, nodding slightly. Was that a good sign? Or was he just being polite? After what felt like both a lifetime and five minutes, it was over and I thanked everyone, walked out of the audition room and took a deep breath. What now? Usually, there would be a debrief in my head; a checklist of all the things I could have done better, moments I stumbled on, words I could have delivered differently, but this time, I felt good, hopeful even. I didn't want to jinx it, but something inside me whispered, that went well.

But in this industry, you never really know. Being an actor is about make believe and half the time we use that skill to pretend we are not crushed when inevitable rejection comes. Being told 'no' after you put your all into something is part and parcel of the job.

You can't return to *EastEnders* in a different role until two years are up and it had almost been that since I had played Meg, so I was crossing my fingers. But I wasn't just holding out for *EastEnders*, as there was something else hanging in the balance too – a big theatre tour with the legendary Dame Edna Everage, the alter ego of Aussie comedian Barry Humphries. I'd done several auditions to be his sidekick and there had been a lot of back and forth between my agent and Barry's team.

I'd been waiting to hear back for weeks and the excitement was unbearable, this could be a game-changer. It was the kind of role that would catapult me to another level, a real turning point in my career. So, I did what all actors do after an audition: I waited. And I waited. And I convinced myself that I must have got the part.

Then my agent called.

"Hello, Cheryl. Barry's people called… they've decided to go with someone else."

The words hit like a punch to the gut and my heart sank. "Did they say why?" I asked, already bracing for the answer.

"Not really. Something about someone else being better for the part." Better for the part. Ouch.

I forced a laugh, pretending it didn't matter, but inside, I felt crushed. No matter how many times you hear 'no' in this business, it still stings. Unless you're Al Pacino, rejection is part of the job, but knowing that doesn't make it any easier.

So, I did what I always do when I feel like total crap, I went to Asda.

As I've said before, food has always been my comfort, my reward, my escape. If I'm happy, I eat. If I'm sad, I eat. It's a cycle I've battled for years and that day, I let myself lean into it. I grabbed a trolley and started throwing in everything I loved from biscuits, crisps, microwave meals, the lot. Screw it, I thought. I deserved a little indulgence.

I wandered up and down the aisles in a daze, the rejection still sinking in, gnawing at the back of my mind. Should I have done something differently? Would it have changed things? Maybe I just wasn't meant for that role. Maybe something else was waiting for me.

I was down by the frozen aisle, staring at a chocolate cake, when my phone rang again. I groaned. What now? I didn't want more bad news so I let it ring for a second before answering.

"Cheryl, it's me again," my agent's voice was breathless.

I sighed. "Howard, I swear to God, if this is more bad news I don't think I can take it."

"It's *EastEnders*," he says. "You've got the part."

I froze. "What? What do you mean?"

Howard repeated, more excited this time, "You got the role on *EastEnders*!"

I blinked. Was he joking? Was this some cruel trick to soften the blow of the last rejection? "You must be winding me up," I say, still staring at the frozen items.

"No joke! Look, it's not much at the moment, it's only for four episodes, they want to see how it goes," he adds. "But you did it. You're in!"

Four episodes? That was more than enough for me. "This is fantastic! I am going to be on *EastEnders* again," I squeal.

I abandoned my trolley right then and there, sprinting out of Asda like a woman possessed, leaving behind biscuits, crisps and that stupid chocolate cake.

I had bigger things to celebrate, I was going to be Heather Trott, whoever she was. I just hoped it was a good part and there was lots to work with. Come on Heather, we can do it!

Chapter Twelve

On my very first day on the *EastEnders* set, Linda Henry, who played my character's best friend Shirley Carter, turned to me and casually asked, "Do you smoke, Cheryl?"

Now, I didn't smoke and never had, but something about the way she said it, so cool and confident, made it feel like a test I didn't want to fail. I was a bit scared of her, to be honest, so I replied, just as breezily, "Yeah, sometimes."

"Great," she said, flashing me a grin. "I'm going out for a menthol. You want one?"

"Yeah, go on then," I said. She handed me this slim, elegant Vogue cigarette, the type that looks like it belongs in a 1970s Parisian film. I took it, lit it and tried not to choke. That evening, I went home and bought my first pack of cigarettes and just like that I became a smoker.

Thing is, that first cig wasn't really about smoking, it was about connection, it was how Linda and I first bonded and became mates, just as Heather and Shirley were. She looked so cool, with her angular cheekbones and cropped blond hair, but the characters she played sometimes scared me. I mean, come on, she was terrifying in *Bad Girls* – proper hard. We'd never worked together before *EastEnders* and of course Shirley Carter was a tough nut too. So I get it, I really do, when people conflate me with Heather, or shout at Steve McFadden in the street because of how Phil behaves, I was guilty of the same thing. You see these powerful performances and think, "Blimey, I bet she bites."

But Linda? Well, she was actually really lovely as well as hilarious; warm, sharp as a tack and so full of life. And what we had on screen became real off screen too, it wasn't forced, nothing about our friendship ever was. You hear stories in this business, actors thrown together who can't stand the sight of each other, who can barely be in the same room, let alone pretend to be best mates and that just seems like hell to me. Imagine doing all those intimate scenes and not getting on. Luckily for me, it was the total opposite.

It might sound cliched, but the *EastEnders* set really is like one big family. When I arrived in May 2007 to play Heather, everyone was immediately welcoming. These were people I'd watched on screen in my favourite soap and adored, from Dame Barbara Windsor as Peggy Mitchell to Linda, as well as Cliff Parisi who played Minty Peterson, Diane Parish as Denise Fox, Steve McFadden and the iconic June Brown who played Dot Cotton.

The list goes on and on. Every single one of them was lovely, including the hardworking crew. There was a real sense of camaraderie, and from the moment I stepped onto that iconic set, I felt like I belonged, even if I was still pinching myself that I was actually there.

The atmosphere was unlike any other job, no one had an ego and no one dominated over the rest, that wasn't the vibe and it went against the ethos of the show. After all, we were portraying everyday people in an everyday world, just mucking in and doing our best. Of course, that's if you exclude the murders, scandals and crime that filled our storylines! There was a lot of laughter off-camera too though. Some of my happiest memories involve giggling in the green room over a cuppa, sharing stories and watching as the cast and crew pulled together to make magic happen on screen. It was a well-oiled machine and I was grateful to be part of it.

The show is filmed in eight-week chunks, but it wasn't long before I grasped the gravity of what being part of *East-Enders* actually meant – it isn't just a TV show, it is a part of people's lives. Early on, we shot a scene down on Brighton Pier with Shirley Carter (Linda), Gary Hobbs (Ricky Groves) and Dawn Swann (Kara Tointon). On the other side of the tape, a crowd of fans gathered, watching us and shouting out the characters' names. "Shirley! We love you! Dawn! Garry!" It was nerve-wracking, knowing people were watching me work in my new job. I hadn't even appeared on screen yet, but I found myself wondering: would they ever be shouting my name?

A lot of people were there for Linda, who had a massive gay fan base thanks to *Beautiful Thing* and *Bad Girls* and Brighton, of course, has a big LGBT+ community. Linda, always generous, didn't let me feel like an outsider. She walked towards a gaggle of fans to sign autographs, but quickly called me over "Cheryl!" she said, her pen nib poised on a fan's poster. "This is Cheryl. She's playing a character called Heather and you'll all know about her soon. You better get an autograph now!" With her encouragement I signed my name on the poster too and as the ink dried I felt like one of the gang. That's just the kind of person Linda is, big-hearted, supportive and always looking out for others.

That scene on the pier was part of a horrible storyline where a man had made a bet with his mates that he could kiss Heather. He'd been chatting her up and she couldn't believe her luck because Heather never really believed in her luck when it came to love, but then he cruelly revealed, "I pulled the pig." Even though it was fiction, it was a harsh reminder of how cruel people can be to those who are different and I felt for Heather.

During the same episode, after belting out some karaoke on the pier, I had to go on a roller coaster while looking for Garry. I went on it twice for the close-up shots, but for the wider ones, they used a stunt double and then the roller coaster broke down! There I was, looking up at someone who vaguely resembles me, stuck in the sky. I felt guilty, to be honest, Imagine landing a gig on *EastEnders* and the first thing you do is put your stunt double in peril.

While originally, I was only contracted for those four episodes, they kept pulling me in for meetings to flesh out Heather's character. They had given me four wonderful meaty scripts – the *EastEnders* writers are the best in the biz – but they always wanted me to come to the table with ideas and give my input.

They told me, "Cheryl, we want you to come to us with a backstory for Heather." That was such an exciting opportunity. I knew that to play Heather convincingly, I needed to give her depth so she wouldn't just be a figure of fun.

The next day, I walked in with this mega backstory. I went all out, where she came from, what her childhood was like, how she knew Shirley. I even gave Heather her signature headbands, which I actually really grew to regret because those hard ones pressed onto my temples ended up giving me headaches for years. I had to switch to softer headbands in the end, as it was hard to concentrate, but those details mattered. I wanted Heather to feel lived-in, like she had history.

In meetings with the writers I told them the story of why Heather wore hairbands which is as follows: Heather's mum was always cruel to her, she was always saying you are too fat, or you're this and you're that. She was a bit clueless as a child and she was easily led, that's why someone like Shirley became her best mate at school. It started because she would get me to go into certain shops and nick make-up for her and I would do it like a little puppy. Heather depended on Shirley and Shirley soon came to depend on me too.

But Heather wore headbands because her dad left when she was a child, he walked out on her and her mum. She remembers the day that he left because she was wearing a headband and he said, "Oh, you look so beautiful. You look so lovely in that headband, how pretty you are Heather" and she never saw him again. That's why she always wore a headband every day after that, because it was the kindest, nicest memory of her dad and then he was gone.

Linda and I would also have long conversations about our characters' back stories, how Shirley, who was tough as nails, would be friends with the naive and jolly Heather. They were chalk and cheese – Heather would have to be the cheese, of course, on account of her obsession – but their friendship worked. I'd also chat with the wardrobe designers, discussing why Heather, who loved frumpy colourful clothing, leggings, ballet pumps and mismatched clothing, would dress like that. A lot of work goes into these characters that pop up in living rooms across the country at tea time and through all of this I was able to build up a vision of a character who became a part of the *EastEnders* family. Just like I had. I wasn't just playing Heather, she was going to become a part of me for the rest of my life.

On 26 June 2007, Heather Trott arrived on the nation's TV screens and she certainly did so with a bang. Okay, not literally a bang, although it did end on a cliffhanger as to whether she had slept with Garry after they woke up in bed together.

My first scene was Heather, all dressed up, tottering along wearing a red anorak with a white handbag and carrying a karaoke machine. She's heading to her friend Shirley Carter's party, knocking on her door at last. She fancies Garry straight away, gets drunk, ends up hitting a bloke over the head with her handbag and then boom! She wakes up in bed with Garry. What an entrance!

I watched the show on the sofa in my council flat I shared with my husband and son. Jay was out, as he often was, but I tried to get Alex to look at Mummy on screen. Of course, he wasn't interested, he was far too focused on his games and given what happened in the episode, that was probably for the best. "Mum," I whispered, after the closing theme tune played. "I told you I would do it."

Chapter Thirteen

"*EastEnders, Eastenders, EastEnders, EastEnders.*" Soon that phrase was whispered wherever I went and I used to say it sounded like a steam train and if you repeat it out loud, you might see what I mean. Although I loved meeting fans of the show, I didn't like the whispering. It sounds a bit like tutting to me and I don't like tutting because it reminds me of being back in the supermarket or somewhere with Alex when he was younger. He'd be having a meltdown on the floor and people would walk past and tut. It made me feel like a terrible mother.

But once you get a big role on a show like *EastEnders*, it's part of the territory that you become the character and you are no longer known by your real name. My life changed almost overnight and every time I left the house people would shout "Oi, Hev! Heather Trott!" at me, but I didn't mind. *EastEnders* is beloved by the audience, they get to know the characters, they follow their stories and they care about their lives, so I was always happy to stop and have a chat.

Dame Barbara Windsor, who has always been a hero of mine, fast became a friend on the show's set. I'd have to pinch myself as I sat in her dressing room gathering all the pearls of wisdom she generously shared. She used to tell me, "Keep your troubles inside your house, darling. When you go out there, when the public are there, just keep smiling. Put on a show and always smile." And she was absolutely right, that kindness costs nothing, but later I did find this to be hard when my heart was breaking and times got tough.

To be honest, all these years later people still call me Heather in the street. It's nice to know that Heather made so much of an impact, that people still remember and love her. It's only in the last five years or so that some strangers call me Cheryl because they know me from my TikTok or Instagram videos. But back in 2007, I was getting recognised a lot and I used to say I felt I was responsible for a lot of the UK's fitness regime because people will walk towards me, do a double take, walk past me, then they would run back and go in front of me, not say anything and then run back again. They were literally doing laps around me!

While it was lovely getting recognised by *EastEnders* fans, I didn't much enjoy it when paparazzi or journalists would make their way onto the estate, but more fool them, as they didn't bargain for the fact that I had many friends in the traveller community who lived in and around the area. There was a fabulous woman called Betsy who lived in one of the flats next to mine and she was sort of the matriarchal figure. She was elderly lady, who was large in both character and size, with a voice like Lou Beale. She had this lovely long dark hair and wore gold around her neck and rings on her fingers and it was her who spread the word to "protect Cheryl".

So when journalists or photographers would come sniffing around saying, "Oh, we hear that Cheryl Fergison who plays Heather Trott on *EastEnders* is here?" they would say, "What do you want? Piss off mate!" They were very, very protective of me, they knew I was on the telly and they liked talking to me about it and they were all very kind. The travelling communities often get a lot of grief, with people saying they are bad apples, but that was never my experience. I had a lot to thank them for and they were true friends.

Although the travellers were able to shield me from nosy journalists when I first started out on the show, it was impossible to protect Alex from navigating his mum's newfound fame. He was just about to turn eight when I first appeared on *EastEnders* and because of his ADHD and learning difficulties he was at a Special Educational Needs (SEN) school. I think he found it hard going to school, with everyone knowing who his mum was and he did get other kids laughing at him and teasing him saying, "Oh, your mum was in bed with someone on telly last night."

He describes it as being very difficult to make friends at that time, because he didn't know who liked him or who liked him because the kids, or the parents of the kids, wanted them to go play at a house where Heather Trott lived. So he had to cope with quite a lot, alongside his own challenges, about who true friends were and who he could trust. His mum was on one of the biggest shows on television, it was set in London and he was living in London, he was bound to get a lot of flack for that and he did. I don't really think I understood that at the time. I tried to protect him, but how do you shield a child from something so big?

And Heather Trott was a larger than life character. There was something about her that just captured people's hearts. Yes, she was naïve, but she was also kind. She was passionate and she wore her heart on her sleeve. She loved cheese so much that she worked on the supermarket cheese counter, until her inability to resist sneaking chunks got her fired. She adored George Michael so much that she went rifling through his bins. Okay, that's not exactly something to be proud of, but Heather's intentions were always good and that's why people loved her.

Heather was hilarious, but she was also a fiercely loyal friend. She had a childlike innocence and I think that's why kids loved her so much too, they saw themselves in her – silly, playful and always getting into scrapes. But life wasn't kind to Heather, she faced more than her fair share of struggles from money woes, carbon monoxide poisoning, asthma attacks, heartache after heartache and yet, through it all, she never let the world crush her spirit. That's what made her special.

While I do truly love Heather Trott, I am not her – although, over the years, that became harder and harder to convince people of. For one, I can stand up for myself; Heather, bless her, never could, she needed her friends for validation. And then there were her body image issues, she never saw herself as beautiful, never believed she had any value because so many people put her down. I, on the other hand, took a different approach. Maybe deep down I still have my own insecurities – and I certainly did when I was younger about my body – but now I refuse to let them show. Life's too short to care about what people think of your appearance and if they don't like it, well, tough.

From the very first episodes, it was clear what Heather meant to people. Take the infamous 'Pull a Pig' scenes. So many people came up to me afterward, telling me it had happened to them. Others were shocked, horrified that something like that could be played for laughs. And that's the beauty of soaps, isn't it? They open up conversations, they challenge people's perspectives, some even asked if I was offended to be acting in that scene, playing 'the pig', but I wasn't. Whenever I put on that headband and looked in the mirror, I didn't see Cheryl staring back at me. I saw Heather.

But from the very first moment I stepped into Heather's ballet pumps people have thought that Heather Trott and Cheryl Fergison are the same person. When I meet people, sometimes I actively try to not be like her. Maybe I've been a little brasher, a little louder, just to prove the point because while I love Heather and I'll always defend her, I also know who I am. Cheryl Fergison. But when I pop to the shops later on someone will probably say "Hi Heather!" and that is okay too.

Things were going well for me in that first year after joining *EastEnders*. I was making money and I mean proper wads of it. I'd never had much before and I certainly hadn't grown up with it. So just like Mum and John used to do with their limited income, I was spending money like the taps had been turned on full blast... water through my fingers.

But I wasn't buying fancy handbags or designer shoes. No, my version of luxury was treating others. I was booking trips for Jay, Alex and me, to Holland to visit Jay's family and to Disneyland Paris because, let's face it, nothing beats watching your kid's face light up when they see Mickey Mouse for the first time.

Being able to spoil Alex felt like a reward in itself. We'd been through a lot, the two of us, it hadn't always been easy and there'd been some tough years. So seeing him happy, really happy, gave me the biggest sense of joy and if he wanted new trainers, I could get them for him. I bought him all the latest gadgets, PlayStations, Nintendos, Game Boys, you name it, every game under the sun and of course, his bedroom was like a shrine to *Doctor Who* filled with figurines, posters, sonic screwdrivers… the lot. You half-expected the TARDIS to be parked by his bed.

Jay didn't go without either. I bought him a motorbike and when he went and wrote it off (don't even ask), I bought him another one. That one cost me about nine and a half grand, which is absolute madness, but at the time, it just felt good to be able to do it.

I was even quietly saving for a deposit on my first proper home, And while there was never a great romance between Jay and me, I felt, for the first time, like my life was starting to come together.

I had an amazing job, proper recognition for my work and colleagues I loved. I genuinely enjoyed going to work every day. We had a holiday booked for Disney World in Florida and I couldn't wait. Everything was going well until one day there was a knock at the door.

I opened it and there stood Michelle, my neighbour Gina's daughter, looking like she'd just walked out of a particularly traumatic episode of *EastEnders* herself. She was crying and clutching a laptop like it was a cursed object. "Michelle?" I said. "What's happened, love?"

She just shook her head and held out the laptop. "I didn't know what to do so I came over," she said, voice cracking. "I saw it on Facebook and I thought… you should know."

I squinted at the screen and there he was. Jay, my husband,

was kissing another woman like it was some giddy teenage romance. I scrolled further down on the computer, and there were more snaps of her and him. A proper timeline of the betrayal.

He had the gall to post it on his Facebook, publicly for everyone to see. It wasn't hidden and it wasn't a secret and I didn't have Facebook, so I'd been completely in the dark. None the wiser, it was like he was making a total mockery of my life and I had just been sat there planning our trip to bloody Florida while he was out playing tonsil tennis with some blonde woman in a low-cut top.

Talk about not even trying to cover your tracks. At least have the decency to cheat in private. I didn't cry or scream or break anything, I just stared at it and thought, Oh my God… he hasn't changed. Because the truth is, I wasn't heartbroken. Not like the first time. Back then, years earlier, when he cheated on me, I genuinely felt like someone had ripped my heart out and stamped on it. I couldn't eat, I couldn't sleep, I cried so hard I thought my ribs would break. I thought I loved him. But this time I just felt… nothing.

Not devastated, just done. "A leopard doesn't change its spots," I said out loud, more to myself than anyone.

Michelle wiped her face. "What are you going to do?" I didn't reply. I just went inside, picked up my phone and dialled his number and he answered on the second ring. "Hello?" he said.

"Hi, Jay," I said calmly, far calmer than I felt. "I've seen the photos on Facebook. Michelle showed me. You know I don't have Facebook, so of course you thought you could get away with it. But let me tell you something, you've taken advantage of me and you've embarrassed me. I have a reputation to uphold now, I am on TV, this is embarrassing."

He tried to interrupt but I cut him off. "You need to make an excuse to leave work. Now. Come and get your stuff. I'm not leaving the house this time. You are. I don't care where you go." He came back like a shot, tail between his legs. There was pleading, there were excuses, the usual promises of change and "it didn't mean anything" nonsense.

But I'd heard it all before. The record was scratched and I was no longer buying what he was selling. "Just go," I said firmly. "Get out. I'm not leaving this time. Off you go."

And just like that, he grabbed his stuff and left.

A few days later I told Jay I was filing for divorce on the grounds of adultery and what did he say? "You committed adultery first."

I stared at him. "What are you on about?"

"You went to bed with Gary," he said, all serious, like he was a barrister in court presenting his strongest evidence.

I laughed. "Jay. That was on telly. It was acting. I didn't actually sleep with Gary, who is a character, we had a scene. There were cameras, scripts, a whole crew!" But he was adamant and couldn't be reasoned with. As if my job on *East-Enders* somehow counted as real-life infidelity. Just goes to show how disillusioned he was, or how desperate he was to wriggle out of the guilt… again!

Anyway, he was out of the house, but he still saw Alex, of course, I wasn't about to cut him off from his son, no matter what had happened between us. As for me, I packed my bags and went to Disney World with Gina.

Now, Gina wasn't just a neighbour, she was like family.

She was a bit older, had helped me out with babysitting Alex over the years and had this warm, no-nonsense energy that I absolutely loved. So we thought, sod it, why not have a proper knees-up with Mickey and the gang?

We had a whale of a time, ate too much, laughed till our ribs hurt, screamed our heads off on the roller coasters. I went from splitsville to Space Mountain in a matter of weeks but when I got back, it was time to focus on the future. Jay was gone and I was ready to start again, properly this time so I threw myself into house-hunting, imagining a little place for me and Alex. I had the money, after all and although the travellers protected me from the press I did still want somewhere calm and private to raise my son.

The first few viewings were… well, disappointing, to say the least.

One place smelt of old fish fingers and marjuana, another had wallpaper that looked like it had survived four different wars, but then, I found it.

A little bungalow, detached and tucked behind another house, so it had total privacy, which, for someone who played Heather Trott, was exactly what I needed. No one walking past my window doing a double take and whispering, "Is that her? The one from *EastEnders*?" It was close to Alex's dad too, which was important, as we were co-parenting, and near his school. I didn't want to uproot his world more than it had already been.

The house itself was perfect.

A big back garden where Alex could run wild and lovely wooden floors. A cosy room for the two of us, a little conservatory at the back that just let the light pour in. The kitchen was tiny, honestly, if you turned around too fast, you'd end up in the fridge, but I hardly cook, so I wasn't too fussed about that.

We had a little puppy, Rosie, a Jack Russell which had been given to us by Betsy and the travelling community. She used to chase Alex in circles through the house, he'd run from the living room to the hall to the kitchen and back again, laughing his head off and watching him like that, so full of life and laughter, made me realise we were going to be okay.

When I finally got the keys, I just stood there for a moment on the threshold, completely still, soaking it in – this was ours, our fresh start. I thought back to our little room in the women's refuge, with the bunkbed and I felt tears in my eyes. How far we had come – I was so happy I could've burst.

I bought Alex a foosball table for the dining room and that became his games den, he had all his consoles in there, all his posters. It was his haven, his little kingdom and the conservatory… that was mine.

I filled it with my instruments, my guitars, my music stuff. I treated myself to two massive white garden chairs; they were ridiculously expensive, but gorgeous. I'd planned to put them outside, but they were too nice for the British weather, so I parked them proudly in the conservatory and perched in one like the Queen of Sheba. Outside, we put in an above-ground swimming pool to splash about in during summer and it was bliss.

Even with everything that had happened, when I moved out of the flat, I let Jay keep it. It was a council place and I wanted Alex to still have access to his old room and familiar surroundings when he visited his dad. I thought I was doing the right thing for Alex and that it made sense, but of course, like so many things with Jay, I lived to regret that.

All that mattered at that time was that Alex and I were safe and happy. We had Rosie, we had each other and we had a lovely bungalow with sunlight and music and a foosball table.

I felt like I was building something. Something real and something ours.

Chapter Fourteen

There are jobs you do to pay the bills and then there are jobs that feel like a gift. Working on *EastEnders* was the latter. It didn't just give me a regular and large wage or the chance to act every day, it gave me a second family, and in that family, my on and off screen partner-in-crime was Linda.

We had a lot of laughs and fun, but we also worked really hard and we later found out the crew called us "the bankers" which meant that they could bank on us. Some actors needed loads of takes, but we'd usually nail it in one or two so they'd schedule us at the end of the day, to help catch up if they were running behind. We were their little safety net.

Although, we weren't always perfect and there was one day, we just couldn't stop laughing. We were filming this really serious scene, meant to be full of tension and one of us, I can't even remember who started it, cracked. Before we knew it, we were like two naughty schoolgirls, sat on the sofa in the Queen Vic, clutching our stomachs, tears streaming down our faces.

The director was fuming because time is money and all that and after a few failed attempts to bring us back into line, he finally snapped and ordered everyone out. "Clear the set!" he shouted. "Everyone out, sound, camera, lighting. All of you!"

We were stunned, but Linda, being Linda, just looked at me

with that mischievous grin… and burst out laughing all over again and so did I.

Eventually, the crew filed back in, faces half-hidden behind their hands, trying not to laugh themselves. We said, "We're so sorry! We're done now! Promise!" but as soon as we started filming again, I caught sight of the boom operator trying to hold it in, his shoulders wobbling like jelly. It was contagious, one of those days where laughter takes over and there's no going back.

We spent a lot of time together off-camera too, she would accompany me for lunch where I would have my "special sandwich" which people thought was disgusting, but I can promise you it was delicious. It was peanut butter on one side, marmite on the other piece of bread and in the middle it was filled with cottage cheese. I would order it every day in the canteen and before you judge, give it a try if you like these ingredients.

Linda's dressing room became our little hangout where we would run lines, share snacks and gossip away. We also lived in the same general direction, Linda in South London and me on the Kent border, so I often drove her home after work.

If one of us finished hours earlier than the other, we didn't mind waiting. She'd say, "What time are you wrapped?"

"I don't finish 'til seven," I'd say, knowing she was done by three.

"All right," she'd shrug. "I'll wait." And she would. We had so many laughs on those drives home. We'd sing along to the radio, prank call daft numbers, you name it. One day, we were driving behind a van that had one of those "How's my driving?" signs with a number to call. Linda immediately grabbed her phone.

"I'm going to ring and tell them how brilliant he is," she said.

"Go on then!"

She rang up and gushed to the poor person on the other end, "I just wanted to say, this driver's wonderful. Absolutely textbook driving. Couldn't fault it."

Next thing we know, the driver pulls up next to us at a set of lights, winds down his window and says, "Oi! Heather Trott and Shirley Carter!" and gives us a big thumbs-up, honestly, we were howling.

Then when David Essex joined the cast as Eddie Moon in 2011, our antics reached another level.

Even though I'd always argued that Donny Osmond was better when I was a kid, I still thought that David was a music legend. I used to do this impression of him and Linda would not let it go, she'd be in fits of laughter and egg me on constantly. "Go on Cheryl, do David Essex in front of David Essex," she'd say, poking me in the ribs.

"Linda, I can't, that's so embarrassing!" I would moan.

"Oh come on! Play your guitar! Sing 'Hold Me Close'!" And before I knew it, there I was, standing there with my guitar, belting out 'Hold Me Close' in front of the actual David Essex. He just laughed and clapped and said, "Go on, Cheryl!" Bless him.

I might've betrayed Donny just a little that day, but I tell you what, it was worth it – definitely a bucket list moment. Those days were the best of fun, full of laughter and joy.

It wasn't all just a big laugh though. One day, when Linda

and I were driving home from work, my car started playing up, you know the kind of spluttering, coughing noise where even the car sounds like it's saying, "I've had enough." We just about managed to chug it into a petrol garage, by the skin of our teeth, but that was it, the poor thing had given up the ghost.

We were in North London, not far from Steve McFadden's house, so after I phoned the recovery people, I gave Steve a quick ring. "Steve, we've broken down," I said. "We're just around the corner from you–" and before I could even finish the sentence, he cut me off.

"Stay there," he said. "I'll be right there." He hung up.

Next thing we know, not ten minutes later, Steve pulls up in his Rolls-Royce Corniche, no less. I mean, honestly, it was like a scene from a film. There we were, two stranded women in a knackered old banger and along comes Steve in this gleaming convertible like a soapland superhero. I was fully expecting, at best a lift home or maybe just a cup of tea while we waited for the recovery truck. But no, Steve hops out and says, "Here, take the Rolls. Use it till your car gets fixed."

I actually laughed. "What? Are you joking?"

"No," he said, totally serious. "Go on. Take it."

I looked at Linda. Linda looked at me. It was like someone had handed us the crown jewels. "Steve, come on," I said. "We can't borrow your Rolls-Royce!"

But he insisted. "Take it. It's just sitting here otherwise. You're not going to leave it at the garage, are you?" Well, I mean... what could I say?

The recovery guy took my poor little car off to the garage, I bundled Linda into the Rolls and off we went, cruising through Peckham like a right pair of celebs. We had the roof down and Linda was doing Queen-like waving at everyone we passed. I was driving like Parker from *Thunderbirds* and she was Lady Penelope, shouting out the window, "Hello darling!" at baffled pedestrians.

"There go the *EastEnders* lot," they must've said. "In a flipping Rolls-Royce now, wow they are doing alright!"

When I finally dropped Linda off and headed home to my little bungalow, I had a dilemma. I couldn't exactly park a Rolls-Royce on the road outside – not in my area. It'd be on bricks by breakfast. So I knocked on my lovely neighbour Doreen's door.

"Hi Doreen," I said. "Any chance I can park a Rolls-Royce on your drive?"

"You what?" she exclaimed. I nodded.

"Yeah… long story."

Thankfully, her drive was long enough to tuck it away safely and for about four glorious days, Linda and I drove to and from work in Steve's convertible Rolls. The whole thing felt so wonderfully surreal but it really showed what sort of person Steve is.

People see this tough guy on telly, Phil Mitchell, all furrowed brows and clenched fists, but in real life, he's generous, grounded and kind-hearted. I mean, how many Rolls-Royce owners do you know who'd happily hand over the keys to two giggling pranksters without a second thought?

As time went on and as Linda and Steve's characters got closer on set, the three of us became a bit of a gang. Steve was the king of *EastEnders*, Linda was the queen and I suppose I was their court jester or lady in waiting, or something like that. I didn't think I was on their level but they treated me like I was.

They were more than just colleagues, they were proper mates. I am even godmother to Steve's daughter Frankie and we support each other to this day. They are good, decent people who looked after each other and me, in a job that could sometimes feel overwhelming.

And no matter how many dramatic scenes we filmed, or how many breakdowns I had (cars or otherwise), it was those moments, the laughter, the unexpected joyrides, the friendships that made it all so special.

There's no doubt the *EastEnders* cast is full of absolute legends and Dame Barbara Windsor was definitely one of them, nothing seemed to faze her. She was funny, warm and totally unflappable, just pure class.

One day, Barbara and I were on location filming a wedding scene for *EastEnders*. It was at a church, though I can't quite remember whose wedding it was. Patsy Palmer was there, Sid Owen was around too and loads of the cast were in attendance, all done up in their wedding gear.

As usual on those days, we'd popped back to catering for lunch. The catering tent was a bit of a walk away from the church so after eating, we were making our way back to the location, walking together, arm-in-arm and nattering about lunch, the scenes ahead and bits of gossip.

We weren't walking alone, there were a couple of security people nearby too. Whenever we filmed outside like that, especially with big names like Barbara around, security was always close by.

We were walking through this quiet little park, taking our

time, when out of nowhere a man, wearing a long rain coat, suddenly leapt out from behind a tree, stood right in front of us and flashed his private bits at us. Now this had obviously been pre-planned, because there was a paparazzi there ready to take that picture of our reaction to it.

I was shocked, but Barbara? She was cool as a cucumber, turned to me and completely deadpan, said, "Oh darling. That's not much to show off about, is it?" I burst out laughing. It was so her – dry as anything, completely unfazed.

Sure enough, the next day, the photo was in the papers. I think the whole thing had been arranged by the flasher and the photographer working together, hoping for a dramatic reaction and a bit of scandal, but you had to get up very early if you wanted to shock Dame Barbara Windsor.

The other true icon of the *EastEnders* family was, of course, the one and only June Brown as the equally iconic Dot Cotton.

She was a complete original, funny and sassy – totally a law unto herself and whenever I picture her, it's with a cigarette in one hand, a wicked smile on her face and a knowing glint in her eye. There was one night in particular that sums her up perfectly. It was 2012 and we were all off to a posh do in London because Barbara had been honoured as a Lady Ratling, which sounds like something out of a *Carry On* film, but is actually a really prestigious honour in showbiz circles. It's part of this old society made up of people from the entertainment business called The Grand Order of Water Rats. Very fancy, very traditional and a big deal in the showbiz world.

The event was held at a grand hotel in London – picture a big reception room done up like a wedding, you had a long top table where the guests of honour sat and since Barbara had invited June and I and some others from the cast, we sat there too. So there we were, sipping on drinks while clapping politely, enjoying the speeches and the laughter, all very civilised.

Now, June, just like Dot, loved a cigarette. That was her thing. Vogue menthols, usually. Elegant, thin, the kind of cig you could imagine Marlene Dietrich holding with a long black glove. But this hotel had a strict no-smoking rule, obviously, so if you wanted to smoke, you had to make a full-on trek, through the banquet hall, out into the reception area, down a flight of stairs and then out into the chilly London night.

But June, well, she wasn't having any of that.

Instead, she slid down under the table, as casual as you like and lit a cigarette right there under the cloth. Next thing I knew, these little curls of smoke started drifting up beside me.

Every so often, she'd pop her head up for a sip of wine, then duck back under again for another drag. It was like she had her own private smoking den beneath the top table. That was June, unapologetically herself, always cheeky, always glamorous and never one to play by the rules if the rules didn't suit her. She was an absolute diamond and I feel lucky to have shared a table and a bit of second-hand smoke with her.

Chapter Fifteen

Awards are awards and I suppose you're meant to say they don't really mean anything, that it's the work that counts, not the recognition. And yes, to some extent, that is true. Every actor on TV is doing the same job and half of it's down to what storylines you're handed. Actors would be nothing without the writers, let's be honest, they're the real talent, they build the world that we get to live in.

But in 2008, I won the Inside Soap Award for Best Comedy Performance and let me tell you, I was absolutely buzzing. It was my little Oscars moment, something I'd dreamt of since drama school, where I'd stand in front of the mirror, gripping a shampoo bottle and practising my acceptance speech in full performance mode.

And there I was, not a shampoo bottle in sight, in front of all these people, in my best black dress and hot pink lipstick, the lights shining bright and my heart doing somersaults in my chest. I felt good, this was my night, but more than anything, I couldn't believe I was there. Me, a girl from a council estate, who grew up in hand-me-downs and with pay-as-you-go electricity, standing on a stage being celebrated for doing the job I loved.

How on earth had that happened? How did I end up on people's televisions, living my dream and winning an award on top of it all? It felt like magic. Pure, dizzying, dream-come-true magic. I wish I could tell you what I said when I got up there, I really do, but it's a blur. All I remember is the noise, applause, cameras flashing and this panicked voice in my head saying, "Don't say anything stupid. Don't embarrass yourself. Don't try and be funny because it might fall flat. Don't hog the mic. Thank your agent, thank *EastEnders*, thank everyone. Don't mess this up."

All I really wanted to say was, "This is fucking brilliant. This is amazing. I wish my mum could see this. I hope I've made her proud. I hope I've made my son Alex proud."

All that night, I was on absolute cloud nine. I don't drink or do drugs but I remember thinking that this must be what being high feels like. Not 'I've lost my tongue on a space cake' kind of high, but that euphoric, floating feeling. I felt like I was underwater, I could barely hear what people were saying, the sound was all muffled and everything was glowing and surreal. I had this award in my hand and I was carrying it around like a baby. I didn't let go of it, not once, it was mine and it wasn't leaving my side.

I laughed, I smiled, I did interviews and I posed for pictures, I was fully in the moment. I had such a good laugh with the *EastEnders* lot, chatted to soap stars from other shows and for a little while, I truly felt like I was part of something special. Then, as the night wore on, people started peeling off; heading to clubs, afterparties, someone's house for drinks. My gang tried to get me to come along.

"Come on Cheryl, just for an hour!"

But I was hungry and for me, food has always been something I could go to for comfort or reward. I was looking forward to treating myself when I got home with a posh ready meal from M&S and some handpicked snacks I'd bought earlier in the week. I deserved some delicious food tonight, surely? It was a special occasion.

Besides, Alex was being looked after by Jay for the night, so the house was all mine. I said my goodbyes, waved everyone off and slid into a taxi with my award still clutched in both hands.

When I got home, the little bungalow glowed softly. I'd left a warm yellow light on in the conservatory and it looked welcoming, cosy and safe. I stepped through the door and wandered through the rooms, smiling to myself, this was my house, I'd bought it and I owned it. How far I had come.

I started thinking about where I should put the award, my little golden moment. Some people put theirs in the toilet, something about not taking yourself too seriously, but I wasn't sure, was that showing off? Too cheeky? I tried the mantelpiece but it looked a bit odd there, like it didn't belong. I took it through to the conservatory, which overlooked my lovely garden, sat down in one of those big white chairs I'd splashed out on, placed the award on the floor by my feet and just… sat there.

The room was quiet and still, it was the middle of the night and the glowing lamplight was catching the shine on the award. I should've felt triumphant and content, but I didn't, instead, out of nowhere, a wave of sadness washed over me, big and heavy. I started to cry, just quietly at first, then all at once came great, gulping sobs. I cried and cried and cried. Because even though I'd just won something amazing, even though I'd been onstage, seen and celebrated, I had no one to come home to, no-one to throw their arms around me and say, "Well done, babe." No one to make me a cuppa or cuddle up to on the sofa and whisper, "I'm proud of you."

It was just me and I was alone in the silence. I got up, went to the kitchen and opened the fridge. I ignored the lovely M&S meal I'd planned, all the little treats I'd lined up. Instead, I just started eating. Cheese, crisps, toast, toast, toast again, then more cheese, then crisps. I was bingeing, properly bingeing, eating past full and ignoring that tight, heavy feeling and just carrying on. I was stuffing down everything I couldn't say out loud.

I would stop to guzzle litres of Diet Coke, the caffeine buzzing in my system like a warning bell. I felt sick and exhausted, but I couldn't sleep, I just kept crying. I didn't know who to call and if I did I would have been too embarrassed to explain. I thought people would say, "What's wrong with you? You just won an award! Why are you down?"

But I couldn't cut myself a break because yes, I'd won, but I was alone. I was divorced, I wanted a special love, I wanted to be happy, I wanted to be married, but that had broken down. All that pain of what Jay had done to me, I felt defeated and there was no comfort in any shape or form – not even in the food I had always used as my crutch. No comfort in my mind, no comfort in my body, no comfort in how I was feeling. It was at that point of complete and utter madness, I just wanted normality. I had given up on a fairytale but I still wanted to be someone's person.

I kept thinking about the other people at the Soap Awards, going home to their partners, their families, their hugs. I was loved by fans of the show and my friends but I was so lonely and I just wanted to be held. That would mean that I was loved, that I was beautiful, that I was worthy of the award. But instead I gorged on food until I passed out in the chair, filling up my insides but still feeling totally and utterly empty.

Binge eating was always something I did in secret. That's the thing; it thrives in isolation. It's quiet. It's hidden. It creeps in when nobody's looking. That's why, when I wasn't giving Linda a lift after work I used to load up on unhealthy snacks at the garage. Anything carby, salty or sweet that I could eat quickly and quietly. I'd eat the whole way home, alone in the dark. Sometimes late at night was another danger zone. When Alex was in bed and the house was still, I'd raid the kitchen like a burglar. All the stuff I told myself I wouldn't eat. I wasn't even hungry, but I couldn't stop. But because no one could see me, I could pretend, for a bit, that it didn't count.

The shame was worse once I was in the public eye. I felt judged all the time. People watched what I ate in cafés, in green rooms, even in the supermarket. If I was shopping, I'd layer my trolley like I was building a lie, salad and bananas on top, frozen pizzas and cakes buried underneath so no one could see what I was buying.

At times I would binge to treat myself after something exciting, like a good day at work or a nice bit of news, but the truth is, if I am honest, it happened most when I was low. I binged because I was unhappy. Because when you're busy and doing work you love, with people you love there's a rhythm, a distraction. But when I was on my own and had no one to share my food with, I would just eat shit.

Afterwards, of course, I'd feel dreadful. It's a vicious cycle, because then you're fed up that you don't fit into your clothes, and you start telling yourself all sorts of horrible things. And once you're in that mindset, you think, "Well, what's the point? I might as well just keep eating."

People used to ask me where I got my clothes from and I'd say, "Millets. Great range of tents." I'd laugh, they'd laugh, but it was always a deflection. Humour has always been my armour. I'm not a vain person, but I knew what I was doing wasn't healthy both physically and mentally.

That's why, when I first started on *EastEnders*, and the writers kept giving Heather all these scenes where she was eating, always munching crisps in the Queen Vic, pining after pies, obsessing over cheese, I decided to say something. I sat down with the writers and asked, "Why is she always eating? What's going on here?"

Because it couldn't just be a joke. Heather's bigness, her eating, it had to mean something. No one just snacks constantly for a laugh. People overeat for a reason. They're filling something, a gap, a silence, a sadness.

So we started threading that into the story. If Heather had a horrible run-in with her mum, or felt rejected or unloved, she'd reach for a bag of crisps. Binge eating, like any addiction, isn't about greed or lack of willpower. It's about pain, shame and survival. And while it might be hard to pin down one single cause, there's always something deeper underneath it. Always. And if sharing this helps someone else feel a bit less alone with it, then maybe all those lonely nights weren't entirely wasted.

Chapter Sixteen

Cliff Parisi played my on-screen husband Minty Peterson in *EastEnders*, though it wasn't exactly a marriage made in heaven. Heather and Minty didn't tie the knot for love, they got married to win a cash prize in a competition and sadly for poor Heather, Minty only ever saw her as a friend.

In real life though, I absolutely adored Cliff. He was born in Poplar, a proper East End geezer who always had this cheeky sparkle in his eye and you just knew he'd have a story up his sleeve. One day on set, Cliff came over to me and Linda and said, "Hello you two, fancy coming round to mine for a brew before work?"

We'd never been to his place before, so we thought, why not? We didn't have to be on set till the afternoon, so one bright morning we hopped in the car and drove over to his place in Highgate, which is a lovely part of north London. Full of chocolate box streets, leafy corners, houses that look like they belong in glossy magazines and just near to the sprawling Hampstead Heath.

We parked up and made our way into Cliff's flat, it was very warm and welcoming, just like him. We sat down, he poured the tea and got chatting, about *EastEnders*, storylines, life, you name it, just nattering away. As I looked out the window, I said, "Oh, it's very posh around here, isn't it?"

Then I asked, "Doesn't Steve McFadden live nearby?"

Cliff nodded. "Oh yeah," he said. "He's about ten minutes up the road." Then, he leaned out the window and pointed. "See that house over there? That's Sting's house."

I gasped, "Is it really? That's cool."

But he wasn't done. "And see that house, next door but one?" he added. "That's George Michael's house."

Well, now, that was really something. As you know Heather Trott adored George Michael, she loved him even more than I once loved Donny Osmond, that deep, aching, obsessive fan kind of love. He meant everything to Heather, but she went one step further than I ever did with Donny, going so far as to name her baby George Michael. I am sure that Alex is thrilled that he isn't named Donny Osmond Saddiqi, although the name does have a nice ring to it.

Cliff saw our faces light up at the mention of the pop icon and said, "Why don't we go for a little walk and have a closer look. It's lovely weather right now."

"Alright then," we said. "Let's go!" So off we trotted, the three of us, like school kids on a day trip. Past the posh houses until we arrived outside a grand Georgian home that belonged to the man himself, George Michael. There was a black iron gate and just beyond it, a bit of gravel and then the front of the house. I thought about how Heather would feel about this, that George Michael lived here. Right here. Then, as we were lingering and admiring, Cliff whispered something to Linda and before I could register what had happened she pressed the buzzer and they both darted off down the street squealing with glee. They left me there like two naughty kids playing knock-down-ginger.

"Where are you going?! What did you do that for?!" I shouted after them.

And I was just about to scarper too, when I saw movement in the window, two hands in yellow Marigold gloves. Then a woman popped her head out of the first floor window. "Hello, yes, can I help you?" she called out.

I froze. My mind went blank. What do you say in that moment? "Sorry to bother you. Umm… is this George Michael's house?" I blurted out. She tilted her head, narrowed her eyes… and then her face lit up. "Oh my god! It's Heather Trott!" she said. "Hold on a minute. Hold on a minute!"

She disappeared from the window. I stood there, stunned, still gripping the gate post.

Further down the road, I could see Linda and Cliff peeking round the corner, doubled over with laughter, watching the whole thing unfold. Before I could gather my thoughts, the woman came down to the gate and opened it with the biggest smile.

"Oh my god, oh hello!" she said, reaching out to shake my hand. "Hello, Heather Trott!"

"Hi," I said, still flustered, "Yes… Yes… Hi… Pleased to meet you. I'm Cheryl Fergison."

She beamed, "I'm so sorry, George isn't here. He's just getting ready to go on tour and he's nipped out, he'll be so disappointed not to meet you, he loves *EastEnders*. He's been to the set and he's absolutely thrilled that your character likes him, he loves your character."

I must've looked like a rabbit in headlights. "Oh… right. Oh, thank you very much," I managed. She smiled even wider. "I'll let him know you called. I'll definitely let him know you called."

I thanked her again, stunned into politeness and wandered back down the road to where Linda and Cliff were waiting, their faces wide with curiosity and amusement.

"Who was it?" Linda asked.

"George's housekeeper, I think," I said, still dazed. "Don't ever do that again!" I added, laughing now, the whole ridiculousness of it hitting me at once.

We walked back to Cliff's place, laughing our heads off the whole way. "I can't believe you turned up to George's house and tried to go inside," teased Cliff.

"Shut up! It's all your fault," I groaned. We finished our tea, still giggling like teenagers, gathered our things and headed into work – just another totally normal day in soapland.

When we arrived at Elstree, we popped into reception, where Angela was working the front desk. She was always there, reliable as clockwork, sorting out mail, answering phones, dishing out parcels. Every show should have an Angie, someone who knows everything before anyone else does and never forgets a name, she was the glue that kept *EastEnders* together.

"Alright, Ang? You alright?" we called as we walked in. She stood behind the desk with her usual stack of envelopes and a knowing smile.

"Here's your post and all that," she said, handing it over. "Couple of packages, some cards... and someone's sent you more headbands Cheryl."

Fans used to send all sorts, from headbands, to knitted booties for baby George Michael, even a crocheted blanket once. Lots of the *EastEnders* characters struck a chord with people, they felt like they knew them, so would kindly write in or spend money on gifts.

But then Angela suddenly pulled a face and said, "I've had a hell of a morning! Just had a weird prank phone call."

"Oh yeah?" I said, raising an eyebrow. "What was that then, Ang?"

She shook her head. "Oh, some bloke pretending to be George Michael. You know what it's like, we get a few nutters ringing up now and then. He says, 'Can you thank Cheryl very much for coming by today.' Like I'm gonna fall for that! So I just said, 'Oh yes, I'll let her know,' and hung up. Just another silly call."

Linda and I looked at each other, eyes wide and then we burst out laughing.

"Angela," I said, wheezing, "it's a good job you're professional and it's a good job you take all those calls seriously no matter how daft they sound."

She frowned. "Why? What's going on? Why are you laughing?"

I could barely get the words out through the giggles. "Because that was George Michael." Angela blinked.

"What?!"

"No seriously," I said. "We went to his house this morning. Well… we sort of ended up there. Cliff showed us where it was, Linda buzzed the gate and then they legged it, but I stayed behind and ended up talking to the housekeeper. She said George wasn't in but that he'd be sad to have missed me. And clearly, he really must have been because he only went and called you to say sorry!"

Angela's jaw dropped. "Oh my god. You're joking!"

"Nope. That was George Michael," I said, grinning. "Next time someone rings claiming to be a pop legend, maybe just write it down, yeah?" We were all howling with laughter, right there in reception. That day just kept getting madder and, later that afternoon, Linda and I were upstairs talking to the storyline producers, telling them the whole story, from Cliff's flat to the stroll in Highgate, to George Michael's gate, the housekeeper, the buzzer, the phone call, everything.

They sat there giggling and not long after that, the real magic happened, because one of the writers took that story and ran with it. A few weeks later, Linda came over to me with a twinkle in her eye and said, "Guess what we're filming soon?"

Turns out, they'd written a whole episode inspired by our little misadventure. In the storyline, Shirley, Linda's character, takes Heather to visit what she thinks is George Michael's house to cheer her up when she's feeling low, except, in true *EastEnders* fashion, it goes a bit... sideways.

There's a gate, of course and a garden and in the scene, Heather tries to climb the wall to get a better look, falls off it and crashes right into the bushes. Absolute chaos. It was hilarious to film and even funnier knowing that the whole thing had come out of a real morning of messing about with Cliff and Linda. That's the thing about *EastEnders*, sometimes truth really is stranger than fiction.

The real George Michael was so kind, honestly, he blew me away with his thoughtfulness. After that day at his house he didn't just disappear back into his pop star bubble, no, he carried on sending little gifts and thoughtful notes to *East-Enders* every now and then. Chocolates, flowers, sweet little parcels that would arrive at reception signed with messages like, "Great episode last night."

Can you imagine? George Michael, one of the coolest men on the planet, watching the show and taking the time to say well done, I was floored. Once, he sent me a CD and he'd signed it: "To a fan, love a fan." It nearly made me cry, it was such a lovely, humble thing to write, like we were on the same level, like there was this shared mutual respect between two artists from very different worlds.

After I left *EastEnders* in 2012, George invited me to one of his concerts. He arranged for me to watch from a private box and it was an amazing night, one of those evenings that just lives in your bones forever. That's where I met his partner at the time, Fadi Fawaz. Fadi was a hairdresser, stylish, charming and so easy to talk to. We clicked straight away and ended up chatting all evening. Later that night, we were invited to an afterparty, it was all quite glamorous and surreal and I was trying to take it all in. I remember standing with Fadi, talking and laughing, when I suddenly saw George across the room. He clocked me and without hesitation, made a beeline straight toward us. He walked right up to me and gave me a big hug and a kiss on the cheek. "It was a fantastic concert," I said.

"Glad you could make it!" he replied warmly.

"Thank you for your gifts over the years. It was so generous of you," I said.

"I loved watching you as Heather," he said, sweetly.

Well, I nearly melted. "Thank you. Thank you for your kindness. It's been a pleasure playing Heather. Honestly, it was one of the highlights of my life and this moment... this is right up there too."

He beamed at me, gave me another hug and we posed for a photo together, one I still treasure to this day. It sits framed in my home and I look at it often, not because I want to show off, but because that picture reminds me of what a wonderful moment it was.

After that night, Fadi and I became close and we'd go out together from time to time, always laughing, always chatting about life and work and everything in between. He had a big heart and I trusted him. Once, I popped round to see him and George was there again, just casually in the kitchen, being lovely as ever. He gave me a big hug, offered me a cuppa. There was no ego, just warmth.

Now, I'm not going to pretend we were best mates, we didn't ring each other every week or anything like that, but George knew me. He knew who I was and he respected me and my work and that… that meant more than I can put into words. He didn't have to be kind, but he was, always.

That was my relationship with George. It was quiet and lovely and very, very special to me. When he died on Christmas Day 2016, Fadi rang me just before the news broke. It was so tragic for everyone and the next day, on Boxing Day, I had to go and perform in a pantomime in Kettering, playing Malevolent in *Cinderella*. I was utterly heartbroken and I remember sitting in my dressing room, staring at the wall, thinking, How do I go out there and make people laugh now?

But I did. Because that's what you do in this business, you pull it together, you slap on the make-up and you go out there and deliver. Even when your heart is breaking. The next day, the press turned up at the venue, shoving a recording device in my face, asking, "What would Heather have thought about George Michael's death?" I was livid.

I thought, This isn't a soap storyline. This is real life. This is a man who was loved, by his friends, by his family, by his fans. This is not the time to turn it into a gimmick. Show some respect. Because George wasn't just a pop legend. He was generous, he was talented and he was kind. He made people feel seen. And it was one of the great blessings of my life that he took the time to care about me too.

Chapter Seventeen

Linda and I were shooting a big wedding scene on *EastEnders* – the Masood wedding, in 2009, when Syed marries Amira, even though he's secretly in love with Christian. One of those big, dramatic soap storylines with all the tension bubbling just under the surface, a real 'what could possibly go wrong' kind of moment.

Shirley and Heather were at the wedding, not guests, mind you, but working as servers at the event, trust us to be running around with trays instead of sitting in the front row. It was a beautiful set-up, though, a traditional Indian wedding with all the colour, music and energy you'd expect and the cast that day was huge.

That morning, I was sitting in the makeup chair next to Linda, going over my script and asking my usual questions about who was who and what was what, ahead of filming.

"Who's playing the uncle?" I asked, flicking through the pages. "He's got a lot of lines. It's quite a big part." Someone nearby casually said, "Oh, that's Ramon Tikaram."

And my heart stopped. I sat bolt upright in the chair. "What? Ramon Tikaram?"

The make-up artist nodded. "Yeah, he's the brother of Tanita Tikaram. You know, the singer?"

"I know who he is!" I gasped. "I used to have a massive

crush on him! That's why I got with Alex's dad because he looked like Ramon Tikaram! He played Ferdy in *This Life*! That's why I got with my ex husband, because he looked just like him!" The room cracked up laughing, but I was completely serious.

I had loved Ferdy. Cool, brooding, stylish, that lush long hair. I used to sit glued to *This Life*, thinking, that's the one. I was obsessed. And just as I was telling everyone this story, in walked the man himself. It was like something out of a film. I hadn't even had time to recover from the confession when he came straight in to sit in the make-up chair next to me.

"Hi," he said, friendly as anything. "I'm Ray."

And what did I say? "Yeah… um yeah I know."

That was it. I was gobsmacked, could hardly get a word out, let alone a normal sentence. The woman who never shuts up was suddenly struck dumb. Linda was sat next to me, absolutely loving it and smirking like the cat who got the cream and I could see her clocking my panic, enjoying every second of my awkward silence.

When Ramon stepped out of the room for a minute, I turned to her and whispered, "Linda, I can't. I can't talk to him, I'm so shy. I mean, Jay, my ex, looked just like him. I literally went out looking for someone who looked like Ferdy and now he's here. In *EastEnders*! What are the chances?!"

Linda was in bits and if that wasn't bad enough, the next day she only went and told him the whole story. "Gosh, that's embarrassing," I muttered, hiding behind my tea mug.

Later that day, Ramon came over to me with a wide grin. "I hear you want to meet me," he said, trying to keep a straight face. I went bright red.

"Oh god," I stuttered. "Yeah... Sorry about that." But he was lovely, so down to earth and so kind about the whole thing. He laughed and said it was flattering and gave me a hug.

Just goes to show, life really can go full circle. One minute you're sitting watching someone on telly, dreaming about them and building entire relationships around how much some guy reminds you of Ferdy from *This Life*... and the next, you're sitting opposite them in a make-up chair on *EastEnders*, trying not to choke on your lip liner. I may have still been looking for love unsuccessfully and it turns out Ramon/Ferdy wasn't the one, but at least life was keeping me on my toes.

Real life is full of *Duff, Duff* moments, and plenty of funny ones too...

"I don't understand why they've given me Bobby Davro as a love interest," said Linda one day, looking genuinely baffled.

"Why?" I asked, half-laughing already, knowing something ridiculous was coming. "Well," she said, lighting a cigarette, "I just can't really imagine myself doing intimate scenes or kissing scenes with that bloke that used to run around with an ostrich."

I nearly choked on my tea. "Linda!" I spluttered. "No! That's Bernie Clifton. You've got Bobby Davro mixed up with the one who rode around on that giant yellow bird! That's Bernie Clifton." Classic Linda. But in all seriousness, when Bobby Davro did join *EastEnders*, he turned out to be absolutely lovely, proper good fun and full of energy and we all got on like a house on fire, well... eventually. His first day, on the other hand, that was a bit of a disaster.

Linda and I were sitting outside on the little veranda where we'd often go for a cigarette and gossip between scenes. We were told Bobby was due to arrive early so he could meet us before shooting and as neither of us had met him before, we were expecting a warm handshake and a bit of showbiz small talk. Next thing we know, an Aston Martin comes veering through the Elstree security gates, it was very flashy and stylish.

"That'll be him," I said, standing up.

We both stood halfway, ready to do the polite thing, when suddenly Bobby pulls up, leaps out of the car and without so much as a glance in our direction, bolts through a side door and slams it behind him.

"Well, that was bloody rude," Linda said, genuinely taken aback. "This is the bloke who's supposed to be playing my boyfriend. This is our first proper introduction and he's legged it past us like we're invisible."

"You're right," I nodded. "It was very weird." We sat back down in the sun, both of us slightly miffed, puffing away on our fags and going over scripts with one eye on the door. About half an hour later, Bobby finally emerged from the building, bouncing with energy, beaming from ear to ear and heading straight for us. "Oh, hello girls!" he said. "I'm Bobby Davro. You must be Linda? I'm playing your boyfriend Vinnie Monks! And I know that you are Cheryl Fergison who plays Heather, of course. It's so lovely to meet you. I'm so, so sorry about earlier."

Linda, arms folded, gave him a bit of a stare. "Yeah? You alright, mate?"

Then Bobby, bless him, launched into one of the greatest icebreakers I've ever heard. "Honestly, girls," he said, "I wasn't

Summer hols:
We took family holidays with my Nanny Beatrice and my granddad Charlie, staying on caravan sites

Family values:
Brian Oldfield, my biological dad and Avril Folly, my mum, in their younger years *(far left, right)*

A star is born: Pictures of me as a baby *(right)* and as a toddler *(bottom right)*

Future Mrs Donny Osmond: Me as an early teenager in the 70s during Christmas time with my first record player, probably playing 'Puppy Love'

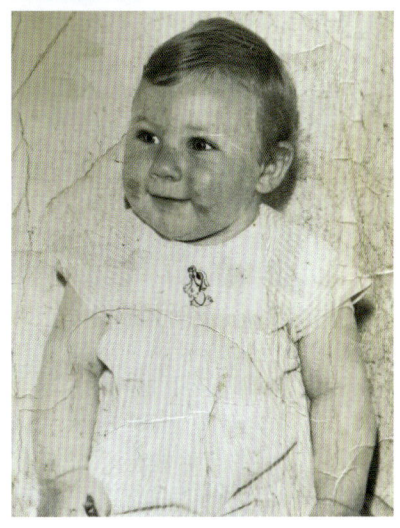

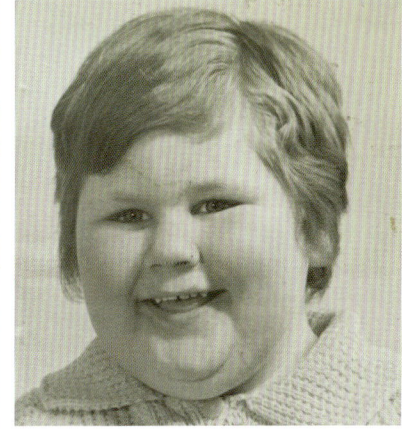

First mentors: My drama teachers from secondary school. Ben Merritt and Yvonne McGuinness, pictured with me at very different stages of my career

Rock'n'Roll star: Me performing with our band Lucy the Cat at the Mean Fiddler in Camden, London in the 80s

First love: Pete Whitfield and I soakir up some rare British sunshine

Missing you always: Me and my mum. I hope I've made her proud

Her Royal Highness: Meeting Queen Elizabeth II after the royal performanc Cyrano de Bergerac at Haymarket Th

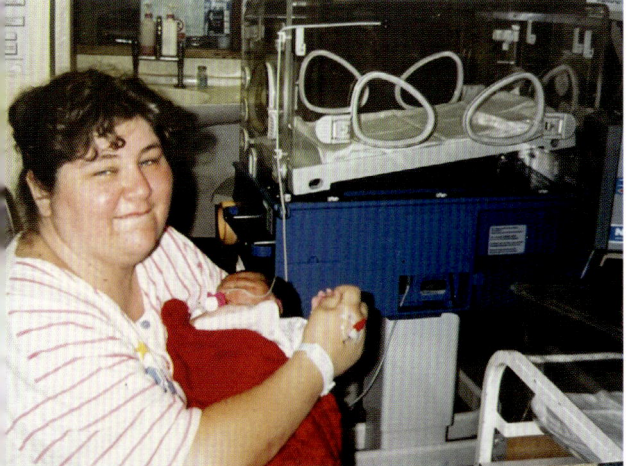

The best day of my life: Welcoming my baby boy Alex into the world. Thank God for him, he kept me grounded, gave me purpose and reminded me every day what really matters

A second family: The Oldfield Family. Graeme, Carol, Me, Lesley and our dad Brian with his wife Pauline. Some things and some people are meant to be part of your life, even if they arrive late

Famous faces: Some pictures of me and some friends over the years *(left to right)* Paul O'Grady, Barbara Windsor and Robert Lindsay

The Enders gang: Myself, Jamie Borthwick, Linda Henry and Cliff Parisi on set at Enfield Lock in 2009

Live on Channel 5: Arriving at the *Celebrity Big Brother* house in 2012, wearing the dress Yas bought me

Albert Square locals: Linda Henry, Bobby Davro and myself at the British Soap Awards in 2008

Friends and co-stars: *(Clockwise)* Myself and my lifelong friend Christine; George Michael superfan and the man himself; me in costume with David Walliams and, lastly, with housemate and friend Julian Clary

y whole world: Everything I hoped for my son, he's doing it. And not just ɔing it, he is thriving. If I climbed a hill, he's scaling mountains

My two boys: My best friend Graeme celebrating Alex's graduation with me

Rosie: The best dog a person could ask for!

Panto: In 2024, Alex and I did our first pantomime performance of *Cinderella* together, The Cresset Theatre Peterborough, *Credit Chris Brudenell*

Proud Mum: I will never stop being proud of him and I'll never stop telling the world what a wonder he is. Alex, thank you from the bottom of my heart for letting me be your mum. *Credit: Joshua Brandwood*

every girl's dream wedding: I
felt like I was playing some sort
of princess in a pantomime, but
this was real life, my life, and it
was beautiful. We sat on thrones
surveying the party and at one
point Yas even came back in on
a horse and honestly, it was more
cinematic than anything I'd ever
done in my acting career

Forever an ally: Being the mum of a gay son and having been surrounded by so many incredible people from the LGBTQ+ community my whole life, I've always been a proud supporter of pride. Heather herself, I think, really resonated with LGBTQ+ audiences because she was the underdog and people root for the underdog. *Credit: Joshua Brandwood*

being rude. I've just had an absolute nightmare. On the way here, I was so nervous about filming, I… well… I shat myself. In the car." Linda and I both burst into laughter.

"I'm not joking," he said, looking genuinely distressed. "The car is full of it. I've had to leave it parked round the back. I ran in to ask if anyone from *EastEnders* had spare trousers and pants I could borrow. I'm waiting for a bloke to come and clean the car out and valet it for me."

By this point, Linda and I were howling – actual tears rolling down our faces.

It was one of those perfect "only in telly" moments – one minute we're sulking because Bobby Davro hasn't said hello and the next we're crying with laughter because he's turned up with a full comedy routine and a ruined pair of trousers.

From that moment on, Bobby was a total diamond. Funny, kind, generous and a brilliant laugh to have around set. He is still a really good friend of mine to this day and we laugh about our first encounter a lot. I don't feel too bad about revealing it either, since he once said to a packed out arena: "I'm not saying Cheryl's big but I got on top of her and burnt my arse on the light bulb." Nothing is off limits with Bobby, which is why I love him.

Aside from making a great mate, meeting Bobby turned out to be more significant than I could have ever imagined. Because of him, I met his dad, Bill Nankeville, who was a famous middle distance runner who had competed in the 1948 Olympics in London. Bill was a real gent and as well as being a legendary athlete, he also had a serious passion for genealogy. One day in 2008 while we were chatting on set, he turned to me and said, "What's your family history, Cheryl?"

I shrugged. "Oh… well, to be honest, I don't really know much about it. I've got my mum's side and I was raised by my step-dad. I've got half-siblings. But my birth dad… I don't actually know who he is. I never met him."

Bill nodded thoughtfully. "Give me what you know. Let me have a look."

I laughed, half-sceptical. "Really? I've got a birth certificate with his name on it and a rough idea of where he used to live, but that's it."

Bill offered a warm smile and shrugged, "I'll do my best." He took it on like it was his own personal mission, not just a favour, but a full-on project and I should've known he'd pull it off. I mean, this was a man who'd run in the Olympics so he clearly didn't do things by halves. The determination, the drive, it was all still there, just channelled into a very different kind of challenge.

Sure enough, a month or so later, Bill approached me in the green room with a spark in his eye and a bit of drama in his voice. "Cheryl," he said, "Guess what? We have found him".

I glanced around, confused. "Found what? What do you mean?"

He paused for effect, then smiled. "I've found your real dad."

I just stared at him for a second, "What?! Are you serious? That's amazing, Bill!" I said, throwing my arms around him in a hug. "I can't believe it. What do we do now?"

He straightened up, that same steady look in his eye. "Leave it to me," he said. And I did.

* * *

It was the night before his wedding when the man who

would soon discover he was my brother opened the door to a complete stranger.

"Hello," he said.

"Are you Graeme? Can I come in?"

If learning he had a half-sister called Cheryl wasn't surprising enough, well, I also happened to be the actress who played Heather Trott on *EastEnders*.

It was a lot to take in. A lot, especially for poor Graeme who was in the midst of the pre-wedding flurry and who – yes, confusingly – shares the same name as my best mate. Between seating plans, cufflinks and vows, he didn't reach out straight away.

Well, he says he did ring me but I didn't answer and to be fair, that does sound very plausible, I've been known to miss the odd call. But the visit had clearly made an impact, because he couldn't stop thinking about what the man – a friend of Bill Nankeville – had told him. At the wedding reception, Graeme told his twin sisters, Leslie and Carol and his dad, Brian, the whole story.

It was Carol I met first. I went to visit her at her house in South West London with Alex. Carol was very thin with dark hair and she worked in a travel agency. Although we didn't look alike I could feel the blood bond. She also gave me the most beautiful gift – a big book of photographs of my dad and my three siblings. It was overwhelming and as I turned the pages, there he was, smiling in the sun, cradling his kids, posing beside Christmas trees and birthday cakes. Moments I hadn't been part of, yet oddly, I didn't feel like an outsider.

We sat together as she gently took me through an oral history of all the life I had missed, stories, faces, memories.

In return, I shared what I knew, filling in some blanks for her, too. It was emotional and strange sitting with this person who was my sister, but it was also warm and familiar somehow.

Next, I met my dad at a carvery in Littlehampton, Sussex, where he lived with his wife Pauline. This came as a shock, as I had been told that my dad looked like Danny DeVito, so I was expecting this little bloke with a bald head. Honestly, all my life when I had seen a bloke that looked like Danny DeVito I had done a double take, wondering if it was in fact him. But my real dad? Well he looked nothing like that. If anything, he looked more like Grandad from *Only Fools and Horses*, played by Lennard Pearce. He was much bigger in stature, but with a friendly look.

As soon as I entered the room, he stood up, before I could see we had the same eyes and his were filled with tears.

"Cheryl," he said, pulling me into a hug. "It's me… your dad." We sat down and chatted about life and all that had happened. He by now, of course, knew I was on *EastEnders* but he didn't really watch things like soaps. Pauline was quite posh so they didn't watch much telly. I told them about my career and it was then we discovered that my dad and Pauline had seen me in a play in Staines when I was touring with the Royal Shakespeare Company. He didn't know that I was his daughter at the time, but he had seen me act on stage. Incredibly he had also kept a black and white picture of me in a wallet and on him wherever he went. It was taken of me as a baby cradled in his arms.

Although my mum wasn't musical my real dad had played drums in a skiffle band, just like I had played drums in the school band years before. It later transpired my dad had been a big drinker, which might have been why my mum didn't want to go out with him. It had been the same when my siblings were young, but after getting with Pauline he had gotten sober. Now, he was everything I could have wanted. Of course, I had a brilliant step-dad in John and siblings I'd grown up with, but still, there was something really healing about knowing that my biological dad was, in the end, a good guy.

I started travelling down to Sussex a lot. It became part of my routine, up and down the A-roads, catching up on years we'd lost. I grew closer to my new siblings, too. Especially Graeme. Nowadays, we see each other almost every day. He lives up north, near me. We bonded so quickly and now we're just in each other's lives.

He told me that there'd been a kind of rumour years ago that there was another girl and she was called Cheryl, but it was just a rumour that one of the sisters had heard and they didn't know if it was true, so Graeme had spent all of his life avoiding dating anyone called Cheryl because they might be his sister. My siblings are different to me, they all have "proper jobs". Carol worked in travel and Leslie is in shipping and Graeme was in the motor industry and now sells antiques. My two 'new' sisters even appeared with me on *Family Fortunes* in 2011 which was lovely.

Sadly, however, by 2014 my dad was very unwell, being treated for prostate cancer and kidney failure at a hospital in Chichester. I was based in South East London at the time and it became this exhausting triangle, working on panto in Redhill, rehearsing all day, then racing across the motorways to see Dad late at night in hospital.

It was miles and miles of driving, often in the dark, with my head full of scripts and my heart full of worry, but I never thought twice about it, I needed to be there. The nurses were incredible. They knew I couldn't always make visiting hours because of work, but they let me come in quietly after hours, as long as I kept the noise down. They were kind, always with a smile and a few of them were *EastEnders* fans, which helped.

They'd ask questions about the show, or about Heather and I could tell Dad enjoyed that. He liked the attention and I could see in his face that he was proud.

Even though he was really ill, we laughed so much. He'd gossip about the other patients, whispering things like, "That fella over there's a right moaner. You should have heard what he said to the nurse this morning!"

It became our little routine, me turning up tired and dishevelled from rehearsals, him brightening up the moment I walked in. I'd pull silly faces, tell him daft stories from panto and we'd swap jokes and memories like we were trying to cram a lifetime into those late-night visits. We had so much to catch up on, but instead of focusing on what we'd missed, we just made the most of what we had right then. It sounds strange, maybe, but some of those hospital visits were the best times we ever had together. Amid all the sadness and the machines and the beeping and the fear, there was laughter, real, proper, belly laughter.

My dad passed away on 15 December 2014, aged 74. I was right there by his side, holding his hand as he took his final breath. The hospital room was so still, it felt like the whole world had paused just for him. I stayed a while after, quiet, present, not quite ready to let go. Then I knew what I had to do next and I stepped outside to call his other children; my siblings.

Just as I got my phone out to ring Graeme, a woman standing nearby, smoking a cigarette, clocked me. "Excuse me," she barked, "aren't you Heather Trott? Can I get a photograph?"

I stared at her, eyes red from crying. "Umm... sorry, now's not really the time," I managed.

She rolled her eyes and scoffed. "You actors think you're special. But you're not special. Don't be so up your own arse." Then she turned and stormed off, leaving me standing there, shaking, still holding my phone, about to make one of the hardest calls of my life.

The truth is, it was sad when my dad passed, of course it was, but meeting him, even for just a short time, changed something in me, something I didn't even fully realise until after he was gone. It was like the jigsaw puzzle of my life had finally been completed.

That last, floating piece, the one I could never quite place, had slotted in. I'd always had the rest of the puzzle: I knew my mum's story, I knew my grandparents, my aunties and uncles. I understood a lot about where I'd come from, but there were still parts of me that didn't seem to belong to anyone I knew. Habits, traits, or an instinct to do things a certain way that I couldn't place. Growing up, I'd always been told I was "just like Mum." But some of me wasn't.

Take this: at around 13 or 14, I started taking myself off to the dentist. I'd discovered I could get free check-ups through school and I made sure I went regularly. I was borderline obsessed with keeping my teeth clean and healthy.

Which, if you knew my mum, was odd. She hated the dentist and wouldn't set foot in one, she used to pull her own teeth out with pliers, bless her. But when I finally met my dad, I found out he had perfect teeth and was proud of them, he even smiled like me.

He was into music too, played the drums, had a love of rhythm and adventure that I realised I'd had in me all along.

When I lost my mum, we weren't speaking – that still cuts me deep and I think it always will, because for so much of my life, especially when I was little, it had been just me and her. She couldn't go anywhere without me and I clung to her like Velcro. It was us against the world and that bond shaped everything about me.

So when she died and I wasn't there to hold her hand or say goodbye, it broke something inside me and I was devastated. I was riddled with guilt and there was no way to make it go away. But with my dad, it was different. I got to be there, I got to sit with him and I got to hold his hand, give it a squeeze and say, "I'm here."

No, it didn't erase what had happened with Mum, nothing could, but it gave me a kind of peace, a quiet balancing of the scales. Life doesn't often hand out those moments, I was lucky I got one. My dad had been the missing piece and when I finally placed it, everything settled and lots of things made a bit more sense.

I often think of my life like a jigsaw puzzle, one of those big ones with odd-shaped pieces, some jagged, some soft-edged. The picture on the front is a bright, messy abstract piece, the kind people scoff at and say, "A kid could've done that."

BEHIND THE SCENES

But I know better, I know where every colour came from. I know every strange curve has a reason, a memory, a moment.

That missing piece – my dad – was half light, half shadow. I turned it over in my hands for years, unsure how to place it. I tried jamming it into corners where it didn't belong. I left it to one side and I wondered if I even needed it.

But one day, quietly and without fanfare, it clicked. Not because I forced it, or understood it perfectly. It just... fit.

And that's the thing about life, really. Not everything has to be neat and not everything makes sense at the time, but some things and some people are meant to be part of the picture, even if they arrive late.

In the end, I didn't just say goodbye to my dad when he died, I also said thank you.

Thank you for letting me find you, thank you for always holding onto my picture and for giving me back the part of me I didn't even know I was missing.

Chapter Eighteen

Back in 2010, things were still going great professionally. At home, Alex was thriving, happy, funny and growing into himself more each day and I had a great social life, full of proper belly-laugh nights with mates.

Some nights the *EastEnders* cast would pile into Little Italy in Soho for dinner and dancing. Rita Simons, who played Roxy Mitchell, was good pals with the owners, so we'd always get the red carpet treatment, even if that red carpet did get more sticky with limoncello as the evening went on.

Obviously, I didn't drink but I did love dancing.

Phil Daniels, who played Kevin Wicks on the show, loved Northern Soul music as much as I did and the pair of us could often be found in the green room twirling around to records, arms flailing, laughing our heads off while everyone else just tried to eat their lunch in peace.

I also got to know the wonderfully eccentric American TV star David Gest, who was once married to Liza Minnelli. I mean, talk about camp credentials. He was a huge fan of *EastEnders* and would often invite me and a handful of the cast to his gatherings, usually held at this lavish, moody restaurant in Camden called Gilgamesh.

David was... well, let's just say he was quite kooky. He had this unique, unpredictable way of being, the sort of person who might call you at 1am just to offload his thoughts.

One night, after one of his events, he invited me back to his place for a little afterparty and I thought, alright, why not? I'm not usually one for after parties.

When we got there, I walked into the living room and who should be sitting on the sofa but Jermaine and Tito Jackson of the Jackson 5 who were staying at his house. I awkwardly said hello, gave them a polite smile, then promptly made my excuses and left. It was all a bit too surreal and overwhelming for me.

But although I had an exciting social life, as anyone who's been single for a long time will understand, I still felt that pang of loneliness whenever I went back home at the end of the day. It hit especially hard when Alex was at his dad's. I'd kick off my shoes, pop the telly on and suddenly feel a bit invisible. I wanted to be held and to be loved, but I only had my dog Rosie to cuddle up to.

The thing is, when you're a bit of a joker and always bring the laughs, people stop looking beneath the punchlines. They see the big personality and the big smile and they just assume that you're sorted, that you are happy. But behind all that, I was lonely. I didn't want fireworks or candlelit dinners or some grand Hollywood romance. I would've settled for someone turning up with a bunch of flowers, even if they were from the reduced section at the Co-op. However, I'd pretty much given up all hope of it actually happening. Even Heather Trott seemed to be getting more action than I was and she was famous for being unlucky in love, so what did that say about me?

At night, after Alex had gone to bed, I started browsing the net. I'd make a cuppa, pad out to the conservatory in my slippers and log onto my laptop, staying up late with the blue screen light. It was my little window to the world. I'd check emails, browse a few music forums and open up MSN Messenger to see who was online. Often messages from random people would pop up from all over the world.

I wasn't looking for love. I was just passing the time chatting to people because I felt lonely and was past the point in my life of hitting bars – besides, my last few attempts at romance had crashed and burned faster than a lock-in at the Queen Vic with no booze behind the bar – but I liked chatting to people and the anonymity of it all. Apart from when I was speaking to my friends, no one knew who I was. No Heather Trott, no *EastEnders*, no baggage, just Cheryl. A regular woman, in her PJs, trying not to fall asleep mid-message.

Some nights, my inbox would ping with those classic one-liners:

"Hi bby."

"Hello, miss beautiful."

"You want to chat wit me?"

Delete. Delete. Block.

But one evening, a message popped up: "Hi. I am Yassine from Morocco. How are you tonight?" I stared at it, eyebrows raised. *Who is this bloke?* I thought and clicked the little X to close it. The next night, he was back: "Hi. I am Yassine from Morocco."

Persistent, I'll give him that. This time, I typed back: "Who are you? What do you want?"

He replied instantly, like he was just waiting on the other

end: "I want to improve my English. I am looking to speak with English people. I work in hotels in Morocco and it is helpful for work. Would you like to chat with me?"

It wasn't a line. There was something refreshingly innocent about it, almost old-fashioned. No creepy compliments or intrusive questions, just polite and honest curiosity and just like that, we started talking.

Yassine, or Yas, as I came to call him, was warm, funny and endlessly curious. He asked questions about everything and he really listened to what I had to say too. He told me about his life, which felt like a different universe to mine. For starters, he was 21 years younger than me. I was a 45-year-old single mum, divorced and juggling work with caring for my kid. He was 24 and living in a suburb in Agadir in Morocco, he fixed computers in hotels, spoke Arabic, French and German and was teaching himself English from tourists, telly, music and now... me. I was basically his human Duolingo, and we started typing to each other late into the night.

"I don't know anything about Morocco," I admitted once, a bit embarrassed.

"No problem!" he replied, as if he'd been waiting for that. "I will teach you." And teach me he did. He sent me pictures of his life, shots of the marina in Agadir, selfies with his mum and sisters, sunsets over the rooftops, giant bowls of couscous the size of satellite dishes. Of course I was struck by his handsome brooding looks with caramel skin and artful stubble, but the chat also felt innocent, like I had a pen pal to write to about the little things in life. He gave me little diary entries of his day: "This is the café where I watch football" or "This is my friend Hamid's shop – he sells carpets and mobile phone covers."

He made me laugh, too. "Today in the souk, one man tried to steal someone else's donkey, so a big fight broke out," he said once, casually, like that happened all the time.

Another day: "There was a car crash, someone hit a camel. How is your day going?"

I'd reply, "Well, slightly fewer camels. But I did burn a lasagne and learn a new song on my guitar." It became this sweet rhythm, two people in completely different worlds swapping stories like postcards.

However, at first, he was doing most of the talking about his life while I was still keeping my cards close to my chest because I was not quite ready to reveal too much about myself. Eventually, I told him I was a struggling musician. This wasn't entirely untrue, I did still pick up my guitar now and again, I just didn't mention the *EastEnders*-shaped elephant in the room.

Soon, we were messaging every single day and it became a little bit obsessive I suppose, but in the best way. I would race home from the set after a long day filming, eager to see if Yas had written and there it would be: a little flurry of messages like modern-day love letters, all waiting to be opened. It was like finding a bundle of handwritten notes stuffed inside the letterbox.

Yas didn't have internet or a computer at the home he shared with his family, so he would spend hours in an internet cafe talking with me. The more we talked, the more we confided, secrets and feelings started spilling out, not in a dramatic way, but slowly and naturally. We were building something.

But still, he had no idea what I looked like or who I really was. Not a clue, but he was very curious; of course he was.

"Can you send me a photo?" he asked gently one evening. "Sorry Yas, I am just not ready yet," I replied. "I need to trust people first."

"Is it because you've been hurt in past relationships?" he asked. I paused, then typed, "No... well, yes. But it's also because of my job. It means I have to be careful about who I share things with."

His next message popped up a second later: "I don't understand. Are you in MI5?" I howled. The thought of me sneaking about in a trench coat with a handgun, drinking martinis and defusing bombs between takes on Albert Square was so ridiculous.

"Something like that," I typed back. "Just kidding! It's not that dramatic, I promise."

And then, instead of continuing to ask for a photo like most blokes would, he just said: "Well then, Cheryl, why don't you just describe yourself as honestly as you can? I want to know you."

There was no pressure in it, no sleaze, no manipulation, just genuine kindness and I think that's when I started to trust him, so I told him.

"I'm a larger lady," I typed. "Much older than you, but very young at heart. I love music and adventure, meeting new people, having a laugh. I've been married before, but he cheated on me, which is a big factor in why we are no longer together. I have a son named Alex. He's just turned 11 and he is my whole world. And yes, I've got trust issues, but I'm working on them."

I told him I liked kind people, honest people. I told him I needed someone who didn't judge me by what I looked like or what I'd been through. I braced myself for the polite brush-off – or worse, the silence.

And you know what Yas said? "Thank you for telling me. You sound so wonderful, Cheryl." That floored me, not because he was saying the "right thing" but because I could sense that he meant it. We seemed to have a genuine connection.

"Okay," I said. "Now it's your turn. Tell me everything about you, Yas. Have you ever been married? Do you have kids? Do you want them? Are you very religious?" He told me he wasn't married, no kids, but he would be open to having them in the future. That he was a practising Muslim, yes, but not in a rigid way. He liked to pray and keep his faith, but he didn't judge others who didn't follow Islam.

The Skype audio calls started after that and we'd speak for hours every night, me in hushed whisper so as not to wake Alex. Some calls were deep and serious, others were downright silly and somewhere along the way, it shifted. It became romantic.

I realised I was developing feelings for a man I'd never even met in person. A man who lived in another country, in fact another whole continent and had never seen my face. Yet, somehow, I felt more seen than I ever had in my whole life.

And I realised... I was falling for him, properly, head over heels. I knew this was totally mad and more ridiculous than any *EastEnders* plot line but despite having not met this person, it didn't feel like a fling. It felt like fate.

He started signing off each call with: "Goodnight, beautiful."

And one night, just before hanging up, he said it, "I think I love you."

I whispered it back, heart thudding, "I think I love you too."

BEHIND THE SCENES

Yas and I spent countless hours on the phone – nearly five months of talking well into the night almost every day. We talked about everything: from childhood memories to what we'd do if we won the lottery, from dreams and daft jokes to what we were cooking for tea. And the more we spoke, the more obvious it became – we weren't just passing the time anymore. I was properly smitten and he was too.

Even though we'd never met in person. Even though he hadn't seen my face.

Somehow, it didn't seem to matter. Or maybe that's why it worked, because we had an emotional connection away from just our looks.

So one night, after we'd finished yet another long, lovely chat about nothing in particular, I shut the laptop, letting the room fall into darkness and just sat there for a moment. And I thought, that's it, I'm going to Morocco. I'm going to meet this man.

It wasn't a mad, spur-of-the-moment decision. It had been bubbling away in the back of my mind for a while and that night, I just knew. I trusted him. And that was the strange part, how much I trusted him. I couldn't explain it, there was no logic to it, really. I just… did.

Maybe it was the way he talked, how he never sugar-coated anything. He'd speak with such calmness, there were no awkward pauses, no red flags, he didn't try to impress me with flashy nonsense, or make wild promises. He just spoke from the heart. My gut said, "Cheryl, this is okay. Go with it."

So one evening I broached the idea with him. "I'd like to come and see you," I said, trying to sound casual. "Obviously you can't come to England just now, you don't have a visa or anything like that, so maybe I could come over there, just for a little holiday. We could meet up in Morocco, say hi in real life. What do you think?"

Without a pause, he said, "That would be very nice."

No panic, or weirdness. No "Oh no, no, don't come." He didn't shut it down, which was a massive relief, but he also didn't leap up and down shouting "Yes! Book it!" either. He was calm and relaxed, like we'd just made a plan to go for coffee down the road instead of crossing continents.

The topic drifted after that, shelved a bit, as if we'd put it on a little side table for later.

He didn't pressure me and I didn't chase it, but the seed had been planted and deep down, we both knew that our meeting was just a matter of time. A few days later, I decided to tell Linda about what was going on.

"I need to tell you something," I said, while in her dressing room one morning.

"Well, go on then," she said, clocking the grin I couldn't hide. "What's going on with you? You look like you've won the bloody lottery."

I tried to play it cool, stirring my tea with exaggerated nonchalance. "I'm seeing someone," I said.

She nearly choked on her biscuit. "What?! Really, Cheryl? Who? Why have I not heard about this?"

"It's sort of new," I replied, bashful now. "Well, we've been talking for a while online."

Her eyebrows flew up. "Online?! Like a dating site?"

"Sort of. It's complicated. But the thing is... he lives quite far away."

She leaned in. "Far like... Brighton far? Or like... Scotland far?"

I took a breath. "Morocco."

"MOROCCO?!"

"Yep," I said, bracing myself.

"Cheryl, you do not mess about, do you? Most people pop down to the pub, you're out there pulling boyfriends off the African continent!" she cried. Linda wasn't convinced at first, but I told her how much I liked Yas and how well we got on and what he was like.

She softened and said, "Well then I am happy for you."

Then I asked for a favour, "Look, Linda, I have to go and see him. I feel like he could be the one and I really like him. I have to give it a shot. I'm going to need to take a holiday. Can you come up with me to the writers and ask about my writing schedule?"

Without missing a beat, she said, "Come on, let's go."

So off we went to the office. "Cheryl needs a week and a bit off," Linda declared, like she was my union rep. "She's got personal stuff to sort and we want to know when it suits in the script for her to take some time off."

The team looked up from their scripts, slightly baffled but a few murmurs later, a flip through the schedule and bam – it was sorted. I had eight days off in a week and a half.

That evening, I rang Yas the second I got in.

"I have spoken to my work," I told him, pacing up and down the living room like I was organising a UN mission. "They've said I can have time off in about ten days. I can come and visit you... if you still want me to?"

There was a pause and then his voice beamed down the

phone. "Oh, that's brilliant. Yes! Yes, I do. I really want to meet you." But then I stopped, because it hit me, he still didn't know what I looked like, not really and he would need to know before I came all that way.

"Well actually..." I said, heart racing a bit, "before we do this. Before I fly across continents to meet you. I should probably send you a photo and tell you a bit more about me. I feel like it's time now. If I'm going to show up in Morocco, you should know who I am and what I really look like."

"Yes," he said softly. "I would love to see you."

So I took a deep breath and said, "Okay, here's what I'm going to do. I'm going to give you my work name. It's not the name you know me by, but it will help you understand the situation. I want you to type it into your computer. You'll find out everything, what I do, what I look like, what my job is. There'll be loads of pictures of me, some snaps where I am me and some where I am dressed as someone else. Then you will understand why I've been so cautious."

There was silence for a second. Then Yas took a deep breath and said, "I am ready."

I smiled, my nerves tangled up with excitement. "Right," I added, "when you've had a look at me online, this is what I want you to do. If you don't like what you see, just give me an audio call to tell me. It's okay, I will understand. I am a big girl. But if you decide that you do still want to meet me, just say, 'Yes Cheryl, thank you' and give me a video call, then we can finally speak face to face. My name is Cheryl Fergison. That's F-E-R-G-I-S-O-N." I hung up.

Now, Yas was good with computers, as he had told me that plenty of times, so I knew he would have found out who I was in no time at all. He'd have typed my name in, hit search and up would've popped a load of photos of me smiling in character on *EastEnders*. Heather Trott, larger than life, wearing a brightly coloured outfit, including leggings and her signature headbands, probably having yet another dramatic day in Albert Square.

What if it was too much? What if he preferred mystery Cheryl, rather than telly Cheryl?

What if he took one look at the online circus and thought, "Actually, no thanks." I started overthinking everything. It had been nearly 45 minutes since I had told him the truth. What was taking so long? Should I have sent a different name? Should I have warned him about the media circus that often surrounds soap stars? Would he fancy me at all?

And then, just as I was halfway through psyching myself into never leaving the house again, my screen lit up.

Yas was calling me and it was a video call.

I hesitated for a second, heart in my throat, then I clicked accept and there he was.

Yas's handsome face, grinning ear to ear.

Finally being able to talk to him properly, face to face, after all this time felt like someone had cracked a window open in a stuffy room. I didn't have to hide anymore. He knew who I was now and he still liked me, loved me, even. "Cheryl, you are beautiful," he said and we started planning the trip.

Later, he told me everything. He had Googled everything he could find out about me in those 45 minutes, forensically scouring the net for information.

"I just wanted to make sure," he explained, "that you weren't one of those people who's always falling out of nightclubs drunk or getting in trouble with the police."

Fair enough. "And I couldn't find anything bad," he said, shrugging. "Maybe just a few people saying not very nice things about you online..." He paused. "...But not many."

We both laughed. "And anyway," he added, "they don't know you like I do. You are lovely and funny and beautiful and intelligent. And I was really proud to see you'd won an award."

Then he grinned. "I wasn't expecting you to be an actor. But it was a pleasant surprise. I can't wait for you to visit," he said.

And neither could I.

Chapter Nineteen

Before I left for Morocco, Linda gave me the rundown. "Right," she said sternly. "If you are booking the ticket, there is no direct flight on the day so you have to go to Casablanca first, then there is a 35 minute flight from Casablanca to Agadir. Call me when you land in Casablanca and if at any point you don't want to go any further, just tell me. Especially when you get to Agadir, let me know if he has turned up and don't leave the airport before ringing me. Ring me every day and if I don't hear from you at each point, I promise Cheryl, I will ring Interpol because I will think you have been kidnapped, do you understand?"

I laughed, nervously. "I am being deadly serious," she said, narrowing her eyes.

"I know!" I replied, popping my arm around her. She pulled me in tight like a mum seeing her kid off to uni. I knew she was only acting tough because she cared.

And a few days later I was in Gatwick Airport ready to fly. I was recognised by lots of *EastEnders* fans, but I didn't mind, if anything, it helped keep my nerves in check. Having lovely chats with people gave me something to focus on besides the colossal leap of faith I was about to take. People kept asking, "Why are you going to Morocco, Cheryl?"

I gave them a polite smile and said, "Oh, just going to meet a friend." A friend. I mean, technically not a lie, but definitely not the whole story.

Even on the plane I kept up the cheerful act, chatting merrily to the woman next to me about everything from telly to teabags, but once I touched down in Casablanca and waved goodbye to that familiar British babble, reality hit me like a dodgy in-flight meal.

There I was, sitting alone in the domestic terminal, waiting for my connecting flight to Agadir – and suddenly, it all felt very real. Gone were the chirpy fans and friendly chatter, around me were men in long flowing robes, women in elegant headscarves and signs I couldn't read. The air smelled different – richer somehow, spiced and warm. My coffee arrived in a tiny glass, thick as treacle and aromatic in a way I couldn't quite place.

No one spoke English, hardly a word and for the first time, I felt like a proper stranger in a strange land. I rang Linda as commanded, trying to act all optimistic but on the next flight, to Agadir, I sat in silence, nervously fiddling with the seat belt buckle, my mind wracked with thoughts. What if I did get kidnapped after all, or what if he took one look at me and changed his mind? Or worse, what if I changed mine?

When I walked out through arrivals, the air hit me like a wall, thick, warm and clinging. It wrapped around me like a wet blanket and instantly I was sweating through my clothes.

The place was heaving, hundreds of people milling about in every direction, calling out in languages I didn't understand. Taxi drivers waved signs in Arabic, people jostled past with bulging suitcases and children weaved between trolleys.

My heart started to pound. I can't breathe. I can't breathe.

BEHIND THE SCENES

What am I doing here? Panic clawed up my chest. It suddenly dawned on me. You've flown to a country you've never been to before, to meet a man you've never seen in person and you don't even speak the language. Are you completely mad?

I looked around for Yas, but I couldn't see him anywhere. I fumbled for my bottle of water in my bag, hands shaking, when my suitcase, my trusty, battered black case with the purple ribbon tied to the handle, toppled over with a thud.

As I bent to grab it, another hand reached down at the same time. It was his hand, Yas's hand. And there he was, just like that, standing in front of me, smiling. He looked exactly like his photos, but broader than I expected and his eyes sparkled with kindness. He was very handsome too and smartly dressed in white jeans, a polo top and nice sandals. I remember thinking, he didn't look his age. He was so much younger than me but he didn't really look that young. For a second, we just stood there, staring at each other in the chaos of the arrivals lounge, like we were the only two people in the world and then we both smiled and he pulled me into a hug.

It felt like I knew him, really knew him, Not from the calls or the messages, but from something older, something rooted deep in the bones, like we had met before in another life. All my worries and concerns melted away, I trusted him completely at that moment and I didn't question it. I thought to myself, I don't know how I know this, but I think I'm going to marry you.

And months later, when I finally told him what had gone through my head in that split second, he smiled and said, "I knew it too. I knew the second I saw you, Cheryl. That you were my future wife and that I was going to marry you."

Of course, I had no idea at the time what he was thinking but as we drove in a taxi to our accommodation, the sun was setting and the sky was pink with promise. I felt like a movie star driving off into the sunset with her true love, like the credits were about to roll following my happy ever after. The windows were open and the warm air was fluttering through my hair, Yas was beaming beside me and life was good.

Yas had organised for us to stay in a little apartment by the beach in Taghazout, a small Berber fishing village about 12 miles north of Agadir. It wasn't five-star, but it had charm. Due to the fact Moroccan law prohibits unmarried Moroccan couples from sharing a room, Yas had booked somewhere with two bedrooms, telling the owner, who was a mate of his, that he had a friend staying from England and she was a woman – but nothing more.

The building was full of surfer types padding around barefoot with sun-bleached hair and guitars slung over their shoulders. It had that bohemian charm and it was like stepping into another life, a far cry from the grey drizzle of England. That first evening, after we had unpacked, I found myself sitting out on the balcony watching the waves roll into the shore, when Yas came out with a pot of mint tea and two glasses.

His smile was as warm as the Moroccan sunset, and we started swapping stories about our childhoods, our families, our dreams. Then, he leaned in and kissed me. It was gentle and electric all at once. And so began our romantic adventure. We spent our days wandering the town, strolling hand in hand along the beach, eating at little cafés in the morning and just talking, laughing and relaxing. At certain points during the day he'd go off to pray in a local mosque or sometimes in the apartment, while I enjoyed the sunshine.

There was a simplicity to those days that made everything feel magical. Just sun, sea, Yas and me. At night we would sit outside under the stars, and soon we became lovers.

Now, I won't lie, being a vegetarian in Morocco was... a challenge. At first, everything felt so exotic and beautiful, the smell of the fragrant spices infusing the hot air and the look of the colourful tagines, but I quickly realised that a lot of the food came with meat.

The waiters were baffled. "Not even chicken?" they'd ask, horrified. Yas would step in, all calm and sweet, explaining yet again, "No, no meat at all. Chicken is meat." So I ate a lot of couscous with veg, but I didn't mind, it was all part of the adventure.

On the second day, Yas turned to me at breakfast and said, "Cheryl, I want to take you to meet my family."

My stomach did a little flip. "Oh wow. That's... big. Are you sure?"

He nodded and said, "Yes, of course. They are excited to meet you. I have told them all about you. I have bought you a headscarf to wear, if that is okay? Just for the neighbours as it is a sign of respect."

I smiled. "Don't worry. I packed a couple myself."

The following morning we drove back through Agadir and out toward Yas's home in the suburb of Dechaira, and the rose-tinted touristy glasses started to slip off. I'd been so wrapped up in the dreamy sunsets, the surfer cafés and the gentle rhythm of our first few days that I hadn't really experienced how people lived beyond the postcard-perfect pictures.

Out the taxi window, the vibe began to shift. Agadir had wide boulevards, modern houses, fancy hotels with fountains in the lobby. It even had a royal edge, the King of Morocco had a residence there. But the further we got from the city, the more that polished gloss faded away, the roads narrowed, the cars thinned out and suddenly, we were passing children weaving between traffic at junctions, selling single packets of tissues for spare change. There were beggars crouched under broken signs, their eyes tired, their hands outstretched. Donkeys and horses pulled carts, not for show or photo ops, but because they were needed. These were working animals.

On the ride over, we talked about where Yas lived and I could tell he was nervous. He said, "Now Cheryl, I need to warn you. While this area is very nice, where I live is very different, but it's our home. It might shock you and you might think, 'Oh my gosh.'"

I squeezed his hand. "Stop apologising for it darling. If it's your home, it doesn't matter."

When we reached Yas's home, the streets were full of noise. Children running round in the alleyways and men shouting to each other about their daily business. Yas opened a large iron gate which creaked with age and gave me a nervous glance before stepping over the threshold into his house. "It's not much," he murmured.

I said, "It's yours which makes it everything."

Yas's home was modest to say the least. It was small and the floors were tiled and worn smooth by years of bare feet and daily living, but if you looked up, in the communal room there was no ceiling, just the sky and this was their only source of light and ventilation. "When it rains," Yas later explained, "the water just comes straight in and drains out over there..." He pointed to a little corner spout. "But it doesn't rain much." And it was true. Most of the time, the sky was clear. At night, that open space offered a stunning view of the stars, but the space was very small. The kitchen was tiny. There was a modest living room and two bedrooms. Yas slept in one, his mum and sister in the other. When his dad was home from working on the fishing boats, he slept in the small living room.

When I arrived, his whole family was there waiting for me. His mum, Khadija; his father, Ibrahim; his sisters, Dounya and Ibtissam; plus all of Ibtissam's children were packed into the tiny front room, shoulder to shoulder, with big grins plastered across their faces.

They'd clearly made a real effort, everyone was wearing their best clothes and the room was thick with the smell of freshly baked goods his family had made especially for the occasion. It was like walking into a warm, bustling hug.

Although they spoke very little English between them, in the three hours that I visited they were all absolutely lovely, their kindness shining through without the need for many words. Yas had told me before I arrived that the traditional way to greet elders was to kiss their hand, as a sign of respect. So, nervously, I leant forward to kiss his father's hand... only for him to whip it away, laughing and saying, "No, no, no, no!" before pulling me into a big bear hug. It completely broke the ice. He wasn't being disrespectful at all, it was the opposite, it was his way of saying: You're family already.

They told me to take my scarf off too, even though his dad was present, which really surprised me. I looked at Yas, wide-eyed, whispering, "Are you sure? Is it okay?" And he just smiled that gorgeous smile of his and said, "You're in the house now. You're part of the family."

I don't want to say that Yas and his family lived in poverty because that word feels like it strips away dignity, but it was a very different life to the one I was used to.

Comparatively, I'd lived like a queen, even back on the council estate in Peterborough.

Meanwhile the El Jamouni family scrimped and scraped and made meals out of next to nothing and made them last. But what they had... it was priceless. Community, family, a sense of hospitality I'd never seen before. It was humbling in every sense. They might not have had much, but they had each other.

And I felt part of it too.

Chapter Twenty

The EasyJet flights from Gatwick to Morocco became like a glorified bus route for me.

The staff at the airport started to recognise me. "Off to Morocco again, Cheryl?" they'd grin as I passed through security and I'd smile and nod like some kind of part-time jet-setter. If I had even three days off from *EastEnders*, I'd be on a flight to visit Yas. I couldn't get there fast enough.

After a while, I started to feel at home there. I loved the smells, the spices, the tastes and the colours of Moroccan life. However, there was one thing I couldn't get my head around and that was the toilet situation when we visited Yas's family house. Mainly that they didn't really have one. It was just a small hole in the ground and it was also used for showering. There were different pans for cleaning and flushing waste – and it was not what I was used to, having to squat in the heat and I would usually wait to use a cafe or something if I could.

One day I was going for a wee, when I saw an infestation of cockroaches swarming in from a crack in the wall. I think someone was doing some work outside and had been hammering on the wall, which disturbed them. I screamed and ran out as quickly as I could without washing my hands and Yas ran in to deal with the insects.

It's really humbling because things we take for granted like having a toilet, a bathroom and a shower is not the case for others. It wasn't long before I had bought his family a sit down toilet and a fridge freezer so they could store leftover food in the heat.

I don't know if I was fixing things that didn't need fixing due to my Western ways, but they seemed grateful and it did help me to feel more comfortable.

It was a totally different way of life and every time I visited I was adapting to it well. I was even starting to dress more Moroccan, in flowy more breathable fabrics. It wasn't because this is what Yas asked me to wear, but more for ease in the heat and the African sun.

I didn't bat an eyelid when I watched a sheep's throat be slit for Eid and I would spend hours shelling peas and preparing food with Yas's mum.

I got used to the noise too and welcomed the traders cycling through the alleys laden with buckets of soap powder and washing up liquid and bleach for us to fill up the bottles, or selling fresh sardines.

It was a simpler way of life and I loaded up on freshly baked bread that was still warm every day I was there. There was lots more dancing too and the kids would spin about having fun.

Yas and I had our favourite haunts, little cafes where the waiters knew us, a stretch of beach we claimed as "ours", even a market stall that sold the best knock-offs. His family were warm and welcoming too and we'd go out for big family meals where I'd tell everyone, "Order what you like!" And they would, plates piled high, fizzy drinks all round and yet the bill would come to about 50 quid for nine people. I was blown away every time.

BEHIND THE SCENES

Eventually, I took Alex with me on one of the trips. He was 10, nearly 11 by then, full of energy and questions. Alex absolutely loved it. He adored the little train that went round Agadir and insisted we ride it more than once in the front carriage only, of course. He tried new food (some of it with his eyes closed), splashed about in the sea and even picked up a few Arabic phrases which impressed Yas's family.

The local kids loved Alex, he was like the pied piper because we had packed a bag full of different treats to share about. Many toys, bubbles and puzzles for the kids to play with. The second time Alex visited he even kindly brought his Wii console for Yas's nieces and nephews to play with and a whole set of games and left it there for them to enjoy.

My selfless boy loved making others happy, but I had to make them all promise that they would only play on it once they had done all their chores and been good for their parents.

It was lovely watching Yas and Alex play together. I remember sitting back one afternoon, watching the two of them playing football on the beach, thinking: This is it. This is my life now. This is my family.

We were falling more and more in love with each visit. And I was sure, completely sure, that I'd found my dream man.

A few weeks later, as Yas and I finished walking round the top of Agadir's famous hill – the one with "God, Country, King" emblazoned in Arabic across its side in huge white stones which lights up at night like a beacon – I breathed a sigh of relief. I hate walking at the best of times and although we'd driven up, trudging around in the heat was too much for me. I was out of breath, puffy and seriously ready for a mint tea and a sit-down. Honestly, I must have looked like I was about to audition for a role as a stranded desert explorer. Yas, meanwhile, was bouncing along like a spring lamb, barely breaking a sweat.

At the top of the hill is an old 16th-century fortress known as a Kasbah, called Agadir Oufella and it's one of the most popular places for both tourists and locals. We stood arm in arm, the warm breeze tugging at my hair, taking in the breathtaking panoramic views of the city stretched out below us – the shimmering coastline, the bustling harbour, the endless maze of dusty rooftops.

It was one of those moments you want to freeze-frame forever. This is what happiness feels like. Just me, him and the world at our feet.

That is, until we were spotted by a coach load of Brits. "Heather Trott! Oh my God, it's Heather Trott!" someone bellowed across the way and before I knew it, I was mobbed.

Suddenly, Yas and I were surrounded by a crowd of well-meaning and sunburnt *EastEnders* fans, waving cameras and calling out, wanting hugs and photos. Yas stood there, gobsmacked, watching the madness unfold and when the crowds eventually thinned and we could breathe again, he turned to me, eyebrows raised. "Is this what it is like for you in England?" he asked, wide-eyed.

"Well, yeah..." I said, a little shyly. "I play a character on a very well-known show. People come up to me often in the street, usually shouting her name first."

"Heather!" he repeated, grinning. "I see!"

That's what I had liked about Morocco, I wasn't well known there. Yas and I were on an even kilter, just Cheryl and Yas, no baggage, no TV cameras, no second glances. And while

BEHIND THE SCENES

I absolutely loved the success and pride *EastEnders* had brought me, sometimes it was nice to just be Cheryl.

But even at the top of a dusty hill in Morocco, you can't really outrun Albert Square. Yas had experienced a small taste of it that day and neither of us knew it yet, but there was plenty more of that to come.

Chapter Twenty-One

Everyone at *EastEnders* feared what we dubbed the Saturday night call, that dreaded ring from the bosses letting you know a journalist was about to drop a bombshell in the papers. And in June 2010, I got one of the worst calls of all from the show's boss Carolyn Weinstein.

I was at home with Alex, curled up on the sofa, just having one of those lovely quiet and relaxing evenings. Telly on, snacks out, feet up… and then the phone rang. I answered, not thinking anything of it, but as soon as I heard her voice on the other end, I felt my heart shoot into my mouth.

A journalist had flown out to Morocco and the *News of the World* were planning to run a front-page story because they said they had a voice recording of Yas. The next day, there it was, splashed across the page in bold, brutal letters: "EastEnder Heather to Marry Penniless Moroccan Goatherd."

According to the article, Yas had told the reporter that I was fat, that he was marrying me because of my money and that it was all just a way to get into Europe. I stared at the paper, unable to believe what I was reading. I was gobsmacked. We weren't even engaged, for starters. As for the rest? It was like being stabbed in the back with a rusty spoon.

The words stung, not just because of what they said, but because of who they said it came from. The newspaper had also said they had a tape. And I thought, oh my god, maybe he is a complete arsehole and I've been duped.

I rang Yas straightaway, shaking, the newspaper still in my lap. "Did you say this?!" I screamed down the phone. "Just tell me now. If you said it, we're done. That is it, it is the end of the road for you and I. And if you got paid to say it, if this was all for a few quid, that's even worse. That is just disgusting."

He was shocked. "No, no," he said. "I love you. If you're ever going to believe them over me, then maybe we should break up, because that means you don't trust me. Cheryl, I would never do that to you. Never."

I remember sitting there, staring at the phone, thinking, God, that's a hell of a thing to say. Then he added, "Ask to hear the tape, Cheryl. Go on, ask them, then you will see. Tell them to send you the recording."

So I did. I went to the team at *EastEnders* and said I wanted to hear the tape, or at least see the transcript. But the *News of the World* refused to send anything. No audio and no proof that he had ever said that. But the damage was already done and printed in black-and-white.

A couple of weeks later, the newspaper quietly slipped out a tiny apology, tucked away somewhere in the middle pages, barely the size of a fag packet. But it was too late. The humiliation had gone national and it cast a long, nasty shadow. It became tabloid fodder, talk radio chatter and worst of all, playground gossip.

Poor Alex was old enough to hear it from other kids, cruel little jokes in the schoolyard about his mum and the "goatherd". It was mortifying. As for the goatherd thing, let's just clear this up once and for all: Yas has never been a goatherd, nor does he plan to become one. He's never herded a goat in his life. I don't know where that came from. Some lazy stereotype to make the story sound more exotic or ridiculous, I suppose. It would be funny if it hadn't been so hurtful.

Even a few years ago, Alex asked an Alexa device to tell him facts about Cheryl Fergsion and the AI speaker replied that "Cheryl Fergison is married to a Moroccan goatherd". The cheek of it! This rumour just won't go away.

Later, Yas told me the truth of what had happened that day. He'd noticed the journalists hiding in bushes, taking sneaky photos of him. He approached them politely and asked them to stop. Then, realising they were clearly going to hang about, he offered to buy them coffee. He thought, if I just speak to them respectfully, maybe they'll treat me with a bit of the same.

He didn't slag me off. He didn't give them quotes, he thought they'd had a friendly chat. He hadn't even answered half their questions, but none of that mattered to them. They had their headline and they weren't about to let truth get in the way of a juicy story. I've had the press write many rude things about me over the years. Often they would write about my *East-Enders* character describing her as "fat Heather" or "George Michael-loving RolyPoly Heather Trott." I mean, there is no denying I am fat, but it is about the way the word is used and the purpose of pointing it out like that. It always felt that it was quite nasty and I'd be lying if I said it didn't upset me. But I am sort of used to it now.

Even so, I did apologise to Yas for doubting him. I felt terrible, but when you're in the public eye, it's easy for the outside world to start poisoning the inside of your relationship. That's what happened. The noise, the pressure, the headlines, they got to me and for a second, I wobbled.

But deep down, my heart knew the truth and my gut never lied about who Yas really was. In the end, the whole horrible experience made us stronger. It reinforced that we had to trust each other, not strangers behind a camera lens or editors with red pens.

Just us, because only we knew the truth of what we had. And we weren't going to let anyone take that away.

That's not to say that there weren't more wobbles in our relationship. Christmas Day, 2010 I found myself sitting there, utterly miserable, alone with Yas's family in Morocco. No one speaks English and they don't even celebrate Christmas – they're Muslim, of course, so for them, it's just another day.

Meanwhile, I'm nursing a cup of mint tea in complete silence, trying not to burst into tears into the sugar bowl.

I can't believe he's left me to fend for myself like this. I feel like a right plonker, sweating in my festive red top like it's gonna summon a bit of Christmas spirit. I miss my son terribly. Alex is back in England, at his dad's. I keep picturing his little face lighting up as he opens his presents and it breaks me a bit more every time I think about it.

Christine's bringing him out tomorrow, thank God, but I already know we'll have to go somewhere else, without my uncaring boyfriend, because at this point, Yas is being a total selfish prick.

Later that afternoon, the door creaks open and he strolls, all casual. "Hi babe, how's your day been?" he asks, like he's just popped down the road for milk.

"How's my day been?" I snap, voice cracking with rage

and frustration. "How do you think my day's been? It's been lonely and boring, thank you very much. All I have done is drink tea. I don't know how to speak to your parents, I didn't know what to do. I am really upset. I can't believe you'd just abandon me like that. You know I am sad about not spending Christmas with my son."

His face creases into this big, smug smile. "Stop smiling, Yas. It is not funny!" I fire back. I'm furious. I've got half a mind to throw my tea at him.

"Calm down love and follow me," he says, still smirking. He took me outside and into a taxi that drove us through the winding streets to a nearby apartment. When we got there, he made me wait in the corridor for what felt like forever – ten whole minutes standing there, stewing in my own festive rage. By that point, I was absolutely at the end of my tether.

Then, finally, he opened the door. The hallway inside was aglow with dozens of tiny tea lights and the floor was scattered with rose petals. Actual rose petals. In Morocco, fresh flowers are expensive because of the heat – they dry out quickly – so I was gobsmacked. I stepped inside, heart thudding.

As I walked into the room, it got even more surreal. More flowers, dozens of them scattered artfully across the floor. On the walls, Yas had written out words in big, bold letters: "Beautiful." "Intelligent." "Adorable." "Kind".

Then I turned towards the bed and there it was. "Will you marry me?" spelled out in rose petals. I froze. And then turned back to see Yas down on one knee. He opened a small wooden chest filled with sand and gently pulled out a ring nestled inside.

"I love you, Cheryl. Will you marry me?" he asked.

"Yes! Yes! Of course I will!" I squealed, as he popped the ring onto my finger.

I burst into tears and we threw our arms around each other. Then, from his back pocket, he pulled out a red Santa hat, popped it on his head and grinned. "Merry Christmas, love."

I started laughing through my tears. Trust him to propose in the most beautiful way but make it funny and silly too. It was, without question, the most romantic thing that's ever happened to me. To top it all of Alex arrived the next day and his eyes lit up when he saw my ring. We spent the New Year celebrating with my friend Christine and her daughter Hollie, who is my goddaughter, in this little happy bubble. All together. I was going to be a wife again. And this time, I couldn't have been happier.

When we got home I couldn't wait to tell my closest *East-Enders* friends the news.

I perched on the edge of the greenroom sofa at Elstree, swinging my legs like an overgrown schoolgirl. Across from me were Linda and Steve and I couldn't hold it in any longer. "Yas and I are getting married," I said, practically glowing through my golden tan.

"Really?" Linda asked, her face lighting up. "Oh, Cheryl, I'm so happy for you!"

Steve gave a low chuckle and stood up to pull me into one of his trademark bear hugs. "Blimey," he said, giving me a squeeze, "it only took you going halfway across the world to find a bloke!" He laughed and shook his head, like he couldn't quite believe it but was made up for me all the same.

"Fancy a cig to celebrate?" Linda said, pulling a packet out of her bag. I smiled and shook my head. "You know what, I've actually quit! Yas doesn't really like it."

Linda raised an eyebrow and gave an exaggerated sigh. "Bloody hell, Cheryl. First you find love in Morocco, now you're giving up fags? What's next, running a marathon?"

We all burst out laughing. Linda flopped back down next to me and gave me a quick squeeze of the hand. "I'm dead happy for you, mate. Properly. You deserve it."

I smiled, feeling my eyes prick with tears. "I'm not going anywhere," I said, dabbing at my face with the sleeve of my hoodie. "Hopefully Yas will come here soon! But we have to get married first."

Steve leaned back in his chair, hands behind his head. "Well," he said with a wink, "You'd better tell the scriptwriters then. Heather Trott getting a Moroccan husband might be the best storyline they've had in years!"

When it came to it the following year, on 2 May 2011, the wedding day itself could certainly have been imagined by a scriptwriter. Honestly, it was the worst wedding I've ever been to and bear in mind, I was there for my first marriage to Jay, so that's really saying something. It was just me and Yas in a registry office in Agadir. Not some grand old building or a romantic little chapel, oh no.

It was a small, tiled room that honestly felt about the size of a public toilet, you could barely swing a cat in there. His mate Youssef came along to act as our witness and the bloke marrying us looked like the spitting image of Mr Bean, complete with twitchy eyebrows and exaggerated gestures.

We did all the documentation, with Yas translating everything for me and then, quicker than you could say "I do," it was done.

I turned to Yas, blinking in disbelief. "Is that it?" I whispered.

"Yes," he nodded. "You are my wife. We are married now."

Married in a tiled toilet by a Moroccan version of *Mr Bean*. Only my life, honestly! You couldn't make it up. It was possibly the most underwhelming 'grand romantic union' you could imagine. But of course, that wasn't the real moment.

Afterwards, Yas bundled me into a taxi and whisked me away to a beach halfway between Agadir and Taghazout. It was the beach we would visit when we were dating and we still call it "our beach". We sat there on the sand, watching the most beautiful sunset I've ever seen and ate salad and tagine.

And then, as if straight out of a film, Yas had organised for two horses to be waiting there for us to ride.

It was magical... apart from one small thing: Yas was a brilliant rider, could ride bareback and everything. Me? Well, let's just say it was giving me flashbacks to the Wigan Way We Were Museum and my tragic attempts at playing Sarah mounting a donkey in Blackpool.

"Yas, I can't get on it," I said, flapping about like a salmon.

"Yes you can, Cheryl," he laughed, gently guiding me onto a rock. Then, with one big lift, he plonked me onto the horse.

With Yas holding the reins for both of us, we trotted off into the sunset as husband and wife. Mr and Mrs El Jamouni. He then pulled out a wedding ring and put it on my finger.

It wasn't glamorous, It wasn't slick, but it was perfect.

Chapter Twenty-Two

Once we had the legal bit done, it was time for the proper celebration. A couple of days before the big event in Agadir, which had taken us months to organise, I had my henna party. Yep, in the UK, brides-to-be go out for a hen do, usually involving pink sashes, L-plates, inflatable willies and enough prosecco to sink a ferry. But in Morocco, it's a much more elegant and spiritual affair. It's all about the henna party, a beautiful female-led celebration that is both meaningful and fun.

If you don't know what henna is, it's a browny-reddish dye made from the dried and powdered leaves of the henna plant. Traditionally, it's used to create intricate, temporary tattoos, symbolising beauty, joy and luck for the bride. And lucky me, I had a proper henna artist come round to one of Yas's mum friend's houses to decorate my hands and feet.

I sat in a throne-like chair in the centre of the room while she painted delicate, swirling patterns across my hands, palms, wrists and feet. She worked with such focus and skill, it was like watching a painter at work. And the designs weren't just pretty, they were meaningful too. Each shape and flower had a purpose, a story behind it. I remember looking down at my hands and thinking, This is it. It's really happening. I'm getting married.

BEHIND THE SCENES

The room was full of women chatting, laughing and sipping sweet mint tea. There was Yas's mum and sisters, his niece, some of their close family friends. My friend Christine and her daughter Hollie had flown to Morocco for the wedding. Alex, who was now 11 years old and had a girlfriend called Britney, who had also come out to Morocco for the wedding with her mum Emma, but they weren't there for the henna party. Alex, however, did not want to miss out. He even wanted to get henna too, but it was just for women so he got his name in Arabic on his arm instead. Very stylish!

I wore a green dress, which is the traditional colour for a Moroccan henna bride, symbolising fertility and growth.

There was no alcohol, no party games and definitely no penis-shaped straws, but you know what? It was absolutely lovely. We ate homemade baklava, melt-in-your-mouth pastries and plates piled high with sticky-sweet Moroccan treats. We sipped tea from little glasses while music played in the background and the women clapped and sang traditional songs as I sat like a giggling statue, trying not to smudge my drying henna.

At one point, I looked around the room, at all these women young and old, all celebrating me and welcoming me with open arms and I got a bit emotional. It was intimate and full of love.

Yas and I also did a pre-wedding photoshoot by the swimming pool at the Sofitel in Agadir for *OK! Magazine*, who were covering our wedding celebrations. It felt very showbiz; a glamorous setting, posh hotel, photographers fluttering around like butterflies.

Yas wasn't overly keen on staying at the hotel. It wasn't that he didn't appreciate it, it was beautiful, of course, but he just couldn't get used to the idea of being waited on hand and foot by fellow Moroccans. For a man from a humble background, it felt awkward.

"I can carry my own bags," he kept insisting. "I don't need someone pouring my orange juice." He found it all a bit too much. But me? I lapped it up. Big fluffy towels, soft lighting, the scent of jasmine and mint wafting through the lobby; I felt like a proper A-lister.

On the day of the shoot, we were both ushered into chairs in the hotel room and a Moroccan woman did both our make-up. Yas, bless him, got the full treatment, they didn't hold back. Foundation, bronzer, highlighter, the works, you name it, they chucked it on him. He looked flawless by the end of it, but also slightly traumatised. "Did I really need all this?" he whispered.

He was dressed head-to-toe in white linen, which looked gorgeous against the poolside setting, while I wore a floaty, white kaftan and trousers and enough eyeliner to scare off a raven. It was hot, we were both sweating, but we smiled and posed like professionals, pretending we weren't melting into the paving stones.

When the photos came back, Yas was shocked. "That doesn't even look like me!" he said, eyes wide.

I had to laugh. I mean, I didn't look like me either! Honestly, I'm sure some of the *OK!* readers were flicking through the pages thinking, "Who is this flamboyant gay man marrying a glamorous transvestite?" But oh well, we were happy. We didn't care what anyone thought. We were in love, we were getting married and we had a magazine spread to prove it.

BEHIND THE SCENES

Then it was the big day and we wanted everything to be just right or at least, as right as it could be with my track record.

However, looking back, we really needn't have worried. Before the wedding, we had to sort out the marriage license properly, Moroccan style. We were ushered into an office and introduced to the man who, apparently, spoke "the best English." By chance, he turned out to be the local police commissioner.

He was thickset with a bristling moustache and had the vibe of a man who hadn't cracked a smile since 1987. He slammed a folder down onto the desk and looked me dead in the eye.

"What is your name?" he barked, pen poised.

"Cheryl Fergison," I stuttered. "Well... actually, legally, Cheryl Campbell. Fergison's my work name."

He frowned, eyebrows knitting together in suspicion. "Work name?" he repeated slowly, like I'd said I was an alien. "What is your job?"

I started sweating and for once it wasn't because of the Moroccan heat. "Um... I'm an actress?" I offered, my voice doing that awkward wobbly thing it does when you know you sound daft.

He looked me up and down slowly then gave a little snort of laughter. Not with me but at me. "An actress?" he scoffed. "What kind of actress are you?"

I could tell he thought I was making it up. Probably thought I was some sort of dodgy cabaret act, trying to sound important. I swallowed hard. "I do TV," I said quickly. "In England. A serial... you know, like a soap opera?" (They call it a serial in Morocco.)

He still looked unimpressed "But who do you work for?" he snapped.

"Oh, I work for the BBC," I offered.

It was like someone had hit him with a cattle prod. His whole face lit up, his posture shot up straight and suddenly he was all smiles and handshakes.

"The BBC?" he beamed. "Wonderful! Fantastic! Very good! Very famous!"

He slapped Yas on the back like he'd just won a gold medal and then merrily invited himself to our wedding celebrations.

The event itself was absolutely epic. The British Consul to Agadir came, no less – which still makes me laugh, because all this fuss was partly thanks to our new best mate, the police commissioner. Because of him pulling a few strings, the whole street leading up to the hall we'd hired was shut down for the occasion. It was surreal, like some grand Hollywood premiere.

When it was time for me to arrive, the police insisted on taking ridiculous levels of precautions. I wasn't allowed to just stroll in all casual, oh no. Instead, I was bundled into a car with a blanket thrown over my head like I was some undercover agent on a top-secret mission. The event itself was a real occasion, with drummers and dancing. I even got carried in on one of those big plinth-throne things, perched cross-legged like a proper goddess. I don't think I could manage it these days without a crane to hoist me up again!

Moroccan weddings are long and fun to attend, but they require a lot of effort from the bride and groom. Seriously, it is like being in an ambitious stage production at the National Theatre. I even had seven outfit changes, which is traditional in Moroccan weddings. Seven! I felt like I was playing some sort of princess in a pantomime, but it wasn't a pantomime, it was real life, my life and it was beautiful. Traditional, magical, like stepping into the pages of a fairytale. We sat on thrones surveying the party and at one point Yas even came back in on a horse and honestly, it was more cinematic than anything I'd ever done in my acting career.

I mean, forget Heather Trott, this was pure Disney princess levels of drama. There were drummers pounding out beats you could feel through your chest, women ululating and clapping, dancing breaking out all around us.

Alex was there too, of course, absolutely loving life. He threw himself into every moment, soaking it all in with wide eyes. He ran around, hyper on fizzy drinks playing with Hollie and Britney. They'd never seen anything like it and I think they were just as gobsmacked as I was. Christine and Emma also mucked in dancing around and it was great to have people from back home here with me, witnessing it all, not just my wedding, but this once-in-a-lifetime cultural celebration. The blending of our families, our histories and our stories.

And then came the tagines. These great big, steaming pots were carried in like sacred treasures. Alex's eyes lit up, he was starving, bless him. He leaned over and whispered, "Finally! Food!" But then the lids were lifted... and instead of couscous or lamb stew, there were clothes. Beautiful fabrics and outfits, a traditional offering to the bride and groom. The look on Alex's face was priceless. "Mum," he moaned, "Where's the dinner?!"

I laughed. "Welcome to your new Moroccan family, love," I told him, patting his hand.

Eventually, we did eat, later in the evening when everything calmed down just a little.

And then came the big surprise. Yas had arranged for my final outfit – outfit number seven! – to be a traditional British wedding dress. It was stunning white lace and it caught me completely off guard and made me well up. I looked at him and said, "Yas, what is this?"

He just shrugged shyly and said, "I thought maybe... you'd like something from home too."

We had our first dance to 'When I Need You' by Leo Sayer. Yas had chosen it himself and was convinced it was going to be the Celine Dion version, so was confused when it wasn't by "that lady singer". My pick for the dancefloor was 'Always and Forever' by Heatwave. A proper slow jam. I've always loved that song and on that night, it felt like it was written just for us. There was something about the lyrics, the softness, the warmth, it wrapped around us as we danced.

Despite there being no booze, the energy in that room never dipped once, everyone danced and laughed and celebrated until 4am. I don't know what they were running on, mint tea and adrenaline, maybe, but those Moroccans have stamina. I was knackered by midnight and still had four hours to go!

By the end of it, Yas and I collapsed into bed. We were delirious and exhausted, but blissfully happy. "Can we sleep in tomorrow?" I asked, already half-asleep.

"No," he groaned, "*OK! Magazine* are coming at nine."

And just like that, the magic turned back into work. But I didn't mind, because I was curled up next to my new husband, after a night I will never forget.

However, unlike most newlyweds, we couldn't simply start

our new life together in the same country. First there was paperwork and lots of it to get through.

It was Friday morning in November 2011 and I was halfway through doing my mascara when my phone started buzzing on the dressing table. I glanced down and saw Yas's name flashing up on the screen. I answered it with one hand while trying to balance the other against the mirror. "Hello babe, you alright?"

There was a pause, then a burst of excitement down the line. "Cheryl, babe, guess what?"

I froze, instantly alert. "What? Tell me!"

"I've got it. My visa. I've got my visa through. I'm coming to England!"

I dropped the mascara wand and I swear my heart did a triple backflip. "Oh my God. Oh my GOD. Are you serious?"

"Yes! I just found out. It's official. I can come over. I'm coming to see you!"

I clutched the phone to my chest for a second, eyes wide, then squealed like a teenager. "Oh Yas! That's wonderful, just wonderful!"

I could hear the grin in his voice as he laughed. "I wanted you to be the first to know."

"I'm so excited. I knew it would happen," I cried. "I just didn't know when!"

We'd been waiting for months. Paperwork, interviews, delays, questions. It had been a slow, frustrating crawl through red tape. It was really expensive, worth every penny, but still they don't make it easy. We'd stayed hopeful, but there was always that niggling fear that something would go wrong. That they'd say no. That it would all fall apart. And now... it was actually happening.

"When?" I asked. "When do you get to come?"

"Soon," he said. "Very soon. I'll find out exact dates this week, but it won't be long now. We can be together properly."

I sat down on the edge of the bed, tears prickling unexpectedly at my eyes. It was the good kind of tears, the kind that sneaks up when your heart's too full. "I can't believe it," I said quietly. "I really can't."

"Believe it, Cheryl," he said, with that calm, gentle certainty he always had. "This is it now. We're going to start our life together."

"I have to go," I said, "but, Yas... thank you. Thank you for sticking it out. I know it wasn't easy."

"For you, I'd wait forever," he said.

I hung up and just sat there for a moment, letting it sink in. He was coming. My husband. My heart. He was really coming. And suddenly, the day felt a little brighter and I floated out the door and off to work feeling like the luckiest woman in the world.

Chapter Twenty-Three

Every couple of months, actors on *EastEnders* would get called up to the producers' office to chat through upcoming storylines, new twists, character development or sometimes just a general check-in. It was all pretty routine, but if you got called in on a Friday... well, that was a whole different kettle of drama.

We'd all clocked it. Fridays were the danger zone. You didn't need a memo, word just travelled. Friday meetings weren't just new scripts or fresh plots, it either meant your character had some top secret storyline, you were going to be sent away for a while or, most probably, that you were being given the boot. They were what we all secretly called "The Culling". If your character was being written out, the hammering blow always came on a Friday – it was a sort of like a soapland death knell.

But when I got into work after learning Yas had his visa that Friday morning, I was on such a high, telling Linda and Steve, that no alarm bells rang when I was asked to pop up to the offices for a chat. I was in a great mood, totally on cloud nine, so I assumed it must be because I was getting a great new storyline and I was even excited to go and talk it through.

Sitting in the greenroom with Linda, I was grinning ear to ear. "I wonder what it will be," I said, stirring my cup of tea.

"Maybe Heather will be getting a new love interest, or finally meeting George Michael in person. Ooh, I really hope it is that. Wouldn't it be amazing?"

Linda gave me a smile. "I am sure it will be exciting, whatever it is. Everyone loves Heather. Maybe they're finally sending her off to Morocco after all, then you can visit your Yas!"

I laughed. "You don't have a meeting today and we are usually a package deal. I hope if it is filming with George you get to come along too. Listen, Linda, I know we are supposed to be going home together, but you can set off now if you like. Otherwise you might just be waiting around for me. It could be a while and you've got the weekend to enjoy."

"Don't be daft," she said, waving a hand. "I'll wait. I want to know the gossip the second you come out!"

I downed the last of my tea like it was a shot of Dutch courage. "Right," I said, giving myself a little shake. "Wish me luck."

"You don't need it," she called after me. "If anyone deserves a new adventure in life it's our Hev!" I walked steadily up to the office, then took a deep breath, straightened my shoulders, and knocked on the door. "Come in," called Bryan Kirkwood, the executive producer, quietly.

Bryan was usually all cheery and full of banter whenever I popped up for a chat. He'd crack jokes, offer you a biscuit, make you feel at ease. He had so many stories and we got on so well. But the second I stepped into that office, I knew something was off. He wasn't smiling. In fact, he looked... gutted. He sighed, like he had the weight of the world on his shoulders.

Then I spotted it: a big box of tissues right there on the desk between us. My first thought wasn't even about me, it was about him. Oh no, I panicked, poor Bryan, something awful must have happened to him. Maybe he'd lost someone, or had some terrible news. I even started thinking, perhaps I shouldn't be here. I'm interrupting something really serious. Maybe I should just go back outside and wait until he was ready to chat to me.

But before I could say anything or make a sharp exit, he simply said, "Sit down, Cheryl."

My heart dropped. You know when you get that gut feeling, when everything in the room suddenly feels about two degrees colder? It was like that. I perched on the edge of the chair, trying to steady my breathing, telling myself not to leap to conclusions. But, deep down, I knew.

Then he spoke. "I'm really sorry," he said softly, "but this isn't great news."

Oh no. He went on, explaining that after lots of discussions with people higher up, they'd made the decision to write me out of the show.

"I want to stress that this has absolutely nothing to do with your acting, or you as a person," he said quickly, like he needed me to understand that. "You're great, Cheryl. A brilliant actress and a real team player. This is purely a story decision, to shock the audience and see how other characters, like Shirley and Phil, respond and grow in the aftermath."

I nodded, trying to process it. I could tell they'd cooked this up with the idea that it would crack Shirley's life wide open. Give Linda Henry the big, emotional arc which I supposed was fair enough.

"Okay," I said lightly. "That's fine." I even smiled. "No hard feelings, Bryan. Honestly, I get it." I think I said it to put him at ease more than anything. He looked devastated, like it was genuinely hurting him to be the one delivering the news. There was a long pause.

Then I asked, just to check, "Wait... I'm not coming back, then?" He looked at me, then at the box of tissues, then back to me.

"We've decided we're going to kill the character off."

My eyebrows shot up. "Heather dies?" I whispered.

He nodded. "Yes." There was another beat, then, "Do you want to know how?" Bryan explained that it was going to be a major storyline, stretched out over months. It would be this big, emotional, headline-grabbing plot. Heather Trott was going to be murdered.

"Murdered?" I gasped. "So, I don't even get to leave in a cab with a suitcase and a sad song, 'Julia's Theme' playing at the end?"

He smiled sadly. "I'm afraid not."

"Well," I said, "I suppose it's more dramatic."

He chuckled, but his eyes still looked a bit watery. "We're giving you a longer heads-up than usual, six months. That should give you plenty of time to plan ahead."

"Great," I nodded. "That gives my agent a headstart. And at least I get to go out with a bang."

"I've no doubt you'll be snapped up quickly," he said warmly. "And on a personal note, I'm really going to miss you."

I stood up, holding out my hand. "Thank you, truly. East-Enders gave me an incredible run. I only thought I was coming in for a few episodes and I've been here nearly five years. It's been brilliant. I've had the time of my life. And it's such a great platform for an actress, you get to do proper acting on this show with so much range, from anger to grief to comedy, romance, tears – the lot."

I meant every word, but if I'm honest, I think I was trying to comfort him more than myself. I knew I still had time left on the show, time to say goodbye to Heather properly.

Now came the hard bit: telling Linda. I walked outside, opened the car door and jumped in beside Linda. She looked at me expectantly, her eyes wide as she practically bounced in her seat like a kid desperate for gossip.

But I didn't say anything, I just stared straight ahead, gripping the steering wheel like it might anchor me to the earth.

"Go on then?" she nudged after a moment, her voice all bright and impatient. "What happened? What is the storyline?" Then, clocking my silence, "Are you okay? What's going on?"

I took a deep breath, still staring at the windscreen. "Nah," I said finally, my voice flat. "It's not good, Linda. Not good at all."

"What? Why? What happened?" she said, properly panicking now, twisting round in her seat to look at me.

I turned to her slowly. "I'm leaving, darling. They're killing me off. Heather's getting murdered."

There was a beat of silence and then she exploded. "What?!" she bellowed, so loud the people walking past probably heard. "They can't do this! That's insane!"

Before I could even blink, she was out of the car, slamming the door behind her like a woman possessed. "Linda, don't!" I begged, scrambling after her, but hell hath no fury like Linda Henry on a mission. She stormed across the car park, head held high, marching straight back up toward the production offices like she owned the place.

"I'm going to tell them they can't do this!" she shouted over her shoulder. I watched her disappear into the building and sank back into the car seat, half touched, half mortified.

About 20 minutes later, she came stomping back, red-faced and breathing heavily, like a furious bull. "They said it's all decided, it's happening, no matter what," she said bitterly, climbing back into the passenger's seat and slamming the door again. "I told 'em. I told 'em if you go, I'm going too. I said, 'If you get rid of Cheryl, you're getting rid of me too!'"

I stared at her, heart swelling but also feeling slightly exasperated. "That was silly, Linda," I said gently, squeezing her arm. "Don't be daft. You love this job."

She turned to me, her eyes glistening with tears now. "They want to see how devastated Shirley will be without Heather? Well, in real life Linda's gonna be devastated without Cheryl!"

I swallowed hard. Tears threatened to sting my own eyes, but I blinked them away.

We sat there in silence for a moment, two mates side by side in a car, hearts broken a little but still stubbornly clinging to the good times we'd had. You see, with Linda, well, a lot of people think she's this tough-as-nails, no-nonsense bird, just like Shirley Carter, but actually, she's incredibly sentimental. She's emotional about people, about relationships. She feels things deeply, she always has. I knew that better than anyone, because over the years, we'd built a real friendship, not just the telly version.

BEHIND THE SCENES

But it was out of our hands now. I was like a turkey waiting for Christmas – or a beloved George Michael superfan with a big heart who in six months time was going to be murdered in front of the nation.

Chapter Twenty-Four

While I was still on *EastEnders* back in 2008, I was asked to take part in a special edition of *The Weakest Link*, an *EastEnders* special. You know the one: Anne Robinson staring people down like a laser beam in a power suit. I was terrified. I thought I'd be off in the first round, tripping over the questions, forgetting my own name, buzzing in at the wrong time, the lot.

But by some absolute stroke of magic, and I mean actual magic because I don't know how else to explain it, I only went and won. Yep. I am the proud winner of *The Weakest Link*.

Even now, I still don't quite believe it. Anne gave me that look, you know the one, where she raises an eyebrow and you expect to be told off, but instead, I was declared the winner. The final link standing. I'd won money for Great Ormond Street Hospital, which made me so happy I could've cried. It was a proper "pinch me" moment. Me, winning a quiz show. Unbelievable.

Now, I wish I could say all my other appearances went as smoothly... but, well... no. Take *Let's Dance for Sport Relief*, for example. A brilliant show, such a good cause and I was thrilled to be asked. But, of course, in true Cheryl fashion, it all went a bit sideways.

I was dressed up as Vanilla Ice. That's right. Full costume.

BEHIND THE SCENES

Hair scraped into a ridiculous style, icy bling, bomber jacket, the lot. I looked like I'd been thrown out of an early '90s fancy dress party for crimes against rhythm.

We were rehearsing the dance to "Ice Ice Baby" which, let me tell you, is not as easy as it looks when your knees click and your hip starts making funny noises, when I took a wrong step, slipped and did myself in. Proper injury and my leg gone. So, when the show finally aired, the only thing that was Ice Ice Baby was the ice pack on my leg.

Very glamorous, well done Cheryl, but luckily they showed my rehearsal performance, and the public seemed to like it as I won the vote to be saved that week. Later on I did *Celebrity Mastermind*. Ah, yes. Emboldened by my stunning victory on *The Weakest Link*, I thought, Here we go again! Quiz queen Cheryl! Let's smash it. Spoiler: I did not smash it.

For my specialist subject, I naturally asked to do The Life and Times of George Michael. I mean, come on, I'd played a character who was obsessed with him, I'd met him, he'd sent me gifts and I knew his whole career backwards.

But no. I was told someone had already done it. Apparently, you can't repeat specialist subjects which, frankly, seems a bit harsh when it's George Michael. He is a national treasure after all. So I said, "Alright, what about Donny Osmond?"

Because, as I've said Donny was my obsession as a child and I knew every cough and spit of his career.

"No," they said again. "Already been done."

I was running out of options. The only other thing I really felt I had a shot at was music.

So what did they give me? Sir Elton John.

To be fair, I do love Elton John. The man is iconic, with great songs, sparkly glasses and big tunes. I mean, I knew he was gay, married, had two kids, wore fabulous suits and once did a duet with Kiki Dee, but that was about as much as I knew.

They gave me a big thick biography about his life to to revise from for the show, but trouble was, I was doing panto at the time and there's only so much Elton you can take in when you're also playing a fairy godmother, singing show tunes and dodging flying foam pies twice a day.

Needless to say, I bombed out. I absolutely tanked on national television. I think at most, I got one or two answers right, which even I was shocked by. The rest? A blur of panic, regret and sheer guesswork.

Then came the general knowledge round, which was just as painful. I didn't want to say "pass" to every question because that looks even worse, doesn't it? You just sit there in silence, looking like you've wandered in from the corridor and no one's asked you to leave.

So I decided to try with every answer, give it a go and have a good guess. Now and this is a secret I've only ever told a few people, one of my friends, who shall remain nameless (but knows who they are), had said to me before the show, "If you can find a way to get the phrase 'four candles' in as an answer, I'll donate £2,000 to your chosen charity."

Four Candles, of course, from the legendary *Two Ronnies* sketch, the one where the bloke goes into the shop asking for "fork handles" and ends up in a full-blown comedy mess. So during the general knowledge round, there came a question I definitely didn't know. No clue. And instead of panicking or passing, I looked deadpan into the camera and said, "I don't know... four candles?"

It made no sense. I looked daft. But I tell you what, we got the donation. And my charity still got their £2,000. So who's laughing now?

Anyway, I enjoyed reality TV and competitions and just as I was starting to look around for what might come next, now that my days on Enders were drawing to a close, I got a phone call. It was my agent, Howard. He didn't even say hello. Just launched straight in with, "What about *Celebrity Big Brother*?" There was a pause. Then he added, "They're offering £100,000 but I think I can push them up."

Celebrity Big Brother. Me? I mean, don't get me wrong, I love a bit of reality telly and I'd watched the show for years. But the thought of actually going on it? Living in a house with strangers, being filmed around the clock, no contact with the outside world? It felt a bit mad. But then £100,000 is £100,000, who wouldn't jump at the chance? Besides, I was starting to worry a bit about what to do for money after leaving the show and Yas and I were talking about building a life together properly and that sort of payday could really change things.

"It sounds good," I finally replied. Howard, though, wasn't done.

"Leave it with me," he said. "I think I can get more."

Over the next couple of weeks, I kept checking in. "Howard, any news?" I'd ask, trying to keep my voice breezy.

"Trust me, Cheryl," he kept saying. "I know what I'm doing."

"Please don't lose it though," I begged him more than once. "It's so much money. This could really set me up after I leave."

He laughed. "Cheryl. Relax. You have to trust me!"

And then, one morning, he rang me up chipper as ever. "How does £175,000 sound?" he asked.

CHERYL FERGISON

I didn't have to think that one over. "When do I pack?" I shrieked. "That is enough money to pay off my mortgage and maybe even get a place in Morocco for me and Yas. Thanks Howard, this is fantastic."

So it was decided, the beginning of my next adventure, the wild, surreal, 24/7 world of reality telly, where the biggest role of all was playing... Cheryl Fergison. God help us all.

Chapter Twenty-Five

Yas came through arrivals, looking around wide-eyed and dragging a battered suitcase behind him. The moment I saw him, my heart genuinely skipped a beat. I ran to him and threw my arms around his neck like something out of a rom-com. Not quite *Love Actually*, but close enough.

He hugged me back so tight, like he was anchoring himself to something solid. He buried his face into my shoulder and for a moment we just stood there, holding each other like the world had gone quiet. It had been a few weeks since Yas was granted a visa, and I could barely believe he had actually made it.

"You're here," I whispered and he nodded, eyes a little glassy. "How was the flight?" I asked, as I pulled back to look at him properly. He looked tired but smiling.

He grimaced. "Terrifying," he said, deadpan. "I prayed the whole way. I thought we were going to crash."

Bless him – this was his first time ever out of Morocco, let alone on a plane. I mean, I complain if I can't get an aisle seat, but my husband had just flown across continents, away from everyone he knew, everything familiar, into a completely new life. That takes some serious guts.

I grabbed his suitcase and led him through the terminal like I was collecting royalty. "You did amazing," I said, squeezing his hand. "And don't worry – if you can survive the Gatwick passport queue, you can survive anything."

We got back to mine and I watched him taking it all in: the traffic, the chimneys, the polite queues. Everything was new, but the thing he struggled with most was the weather which is understandable when you have just come from sunny Africa. He kept shivering, rubbing his arms and saying, "Cheryl, it's so cold here. It's so cold. I don't know how you do it."

So once he'd unpacked and settled in, our first official outing was to buy him a winter coat. A nice thick wool one, with an upturned collar. He looked so handsome in it. Then we did the sights, of course. We drove down The Mall, with him wide-eyed like he was in a film, wandered around Leicester Square and down the South Bank, stopping to watch the street performers and take it all in.

We went to the Trocadero in Piccadilly and explored the arcade, fascinated by the lights and noises and general British madness. Seeing London through his eyes was like seeing it for the first time all over again. I imagine his expressions were just like how I must have looked when he showed me around Agadir, full of wonder and cultural curiosity.

Yas liked a slow start in the mornings, so he'd often still be curled up in bed when I left for work. I'd peek in at him before heading out, watching the sunlight sneak through the curtains and light up his sleeping, peaceful face.

At dinner time, the western food was often met with confusion. There was no tagine bubbling on the stove at first. Instead, I introduced him to the delights of British cuisine, fish and chips, pizza, baked beans and crumpets were his favourite. He was incredibly polite about it all, but

I could tell his tastebuds were calling out for the spices and flavours of home. Still, Yas threw himself into every new thing I gave him, smiling and saying, "Yum...Very British," before reaching for the ketchup. But a few weeks in, he started filling my home with the smell of rich Morrocan food.

In between sightseeing, cups of tea and cuddles, we threw ourselves into planning the UK leg of our wedding celebration. There was so much to do, dresses to pick, a venue to book, invites to send, menus to choose and flowers to think about. Yas had done so much of the organisation for the Moroccan celebration and he was just as keen to be involved in every detail, which was adorable. We were building a life together, day by day, as husband and wife.

"You are invited to celebrate the marriage of Mr and Mrs El Jamouni at the Hunton Park Hotel on 2 September 2011. Dress code: Black and White."

It looked so posh on the invite, like we were throwing some kind of celebrity gala, which, in a way, we were. *OK! Magazine* were covering the whole thing again, which added a layer of glitz I'd never imagined for myself when I first met Yas on MSN in my pyjamas, probably eating biscuits and chatting about Moroccan life. Now here we were, having a party to celebrate our recent marriage in a stately manor in Hertfordshire, with our own spread in a glossy mag. Life, eh?

The venue was stunning, Hunton Park Hotel, all grand staircases, chandeliers and perfectly manicured lawns. The kind of place you half expect to bump into Mr Darcy behind a hedge, clutching a bouquet. Everything had that soft golden glow you only get from proper wedding lighting and expensive candles. We wanted it to feel like a fairy tale and honestly, it did.

The theme was monochrome, very classy. I had two dresses, one white, one black, identical in shape, both lace, fitted just right to make me feel like the leading lady. I wore the white one for the ceremony, then did a quick-change into the black one for the evening do. I felt like Madonna, doing my own little wardrobe swap halfway through the show. Well, if you're going to do it, do it properly and after seven dresses in Morocco, one switch seemed very understated.

Most of the *EastEnders* cast came. Linda Henry, June Brown, Steve McFadden, Perry Fenwick, Tanya Franks, Diane Parish, Ricky Groves, Cliff Parisi, plus a good chunk of the crew too. It was like the Queen Vic had packed up and gone on holiday to Hertfordshire. Linda and Steve sat up on the top table with Yas and me, looking like proud Mafia bosses surveying the room.

Linda was very chic in a tailored black suit with matching tie and Steve was holding court with a pint of lager in hand. They'd been with me through thick and thin, on and off the screen and to have them there, not as castmates but as friends, meant the world.

My best friend Graeme was never one for subtlety but he had put together a video montage. I'd been dreading it, thinking he might include one too many dodgy karaoke clips or talk about that time I ate the weed cake in Holland.

"It's not too embarrassing, is it?" I asked.

"Course not," he said with a wink, which usually meant I should brace myself. But actually, it was perfect. Funny, heartfelt, full of moments from my life that made people laugh and cry in equal measure. Even Yas's face lit up watching it, which made me even more emotional.

Yas, bless him, had stayed up all night before the wedding writing his speech. He was so nervous. This was a young man from a deprived suburb on the outskirts of Agadir, now standing in a big English manor, surrounded by people off the telly and trying to find the words to express how he felt. He stood up, hands shaking, suited and booted, holding the microphone like it might electrocute him.

"I love you so much," he said and then his voice cracked. Tears started to fall. He had to sit down, overwhelmed by the emotion of it all. People "aww"-ed and dabbed their eyes. He kept whispering, "I'm sorry, I'm sorry," and I just grabbed his hand and said, "Stop it. You were perfect." Because he was.

Then Steve stood up, doing his unofficial Father of the Bride bit. Pint still in hand, naturally.

"Now listen," he began, fixing Yas with a look that could strip paint, proper Phil Mitchell style. "I've known Cheryl a long time. She's family. So you'd better look after her, alright? Cause if you don't..." The room burst out laughing. Yas looked like he might pass out. Then Steve broke into a smile and gave him a wink. "Only kidding, mate. We're all chuffed for you both."

It was a beautiful moment, but I could see how overwhelmed Yas was. He looked like a lamb heading for the slaughter. No family with him, not one familiar face from Morocco.

His mum and dad and sisters were all thousands of miles away and that broke my heart. But to his credit, he handled it all with such grace. Everyone made an effort to talk to him, to welcome him in and he responded with warmth, humility and that big gentle smile that had made me fall for him in the first place.

The food was lovely, proper posh wedding grub and the flowers were like something out of a magazine – which I suppose they actually were! Richard and Judy's daughter Chloe Madeley turned up with her boyfriend at the time, Sam Attwater. It was a proper *EastEnders* knees-up, full of laughter, music, clinking glasses and hugs. My drama teachers Ben Merritt and Yvonne McGuinness, who had inspired me back in Peterborough were also there and it was special to share the moment with them. Yas and I danced to 'Always and Forever' again, just like we had in Morocco. It was our song by then. And as I looked around the room at all these people who meant so much to me and at Yas beside me, smiling through the chaos, I thought: We did it. We actually did it.

Chapter Twenty-Six

Watching the coffin being carried into the church, the tears came unbidden. I felt a wave of sadness rush through me and my knees buckled slightly, like the emotion had hit me physically. She was dead. She was actually dead. I mean, I knew it was coming, I'd read the scripts, I'd filmed the scenes, I'd had the meetings. But nothing quite prepares you for the moment when you see the pink prop coffin being carried in like the real thing. It suddenly all felt horribly final.

But then I thought to myself, hang on a minute... there's no chance I would've actually fit in that tiny coffin! It's far too small. And I burst out laughing through the tears. Trust me to be cracking morbid jokes at my own on-screen funeral. That was the surreal thing about it, few people ever get to watch their own funeral, like some loitering ghost surveying the scene. But there I was, on location, off-camera, watching the whole thing unfold like some bizarre out-of-body experience.

EastEnders doesn't film in chronological order, but Heather's funeral was one of the last scenes I was involved in. I wasn't in the episode – obviously, being dead and all – but I still came in to be part of the day. I didn't want to miss it. I suppose, deep down, I needed closure, it felt like a proper goodbye to this character that had been a part of me for so long.

I watched as Joshua Pascoe, who played Ben Mitchell, sobbed over my coffin with a look of such despair on his face. He was brilliant, committed and teary-eyed and full of angst. But all I could think was, "You little liar! You're the one who hit me over the head with a photo frame!" Of all the weapons. A photo frame!

And Linda. Oh, Linda Henry, she broke me. She stood there as Shirley, my best mate, delivering this gut-wrenching eulogy with so much truth and vulnerability in her voice that everyone on set had a lump in their throat. She said, "I'm going to miss your smiles, I'm going to miss your cuddles... but most of all, I'm going to miss my best friend." And even though we were acting, it was real and I stood quietly behind the monitors with a tissue in hand, watching them all say goodbye. Watching the extras sob. Watching the black suits and funeral flowers and mourners file into the church. I watched my on-screen life get laid to rest. And it was beautiful. It was heartbreaking. It was weirdly peaceful. And I knew then, I was going to miss them all too.

How could I not with such icons of the small screen as my workmates and friends? Take June Brown for instance, she was a proper professional and an absolute legend. She acted in *EastEnders* as Dot Cotton until she was 91 years old and she was epic. Even pop star Lady Gaga was in awe of her when they appeared together on *The Graham Norton Show* in 2013, inviting her to a nightclub after they were interviewed. But let me tell you, she took her job very seriously even in her old age. June knew everything about her character, from Dot's favourite tea bags to her great aunt's neighbour's cat. She was on it. And when it came to the set, June was the queen of continuity. You could have moved a coaster half an inch and she'd notice. If there were two apples and a banana in Dot's fruit bowl during one scene, you can bet your last sausage roll she'd spot it if there was only one apple the next.

"No, no," she'd say, her voice thick with authority. "Last time we were in here, there were two apples. We must keep continuity!" Nothing got past June.

So, on my last day filming *EastEnders*, when Linda suggested I take a small memento from the set to remember my final scene, I wasn't convinced. Not just because it felt a bit cheeky, but because we were filming in Dot's house. And that, in *EastEnders* terms, was sacred ground.

"It's not my front room, is it?" I said, trying to play it cool. "This is June's house. It's Dot's house. She'll know something's gone the minute she walks in."

Linda grinned. "Come on, Cheryl. You've been part of this family for years. You should take something to remind you of your last scene, where you were, what you did. No one will mind."

I raised an eyebrow. "June will know," I protested. "She always knows."

Linda just laughed. "Oh, come on. She won't notice one tiny thing's missing."

Now, in the corner of Dot's lounge there was this glass-fronted cabinet, proper old-fashioned, full of little trinkets and ornaments. Among them was this tiny ornamental teapot. Nothing flashy, but it had a charm to it. Linda had clearly had her eye on it.

When nobody was looking, she crept over, opened the cabinet and slipped the teapot into her coat pocket. She then turned and passed it to me, with this naughty glint in her eye. "What are you doing?" I hissed.

She shrugged, all casual. "Take it. Then you'll always remember your last scene in Dot's house. It'll make you smile when you see it on a shelf at home." I was still dithering about the ethics of it all when Linda did what only Linda could get away with, she marched right over to the props assistant.

"Listen," she said, "I've just given Cheryl that tiny teapot figurine from Dot's cabinet to keep as a memory. Can you replace it with something similar?"

He looked up from whatever he was fiddling with and smiled. "Totally fine. Don't worry, I'll sort it."

Crisis averted... or so I thought. Weeks later, after I had left, Linda rang me up. "You'll never guess what happened the other day," she said, already snorting. "You know the teapot?"

"Of course," I said, "the Great Teapot Heist of Albert Square."

"Well, the props lad who covered for us. He was on set with June the other day, filming a scene back in Dot's house," she revealed.

"Oh no," I said, my stomach already tightening. "Don't tell me..."

"She spotted it!" Linda squealed. "She clocked the new one straight away." I groaned. "Of course she did. Go on..."

"So they're setting up the shot, everything's fine and June's chatting away. Then she goes all still and says, 'Where's my little teapot?' Just like that. Dead serious. Everyone froze. The props lad kept it cool, 'Oh June, I meant to tell you. I was dusting and it... erm... it fell. It smashed. I replaced it. Sorry.'" What a hero!

But back to the final scene: Linda was in tears and had to

leave the set, while everyone was giving me hugs and congratulating me. She was just in bits. "I am just going to miss you so much," she said later in the dressing room. "I am going to miss you too," I croaked, swallowing hard. On *EastEnders*, they have a rule: you have to be there five years to get a leaving party.

So I wasn't expecting one as I was a couple of months shy of that point and while I'd been flooded with hugs and cards and lovely words from the cast and crew, I assumed that was it. No fuss, no fanfare, just a quiet goodbye. After all, rules were rules.

I'd packed up my dressing room that day with a heavy heart. Took one last look at the room that had played host to so much fun, joy and creativity. It was a surreal feeling, closing that door for the final time. I'd spent nearly five years living and breathing that building and suddenly it was all done.

Afterwards, I was sitting with Linda in her dressing room, chatting about old scenes and laughing about all the great times we had, when Perry Fenwick, who plays Billy Mitchell, and Steve McFadden popped their heads round the door.

"Fancy going for a quick drink at the pub down the road, Chezza?" said Steve.

"Hmm, I don't know," I replied. "Maybe I should have a quiet one. It's been a long day, I feel a bit tired." Perry piped up, grinning. "Don't be daft. One last post-work drink! You have to."

I gave in. "Go on then."

So the four of us piled into Steve's car. It felt weird, driving out of the Elstree gates, knowing it might be the last time I ever did that as a cast member. The buildings I'd walked into day after day, the security guards who'd always given me a smile, the canteen staff, the make-up girls, all of it was fading into the rearview mirror. I was saying goodbye to Heather Trott, to the Square, to the show that had changed my life.

But then, as we turned the corner, Steve suddenly pulled a U-turn. "Sorry Cheryl," he said over his shoulder. "Perry has forgotten something. He is just gonna nip back in." I raised an eyebrow but didn't think much of it. We parked up again and Steve turned to me.

"Actually," he said, "why don't we just have a drink in the BBC bar? Since we're already here."

"Sure," I said. "Why not?"

We walked back in through the familiar doors, up the corridor and into the bar. And as Steve pushed the door open... "SURPRISE!"

The room erupted. I blinked, stunned. Everyone was there. Cast, crew, makeup, costume, runners, writers, even Barbara Windsor and Pam St Clement had come back just for the party. I was gobsmacked.

The whole bar was filled with all the people I loved, all there for me. I stood there for a second, not quite believing it. My eyes welled up with emotion, full of happy tears.

Linda came up behind me and gave me the biggest hug. "You didn't really think we were going to let you leave without a send-off, did you? Not a chance!"

Turns out, the cast and crew had decided to throw their own party for me, rule or no rule. They'd planned it all in secret, pulling strings and calling in favours. Even the bar staff were in on it.

It was all so overwhelming. Bittersweet, yes, but mostly

just beautiful. That feeling that I had meant something. That I'd made real friends. That I had made an impact not just through Heather Trott, but as Cheryl.

This wasn't just the end of a job. It was the end of something magical. But I walked away with more than a storyline. I walked away with lifelong friends... and a tiny stolen teapot full of memories.

Chapter Twenty-Seven

I arrived at the hotel, wearing a black balaclava and dark glasses, it was five months after I'd left *EastEnders* and I needed to go incognito.

I jumped out of the taxi, holding a plastic Co-op shopping bag and the camera bulbs flashed.

No, I was not here to rob the place, although if I was, the paps would have rumbled me. Instead, I am headed inside to prepare for my stint in the *Big Brother* house. The producers had told us we had to go in disguise, wear a hat and glasses, but I thought screw that, I could do better. Which is why I chose the balaclava and glasses. I look a bit stupid and it's obviously me, but give them a show I thought – I am a performer after all. All the celebs were given code names by production, named after chocolate bars and I was Crunchie – which was funny. We had to stay in the hotel a few nights and my phone was taken away from me, so I was only allowed one call to Alex and Yas in the evenings. It was a bit like prison really and I was only allowed to watch certain programmes on the TV, so that I was kept in the dark as much as possible.

The production team went through all my suitcases to look at my things. If any of the clothing was branded I wasn't allowed to wear it and stuff like shampoo and bodywash had labels stuck over it so you couldn't see the brand. I'd heard a rumour that Julian Clary might be going into the house, too. Oh, please let that be true, I thought. I've always fancied meeting him, someone with a proper sense of humour, a bit of camp, a bit of mischief. He was the kind of person who, if you were going to be stuck in a fishbowl for a fortnight, you'd want him there with you.

Before I left, Yas had sat me down in the kitchen and said, "Do you want me to take Alex to Morocco, just while you're in the house? I know what the press are like, maybe it's best for him to be away from it all." That's the kind of man he is, always thinking ahead, always protecting us. And I agreed, I knew Alex would be safe and spoiled rotten by Yas's family and that gave me peace of mind.

Meanwhile, my friend Christine had come round and said, "Well, while you're in there, why don't we give your house a bit of a spruce up? Paint the living room, sort the bathroom, make it nice for when you get back." Bless her.

The *Big Brother* prize was feeling more and more like a holiday. A weird one, mind you, where you share a house with strangers and millions of people watch you eat cornflakes. But a break all the same.

I kept telling myself, "This is a laugh, Cheryl. A game. Just go in there, be yourself, have a bit of fun. And at the end, you come out with a cheque big enough to set you, Yas and Alex up properly." I sat at the hotel munching on snacks and watching telly and thinking, what on earth have I signed up for? But also... I couldn't wait. It was going to be fun.

Then it began. 15 August 2012. The telly flickers on, the *Celebrity Big Brother* theme blares and there I am, Cheryl Fergison, beaming out to the nation, giving it my best energy in the pre-recorded VT, shot under bright studio lights. Hair freshly done, lipstick on, ready to take on the challenge.

"Hello, my name is Cheryl Fergison," I say beaming. "You might know me as Heather Trott from *EastEnders*. Heather had some amazing storylines before she died. I was done for nicking cheese in a minimart, I got pregnant by a teenager and then I got hit over the head with a picture frame. Since being in *EastEnders* it's been amazing, people's reactions on the street. I get shouted at, 'Heather! Heather!' I get proposals of marriage, dinner and go to George Michael conventions. I love singing. I might be a bit annoying sometimes. I think I am a nightmare to live with. If there is any conflict in the house I will probably just try to walk away from the conflict. I don't know if I will be a great housemate, I just hope I am a happy housemate. Probably, you will find me weeping in a dark room a lot."

Cut to me, live on Channel 5, stood outside the *Celebrity Big Brother* house, heart thudding so hard I could hear it in my ears. The crowd's roaring, the music's pounding, host Brian Dowling is shouting over the din and I'm waving like the Queen at a Jubilee.

I take a deep breath, plaster on a smile and walk down that runway, up those famous steps and into the house...

Being in the *Big Brother* House is weird, because it doesn't seem like a house at all. Really, what it reminds me of is being in an Ikea set. It's not a real house. You know when you go shopping around a superstore and you see all the different items that aren't yours, but you might want to buy? It just felt like that, very fake, like play acting. It was also obvious that we were in a film set as you could hear the cameras behind the walls and then the whirr of them moving on dollies when something interesting was happening.

If something was going on in the garden and you were in the kitchen, you knew that there was something going on somewhere else, because there would be a stampede of the cameras. I didn't expect to be centre-stage on the very first night in the *Celebrity Big Brother* house, but oh boy, was I.

Talk about being thrown in at the deep end! I hadn't even unpacked my toothbrush before I was smack bang in the middle of an almighty bust-up, with none other than soap royalty herself, Julie Goodyear.

Now, let me set the scene. Julie, aka Bet Lynch from *Coronation Street*, wearing leopard print cat ears and armed with razor-sharp wit, was the first celeb to walk into the house that night. I came in shortly after, all nerves and excitement, wearing a gorgeous dress my husband Yas had bought me from Morocco. I loved that dress. It was a floaty black kaftan embroidered with brightly coloured jewels across the front. I felt like a goddess in it, but that feeling didn't last long.

The minute the two of us were in, we were summoned to the Diary Room. It was all very hush-hush, very cloak and dagger. And there we were told, live on air, that we'd been chosen for a secret mission: The Battle of the Soaps. Our task? To stage a massive, no-holds-barred, rip-roaring row the moment the other housemates walked in. We had to make it believable. Like proper telly gold for the people back home. No pressure then.

So, we strutted back into the living area, our minds whirring with what to say and took our places. Next came the rest of the housemates, filing in one by one under the bright lights away from the roar of the crowd outside. I clocked them as they arrived. Singer and presenter Coleen Nolan, warm and chatty as ever; Spandau Ballet bassist and ex *EastEnders* actor Martin Kemp looking like a rock star off-duty; MC Harvey from So Solid Crew; *Jersey Shore*'s Mike 'The Situation' Sorrentino; journalist Samantha Brick; glamour model Rhian Sugden; model Jasmine Lennard; page three girl Danica Thrall and Julian Clary, whom I had been a fan of since forever.

It was a real pick 'n' mix of personalities, like someone had shaken up a snow globe filled with British telly and let the flakes settle in one very chaotic house. Once everyone had started mingling, I turned to Julie, eyes blazing, channelling every ounce of my inner soap opera diva into a meltdown.

"Can we sort this problem out seriously," I snapped, my voice sharp and cutting across the room, "because you keep giving me looks and they are not very nice. These guys don't know the history, okay? They don't know the history, alright?"

Julie didn't flinch. She narrowed her eyes and replied coolly, "I am not, Cheryl."

"You are," I fired back, "you are giving me looks across the way and I don't like it very much. And you know the situation and you know what you've done."

"Cheryl, I haven't done anything."

"No, you have," I insisted. "You keep looking at me across the way."

Julie scoffed. "Don't be ridiculous."

"You do," I said, refusing to back down. "You keep giving me evils across the way."

"Don't talk stupid."

I took a deep breath, managing to stay in character even though I wanted to crack up.

"The problem is, Julie, these guys don't know the history or nothing of what you've done."

Julie raised her chin defiantly. "Well, why bring it up now?"

"Because you keep giving me the evils!" I bellowed.

That was when she exploded. The switch flipped and Julie transformed into a full-blown soap diva right there in the living room.

"Don't talk shite!" she roared. "Now leave it, alright? Just leave it, Cheryl!"

The rest of the housemates, all of whom were now frozen in horror, eyes wide, jaws dropped at the drama kicking off within minutes of arriving.

"I knew there was going to be a problem with you coming in," I said, my voice rising. "I knew there would be. Sorry guys, I am so sorry. There is a slight bit of history and it's not even fucking funny. It's not even funny and I am not having the looks you are giving me across the room."

And then, right on cue, the final act came when Julie, clearly gunning for her BAFTA, ended the argument by chucking a drink over me. I kid you not. One minute I'm standing there defending Heather Trott's honour and the next I'm dripping with prosecco and it's all over my beautiful Moroccan embroidered dress. The new one Yas had bought me so lovingly was soaked.

"Shut up!" she shouted. "Shut up now! Leave it!"

There was a beat of absolute silence. You could practically hear the nation gasp in unison. The housemates were horrified. The looks on their faces ranged from "oh my god she's gone too far" to "someone get me out of here!" It was really dramatic and telly gold, just like the producers wanted.

Inside though, I was raging. My brain was going at a hundred miles an hour: Do I cry? Do I scream? Do I chuck something back? Do I hit her with a throw cushion? Do I burst out laughing? I couldn't blow the cover. This was a task. We had to keep the argument going, pretend we hated each other's guts and hope that no one twigged it was all an act.

So I did the only thing I could think of: I burst into tears. Fake sobbing and blubbing and bless the housemates, they rallied round, comforting me like I'd just lost a loved one. I was getting all the sympathy. Meanwhile, Julie stomped off like the villain of the piece.

Hours later, once the live show had gone off air, we were finally allowed to let the cat out of the bag. The *Big Brother* voice of doom summoned us all to the sofas. And then it was revealed: "Earlier this evening, Cheryl and Julie were given a secret task..."

There were lots of gasps and laughter and a fair bit of side-eye. I looked around and saw a few faces fall, not because they were angry about the task, but because I'd managed to fool them. I'm not a game player, I wear my heart on my sleeve, or in this case, all over a damp new dress. I remember thinking, oh god, they're never going to trust me again.

In the end, people saw the funny side and the clip went a bit viral. "Julie Goodyear throws a drink on Heather Trott" isn't exactly something I thought I'd be associated with in life, but hey, if you're going to go in, go in with a splash. Literally.

Julie and I had a right laugh about it afterwards. We became mates in the house and that mad mission bonded us in a weird way. It might have been fake fury, but it created real friendship.

And the dress? Well, it dried.

Chapter Twenty-Eight

If you sing songs in the *Big Brother* House that they can't get the copyright to, they won't air the scene. This is because they have to get permission from the owner of the song and pay lots of money. Once I'd learned this I thought, brilliant, that's how I'll get a bit of privacy! If I don't fancy being on telly for a bit I can just sing along to something that will be too expensive for the show to afford.

Martin Kemp, who played Steve Owen on *EastEnders* before I joined, also cottoned onto the same trick and the two of us would sing along happily during the long brightly lit days. What I didn't realise until after I left the house was how much Julian Clary had found my singing really annoying, apparently. He'd been slipping into the Diary Room, telling *Big Brother* and everyone at home, "Oh, Cheryl sings all the time. It's rather irritating, actually."

I mean, fair. I probably was annoying to be around. But I was also completely thrilled to be in there with Julian because I was so in total awe of him, he was one of my heroes.

I'd adored him back when I was a student, with Fanny the Wonderdog, his outrageous cabaret acts, his sharp tongue and eyeliner flicks. I just thought he was fabulous.

So when he actually walked into the house, in his blue and black satin suit, heavy eye make-up and pink lipstick, I was over the moon. As I've said before, I'd heard rumours that he might be going in, but I didn't want to let myself believe it. Then there he was, sashaying in like a glamorous raven in a silk scarf. I was like a little puppy dog around him, trailing him from task to task, hoping I'd get a moment to chat.

I just found him so fascinating. He had this old-school showbiz glamour that's rare now and was funny, strange and bitingly clever, with this dry wit that could cut through a room like a scalpel. I wanted to hear all his stories, about the clubs, the telly years, the stage. Him and Julie Goodyear were close from the start and I'd often sit myself nearby in the hot tub, pretending to relax in the jacuzzi, but really just ear-wigging on their fabulous conversations, soaking up every syllable like I was eavesdropping on royalty.

And I know they say don't meet your heroes, but Julian lived up to the lot. He was everything I'd imagined and more. And yes, okay, he might've moaned about my singing behind my back, but honestly? That only makes me love him more.

I spent most of my time in the *Celebrity Big Brother* house floating about in the pool like a content hippo in a heatwave. Proper luxury for me, that was. And then there was the house bowling championship. Honestly, we got so bored between tasks that we started rolling balled-up socks at random bottles of suncream, trying to knock them over. It became a proper competition. And guess who won? Yours truly. Champion bowler of Series 10.

So yes, I was having fun. Which made it a bit of a blow when I was evicted on the 10th day. I remember hearing the announcement and thinking, really? Already? Christine and my mates hadn't even finished painting my house yet, they thought I'd be in there for at least a couple more weeks. I think Christine was more shocked than me!

Someone later told me I might've been out earlier than expected because it was the year they changed the voting system from "Vote to Evict" to "Vote to Save". They may have just been trying to spare my feelings but still, I couldn't be too upset, because as I headed out to the top of the steps, a new thought hit me: I was finally going to start my life with Yas and Alex. The show was fun, yes, but real life, with the people I loved, was waiting for me outside those sound-proofed, mirrored walls. Who knew what would come next? The world felt open again.

I walked down those famous stairs and waved at the cheering fans in the crowd. It was surreal, flashbulbs going, people screaming my name, the whole world feeling a bit brighter and madder than I remembered it.

Then I sat down across from Brian Dowling, who was lovely as ever and had my big exit interview. And just like that, my time in the *Big Brother* house was over, but a brand new chapter was just beginning. I was going to live my happy ever after, with my new husband and my son and hopefully a new great acting role. I was excited and positive, but then it all came crashing down, when I was finally given my phone back.

I turned my mobile on and within seconds it was like a digital assault: *ping! ping! ping! ping!* One notification after another lighting up the screen like a slot machine on a winning streak. Some of the messages were from friends or family saying how much they'd enjoyed watching me, but lots of them were something very different.

What I saw were a string of urgent, panicked messages from a few people whom I won't name who were suddenly falling over themselves to reach me.

"Cheryl, please ring me ASAP."

"You need to call me immediately."

"It's serious. It's bad news.."

Then one message stopped me cold. It read: "Shit. We are in big trouble. Ring me. It's about our accountant."

My accountant had seemed so normal. Nothing about him screamed dodgy, in fact he seemed very ordinary, quite boring, even. The kind of man you'd forget five minutes after meeting. He wore glasses and was always neatly turned out in a suit and tie and gave off a quiet yet capable vibe.

I was introduced to him by others in the wider film industry and he was highly recommended as a good accountant, a safe pair of hands. He spoke softly, didn't overcomplicate things and seemed to know what he was doing. I was so busy with *EastEnders* and everything else going on that I was relieved to have someone just "deal with" the tax side of things. By the final year I was on *EastEnders*, he had moved abroad, but he still made the trip back and forth for our meetings.

At one point, he told me his daughter was seriously ill with cancer. He said he needed me to file my taxes earlier, as he was caring for her. What could I do? Of course I believed him, I sympathised with him and I handed it over without a second thought.

For five years, I paid him. For five years, he pocketed the money and didn't pay a single penny to HMRC. When I found out, it was like someone had pulled the rug from under me. Everything I had built, saved and worked for was gone.

I was planning to start a new life with Yas and Alex, we were finally ready. The cheque from *Celebrity Big Brother* had just come in, that was meant to be our new beginning, instead, it went straight to the taxman. Every last penny of it. And all my savings? Gone too, completely wiped out.

The police got involved. There was an investigation and there were other victims who had been fleeced too. It turned out his address was just a PO box and his daughter was never sick. I was told a warrant had been issued for his arrest, but he'd vanished.

The policeman who dealt with the case, who has since retired, later told me that Interpol had picked him up in connection with a completely different fraud. But even now, we don't know where he is. He disappeared, leaving a trail of destruction behind him. He ruined my life.

I had already paid him hundreds of thousands; money I worked hard for. And now I owed more than the same again to the taxman. I had no idea how I was going to come up with that. They wanted to make an example out of us actors and even though I was a victim I had to repay the money. I was beside myself and I just did not know what to do.

I'm not a law-breaker and I never have been. What the hell had gone on here? Why had it gone wrong? This should have been a really happy time in my life, but I felt so angry, so sad, so pissed off, so annoyed with myself that I trusted this man. What was I going to do? How could I get out of this? Who could I trust anymore?

I was devastated and I felt humiliated. I'd been conned in the worst way. No one wants to feel like they can be duped, but worse than that is the guilt and the shame that follows.

BEHIND THE SCENES

How could I be so naive? But then again, how was I supposed to know?

You hire a plumber because you think they can plumb and you don't fix the pipes yourself. You trust them to do their job. You hire an accountant for the same reason, because it's not your area of expertise. You assume they'll do what they say they will, that they'll look after your money and that they won't steal it. It's not stupid, it is human, but money shame is cruel. It makes you feel worthless, it makes you question everything, your judgment, your intelligence, your ability to protect your own family. And worst of all, it isolates you. You don't want to tell people, because you're embarrassed.

You think they'll laugh, or judge you, or think less of you. And maybe some of them do. At least I had my husband to lean on. Yas was supportive, of course, but he was so young, from a different world and didn't know how to help. But he listened, which is all he could do. I couldn't tell Alex, he was too young, but I confided in my friends like Graeme and Christine.

As for the accountant? I wanted to pulverise him, really I did. I wanted to grab him by the collar and scream in his face. I wanted him to feel the crushing panic I'd felt, the betrayal and the grief. I wanted to beat the living daylights out of him. I wanted him to suffer. Not quickly, not in one clean blow. Slowly. Painfully. I wanted him to feel every ounce of hurt he'd caused me, to feel the ripples of damage he'd sent through my life.

I don't use the word hate very often. It's a heavy word, one you can't always take back, but in this case, I meant it. I hated him. Not just for what he did, but for how he made me feel about myself. For the mess he left behind. For every sleepless night, every tear, every humiliating phone call to the tax office, to banks, to friends trying to figure out how the hell I was going to keep my head above water.

Going broke when you're famous is the worst because everyone expects you to have lots of money. People assume that you're minted and set for life, dripping in cashmere and cruising about in a top-of-the-range Range Rover with a handbag full of crisp fifties.

They don't imagine you're juggling overdrafts, maxed out credit cards, payday loans and mountains of bills. But that was exactly where I found myself.

I'd just come out of one of the biggest soaps in the country, I'd done *Celebrity Big Brother*. I was still in the papers, still recognised in the street, but behind the scenes, I was totally skint.

The worst part? You still feel like you've got to keep up appearances and pretend because if you don't, the shame feels double. You're not just broke, you're publicly broke. People don't understand how that could happen to you when you have a huge platform and great opportunities. But it does, anyone can get into debt. I tried my best to hide it and I was still paying for others.

I was still going to my local Turkish restaurant and bringing along friends who were on low salaries.

I'd say, "Don't worry, I'm paying. I've got a job next week." I'd tell myself it was fine, that something would come in. That I just had to keep the momentum going, keep people thinking I was doing well. When you're well known, the bill doesn't even get passed to you. It just appears in front of you. The assumption is always: "She's off the telly, she'll be paying."

I couldn't stop. I couldn't bear the thought of people thinking

I was struggling. So I kept covering bills, kept spending and kept pretending. But behind the scenes, I was drowning. I got into a spiral of debt, taking out loans to pay off other loans.

It all crept up on me. I think, subconsciously my spending was tied up in the grief from losing my mum so young. She always used to say life was short. She was gone at 52.

That idea really stuck with me, that you had to live for today, make the most of things while you still could. So if I had £50 in my pocket, I didn't think to save it. I always thought: Who can I treat with this?

It could be a little something for Alex, or a trinket for Yas, or a meal out with friends. If I saw something that would make someone else happy, even just for a moment, I'd buy it. I didn't think about the consequences, or at least I ignored them.

I was partly to blame for this because I had thrown money around like confetti when I was on *EastEnders*. Taxis? On me. Dinners out? I'd cover the bill. Presents, drinks, little treats for the people I loved, I never thought twice. I'd pay for friends who were struggling, family members who were skint, or those who just needed a leg up. That generosity came from a good place, of course, it always did. I wasn't doing it to show off, I think I just wanted people to feel cared for and loved. Maybe because I'd known what it was like to feel like you had nothing.

But while my heart was in the right place, my bank balance was not and I wasn't ready to face the truth of the fact that I was in a deep financial hole. And fame, contrary to what most people think, wasn't going to dig me out of it.

Chapter Twenty-Nine

Yas was back and forth to Morocco, trying to balance being caught up between two worlds. He wanted to care for his grandparents and his sick father and also be there for his wife. He would come and stay for long stints at a time and one day, in October 2013, we went up to Liverpool because I was an ambassador for the Health Lottery and was set to visit a Tesco Superstore which had raised money for charity. It was part of a public event and I thought why not make a weekend of it? Yas's dad was a die-hard Liverpool fan, so I suggested we tack on a little visit to Anfield Stadium while we were there.

"That would be great," Yas said, his face lighting up like a kid at a carnival. He was buzzing with excitement all morning. So off we trotted to Anfield, hand-in-hand, like a couple of tourists. The place was packed with fans doing tours, taking selfies and staring in awe at the huge stadium. We wandered into the gift shop which was crammed full of Liverpool branded water bottles, socks, key rings and shirts.

Yas was absolutely in his element, pointing at shirts, going "My dad would love this!" and "Look at the price of these boots!" when suddenly I saw two massive security guards pointing at us. They then started heading towards us. I braced myself, thinking, oh no, someone's clocked me from

EastEnders. Here we go again. I stepped forward to say hello, But no, they walked straight past me, without even glancing my way and went straight for Yas. One of them put a firm hand on his shoulder. Yas turned around, all wide-eyed and startled. The guard looked shocked, "Sorry, mate. Sorry. We thought you were Luis Suarez. People were saying he was in the shop."

Yas just froze and held his hands up like he was being arrested. "What?" he asked.

"You know," I chimed in, laughing. "The famous Liverpool footballer. The one from Uruguay."

Yas burst out laughing. "I know who he is!" He said, "I am not Suarez!"

Honestly, I could've keeled over. The guards were all flustered, apologising profusely, but I was loving every minute. To be fair, Yas was a dead ringer for Suarez back then and I couldn't help but wonder what the poor shoppers were thinking. Luis Suarez and Heather Trott from *EastEnders*, casually browsing keyrings together in the Liverpool FC gift shop.

What a crossover episode that would've been. We laughed about it afterwards and I told Yas he should've signed a few shirts and done a fake autograph session. "You missed your moment!" I teased. "Could've made someone's day."

We had so much fun together, so it was sad when Yas went home a few months later, but he felt he had to. He found it hard to settle into life in the UK, not because he didn't love me or Alex, but because it was all so different for him. The language, the culture, even the weather. Then, one thing after another hit him, his grandfather passed away, his father became seriously ill and suddenly, his place was back home. He needed to be there for them, the way I was for my family once. And I understood that, I truly did. But it made things tough for me. Really tough.

While I was trying to keep a brave face and juggle auditions, bills and raising a teenage son, I had to do it alone a lot of the time. Alone and secretly battling debt. But I am not someone who just sits and wallows. Chin up, Cheryl, I thought, a positive attitude will see me through. I love my husband and at least I can be thankful for the fact he doesn't bite people – not like the real Luis Suarez!

And despite everything, at least I still had work to do, which I was grateful for. One of the most fun jobs I landed in 2013 after *EastEnders* was a guest role on *The Spa*, created by the brilliant Derren Litten who also was the brains behind *Benidorm*. It was set in a Hertfordshire spa that proudly boasted it could cure anyone; the fat, the thin and the lazy. It was a proper laugh from start to finish. I played a character called Bergita Wilde, who was a customer at the spa. In one scene, a member of the staff writes her name down phonetically as "Big Eater" – which, when you hear it out loud, sounds exactly like "Bergita". Cue absolute chaos. It was a classic Derren gag; cheeky, daft and full of heart and it was exactly my cup of tea.

What made it even better was the people I got to work with. There were some cracking guest stars on that series including cricket legend Freddie Flintoff and the one and only Chesney Hawkes. Although the show was fantastically funny, it was even more hilarious larking about off-camera with those two. You'd think they'd be a bit aloof or "celebby," but they weren't at all, just down-to-earth, easygoing and up for a bit of fun, exactly the kind of people you want to be around when you're filming long days.

My character, much like Heather was with George Michael, was absolutely obsessed with Chesney. So when I found out I'd be doing a scene where I got to sing 'The One and Only' with him on stage I was thrilled. I mean, come on! What a moment. We belted it out with full dramatic flair, the audience (and crew) in stitches.

Around the same time, I also landed a role in *Big School*, created by my hilarious mate David Walliams whom I'd met on *Little Britain* all those years ago. It also starred the inimitable Catherine Tate, who is as talented as she is kind. I played Jo, the school's quiet lab assistant who hardly said a word for most of the series, but in one standout moment, she sang 'Ave Maria' at a funeral in front of all the other teachers, leaving them (and viewers) completely gobsmacked. It was one of those beautiful, bizarre, unexpected turns that only a show like that could get away with. I loved it.

Life was still full of pinch-me moments, even if I was having to pinch the pennies. I was skint and still dealing with the fallout from everything financially, but when I look back on that time, I like to think I was experience-rich. Not every role fills your bank account, but some of them fill your soul. And that, in a way, kept me going.

One job I relished involved me and my dear friend Julian Clary who, as I've already mentioned, found my constant singing in the *Celebrity Big Brother* house quite irritating. He'd march into the Diary Room and grumble about how I was forever warbling away like a broken jukebox. So you can just imagine his sheer delight when, in 2013, he found himself in the privileged position of having to sit through my singing again. This time not only watching, but judging me on national telly.

That's right. In July 2013 I appeared on the ITV show *Your Face Sounds Familiar* and Julian, bless him, was one of the judges. He was joined on the panel by none other than the absolute icon that is Emma Bunton, a.k.a. Baby Spice. It was like a fabulous fever dream of mine had collided into one glittery, slightly bonkers talent show.

The show itself was a riot. Each week, I had to transform into a different musical legend and perform one of their songs wearing a full costume with total commitment and no holding back. One week I was Adele belting out 'Someone Like You', the next I was Lulu screaming 'Shout'. I got to be Meat Loaf (complete with a sweaty ruffled shirt and long greasy wig), Madonna in 'Material Girl', Cher doing 'The Shoop Shoop Song' and Anastacia in 'Left Outside Alone'. Honestly, it was a proper musical identity crisis and I absolutely loved every moment of it.

The very first week, I was preparing to perform as Dusty Springfield. My number? 'You Don't Have to Say You Love Me'. I was in rehearsals all week, getting to grips with the vocal stylings and perfecting the sultriness that Dusty was so famous for. After one particularly long session, a producer came up to me, grinning from ear to ear and said, "You're not going to believe who the guest judge is, Cheryl."

I looked at her nervously. "Who is it?" I asked, clutching my water bottle like a stress ball.

"Are you sitting comfortably?" she said

BEHIND THE SCENES

"Just tell me!" I begged.

She smirked. "It's Donny Osmond."

My jaw dropped. I couldn't speak and my eyes filled up with tears. "You're joking. You must be joking." But she wasn't. It was really true. My childhood icon was going to be watching me sing.

The next day, Donny and his lovely wife Debbie arrived at the studio and he started doing the rounds, popping into dressing rooms to say hello. What did I do? Well, of course I did what any self-respecting adult woman would do in that situation; I legged it.

I wasn't in my dressing room when he came to say hi, I just couldn't face it, it was too much to handle and my inner 11-year-old was screaming.

Later that day, during the technical rehearsal, I saw him. He was sitting with his wife and son in the judging area, looking just as I remember. The years had barely touched his face, he still had that thick head of hair, megawatt smile and cheeky grin. But it was a marvel I clocked any of this, considering I could barely look at him. I'd glance his way and then look away again immediately, acting like I was deep in conversation with someone, anyone, just to avoid locking eyes.

I must have seemed rude, but honestly, I felt I would explode if we had eye contact. I am sure he realised what was up, because eventually word got around: Cheryl can't cope. She's in love. She's actually gone full fangirl.

It wasn't until that evening, before the live show that we actually spoke. He came into my dressing room to see me as the final touches were being added to my Dusty Springfield smokey eye make up. "Good luck with everything tonight, Cheryl," he said with a smile.

I looked at him, sheepishly. "Thank you. I'm so sorry I couldn't talk to you yesterday," I said.

"I know," he replied kindly. "They told me I was your crush years ago."

"Oh Donny," I said, half-laughing as I finally made eye contact. "You still are. You've still got it, mate."

And then it was showtime. On the stage the lights went down, the smoke machine fired up and the stage lift slowly brought me up into the spotlight. There I was, Dusty Spring-field, full beehive, cat-eye liner, sparkles and a microphone in hand, singing 'You Don't Have to Say You Love Me' while looking into the eyes of the man I'd loved since I was a girl.

But I wasn't clutching a hairbrush in my bedroom this time. I wasn't daydreaming about him while singing to posters on my wall. I was on a real stage, holding a real mic, with the real Donny Osmond right there, smiling back at me.

And you know what? I won that week.

When they announced my name, Donny came up on stage and gave me a hug and a kiss. I could've dropped dead right there and I'd have died happy. Just goes to show everyone was wrong. It wasn't just a Puppy Love after all.

Chapter Thirty

Alex and I were in the car, driving back home from school one afternoon, just the two of us. We were listening to music and I was humming along to whatever was on the radio, and tapping the steering wheel in rhythm, then, out of nowhere, he reached forward and switched the music off.

He turned to me, his voice soft but certain. "Mum, can you stop the car? I need to tell you something."

"Sure son," I said, glancing over and noticing how serious his face was, creased with worry, his eyes darting nervously between me and the dashboard. My beautiful boy was growing so fast.

At 14, he'd grown into such a handsome teenager, still full of cheek and mischief, but with a newfound confidence settling into him.

He was doing brilliantly at school, especially in music and drama, where he was really thriving. He had made good friends, especially a nice group of girls and they were the kind you hoped would stick around for the long haul. What could be the matter? I parked the car down a side street and faced him.

"What's up, Alex?" I asked. He took a breath, looked down at his hands, then said it in one quiet exhale, "I am gay. I like boys"

"Oh," I said, the corners of my mouth lifting instinctively in a smile. "Yeah?"

And then he burst into tears. "Are you upset with me?" he asked, his voice cracking through the emotion.

"No, I'm not," I said, reaching across the seat and pulling him into a hug right there and then, parked up on a side road. "To be quite honest, Alex... I'm actually quite happy." He looked at me, confused.

"I mean it," I said, brushing his hair off his forehead like I used to when he was little.

"Now we can go to Pride together. You know I've always been an ally of the LGBTQ+ community. I've been going to Pride for years with your Uncle Graeme." He looked completely horrified. "Mum! You can't come to Pride with me. That would be so embarrassing."

"Oh, alright then," I laughed, clutching my chest. "Now I am upset with you!"

He giggled, wiping his eyes.

"Only joking," I added, my voice softening. "I am so proud of you, son. I love you so much."

We stayed like that for a bit, arms wrapped around each other, both a little teary but feeling lighter. That moment, that honest and brave confession, changed everything, and nothing at all. He was still my Alex. Still my beautiful, kind, clever, musical and funny boy. He was just a bit more himself now.

We talked about how he had told me a few months earlier that he was bisexual because he had been too scared to say he was gay and how he'd dated his friend Britney to stop his schoolmates from finding out. It broke my heart a little, knowing he'd carried that fear. But it also filled me with pride, watching him shed it, piece by piece, with every word he spoke.

Eventually, after the hug had loosened and the tears had dried, we talked about telling his dad. Alex was nervous, understandably. Jay had never been the most open-minded, but I told Alex it was important that he was true to himself. That he didn't hide who he was for anyone.

He nodded, still anxious but determined and we decided he would make the call on speaker. I sat beside him, my hand on his knee.

"Hi son," came Jay's voice. "You alright? Are you still coming over tomorrow?"

"Yes, Dad," Alex said, his voice shaking slightly. "I, err... I've just been talking with Mum, and I've got something I need to tell you."

"What is it, son? What's going on?" he asked. Alex looked at me. I smiled and gave a small nod. "I just need to tell you that... I'm gay. I like boys," he said quietly. There was a pause, the kind of silence that slices through the air like a knife.

Jay laughed, a sharp, joyless bark. "You're kidding, right?"

"No, Dad," Alex replied, steadier now. "I'm being serious."

And then, the explosion. "This is all your mother's fault, isn't it? She's made you gay! With all her gay friends. She's brought you up to be this!" he yelled, voice rising.

I stepped in, calm but firm. "Come on, Jay. Aren't you happy that your child's happy? That he's brave enough to be honest? It doesn't matter, he's your son, for God's sake!"

But he wouldn't hear it. The argument grew and grew until finally Jay spat out, "I don't want to see you again, so don't come round. You are not my son." The line went dead.

Alex stared at the phone for a moment, tears brimming. He was heartbroken, of course, but he was angry too and rightly so. That was the last time my son spoke to his father.

Alex tried to reach out a couple of times after that, but the silence was louder than any words. Jay had made his choice and it was the wrong one. He had chosen to miss out on what was mine and his greatest achievement. This wonderful, smart, kind and talented young man.

From that moment on, Alex never looked back. Years later, he discovered that his dad had remarried and had two more children, on Facebook of course, just like I had discovered Jay's cheating all those years ago. Some people never change.

But Alex? He had someone far better than a dad like Jay. He had Graeme, my best friend for over 40 years. A brilliant, kind-hearted, wise man who fostered LGBTQ+ youth and gave them shelter, warmth and love when they had nowhere else to go. He'd always been there for Alex, since he was a baby. And really, he'd been the true father figure all along.

Graeme taught Alex everything. How to love who he is, how to laugh and how to own who he is with confidence. They share a beautiful bond, one rooted in care, humour, and mutual respect.

When Alex turned 18, I took him to Belfast for a play I was in and we ended up in a drag bar, his first time at one. The queens were fabulous, the music was pumping and I was having the time of my life, then I clocked some blokes eyeing up Alex. Protective mum mode kicked in instantly.

Two drag queens swooped in and said, "Oi, back off, that's Cheryl Fergison's son. His mum's here and she's not playing around!" One of the two queens then came over to us and we chatted about Pride and she asked Alex, "Does your mum go with you to Pride?"

He looked horrified. "Oh, no, no, no, I don't want her coming to Pride!"

The drag queen shot him a look and said something I'll never forget, "Alex, if your mum wants to come to Pride with you, you need to celebrate that. Most of us didn't have parents who supported us. We would have given anything to have a mum like yours. Let her come, even if it's just for the first hour, let her show her love."

That hit him and you could see it sink in. Now, I proudly go along to Pride with Alex every year. Me and my pride and joy.

Chapter Thirty-One

Being in debt is so stressful. I was acting in shows but still my money worries were a dark undercurrent running beneath everything, the shadow that followed me around day and night. I now understand how Mum must have felt when the Provident man knocked on our front door as kids. That heavy thump in the chest, the dread you can't shake, no matter how many times you try to convince yourself it'll all be alright.

But it wasn't just the finances. Deep down, something wasn't right within my body either. I was bleeding again and my lower back was sore. I'd been fitted with a Mirena coil to help manage my heavy periods and the constant bleeding I'd had after having Alex. But somehow, this felt different. It wasn't just the discomfort, it was a deep, instinctive sense, a knowing whisper in my gut that something was wrong.

I tried to brush it off and tell myself it was the stress getting to me. I was juggling so much, trying to hold my life together, working when I could, worrying about the bills and keeping the household afloat. When I went for a smear test, it came back clear so I let myself believe that was the end of it, that I was fine. Nothing to worry about, just hormones, just stress and just life.

But still, that nagging feeling wouldn't go away. Yas and I had talked about having children, he was still so young and wanted to be a dad. We both knew I was approaching 50 and the chances were slim, but hope's a stubborn thing, isn't it? I'd been told years ago that I probably wouldn't be able to have children and yet here was Alex, my miracle, living proof that sometimes the odds don't matter. So I thought, maybe, just maybe, it could happen again, maybe I had one more miracle left in me.

Eventually, I went back to the doctor and told them that I was bleeding, so they fitted me with a new Mirena coil. It didn't work, I was still bleeding so I booked another appointment. This time I expected another reassuring pat on the hand, another, "You're fine, Cheryl, it's just your body doing strange things." But the doctor nodded as I spoke, asked questions, scribbled notes, then he referred me for a series of tests and a biopsy at the local hospital.

It all felt like a blur, blood tests, scans, poking, prodding, paper gowns that never quite tied at the back. I told myself it was just precautionary and just a box-ticking exercise.

Still, somewhere deep inside, I knew.

A few weeks later I got the call. They wanted me to come into the hospital for an appointment. I knew then it wasn't good. Doctors don't call you in for nothing. I sat in the small, sterile room, hands knotted in my lap, staring at a faded poster about how to quit smoking. I had brought my friend Trudie, who is a nurse, along for moral support. The doctor came in, closed the door gently behind him and gave me that look. The one that says, "I don't want to be the one to say this." He sat down and cleared his throat.

"Cheryl," he said softly, "I'm really sorry. It's not good news. You have cancer. Stage II womb cancer."

For a moment, everything slowed. The words didn't land. It was like hearing them underwater. I blinked. Swallowed. Blinked again.

"What?" I said, though I'd heard him clearly.

"I know it's a shock," he said, gently. "But we caught it early. It's Stage II. You'll need a hysterectomy within the next few weeks. We'll move quickly."

I stared at him, mouth slightly open, trying to compute what he'd just said. Cancer? Me? It felt like a soap storyline, like I was watching myself on an episode of *EastEnders*. Like I wasn't even in the room, perhaps it was Heather. I felt outside of my body.

My first thought was, am I going to die? My second, how do I tell Alex? Then Yas popped into my head. He was in Morocco. What would he say? Would he not want me when he knew kids were totally off the table? It had been a dream of ours, that was out of reach, but this made it final. A full stop, a slammed door and a womb-shaped hole where hope used to be.

"Oh god," I whispered, more to myself than the doctor. "What am I going to do? How do I tell them? My son, my husband? And what about the money? The job offers? Am I going to die?"

The doctor's voice broke through my thoughts, calm and steady. "You're not alone in this, Cheryl. You've got a treatment team. We're going to support you. The prognosis is good. But you will need time to rest and to recover."

I nodded, numb. I wanted to cry. I wanted to scream "Why me?" I wanted the director to yell cut and for the scene to be over and for me to be able to walk off set and into the green room to have a cup of tea. But instead, I just sat there blinking at the blue tiled floor, wondering how my life had come to this.

All the things I had gone through, all the shame and pain and now this? I don't like to feel sorry for myself, but this felt too cruel. Like it was a horrible cosmic test with the universe saying, "Let's see what else she can take."

But somewhere underneath all the shock and sadness, something flickered deep inside. A tiny ember of strength that hadn't gone out. I'd been knocked down before and every single time, I'd stood back up. I could do it again.

I just wished Yas was here in England. I wanted his arms around me, his calm voice, his kindness. But even without him by my side at that moment, I reminded myself: this was my body. My life. My womb. My future.

Cancer might have come for me, but I wasn't going to let it take everything. I wouldn't let it steal my hope, my humour, or my fight. The reality of course was not so simple and what followed was one of the most difficult and surreal chapters of my life, a stretch of time that felt like I was suspended in mid-air, watching my world tilt and shift beneath me. I was scared, confused, angry and exhausted, but I also found moments of strength, flashes of clarity and the tiniest bits of light in the darkest places.

At the time, I started keeping a diary. I didn't really plan to, it just happened. I typed on my laptop on the day I was diagnosed to share my private thoughts and fears. I logged my medical appointments, my heartache and everything in between. It wasn't for anyone else, it was for my eyes only, as a way to make sense of it all, to get it out of my head and onto the blank page. Looking back now, those pages feel like a time capsule from a version of myself I didn't know I'd need to meet. The following entries are taken from that diary. They begin on the day I found out I had cancer and carry on through the long, strange, emotionally draining summer of 2015.

2/6/2015 – Tuesday

I heard the news today and oh boy. A hospital appointment with Dr McDermott. Stunned to the core to be told I have cancer inside me, inside my womb. I have a full hysterectomy booked in on 29th June. MRI scan and chest X-rays on 11th June. I am in shock.

3/6/2015 – Wednesday

Still in shock, I went to Kennedy's to keep my hair appointment with Rikki.
Couldn't appreciate his amazing work. I am just numb.
I know the logic of all the surgery and that they will get the cancer out but all I can think of is I'm walking around with this inside me and I want it out. Like yesterday. I feel bad I'm lying to Alex but just protecting him. He's smack bang in the middle of his GCSE exams. Bloody brilliant.

4/6/2015 – Thursday

Bad day today. Hibernating. Wake me up when it's all over!

5/6/2015 – Friday

Went to my friend Brendon's house today. He has horses so we went to the field and fed the horses and it was extremely therapeutic. Then we went for some lunch in Chatham Dock the day was beautiful and the sky was cloudless but despite this my heart was heavy.

After leaving Brendon I went to "Ellenor" the hospice. Ironic but I felt really blessed being there – it was the Volunteers Awards in the garden and one of the patients was well enough to join us in the garden she had such an amazing spirit and wasn't fearful that her life would end in this, her now final home and the staff well everyone there do the most amazing care work. It's all so dignified and happy ... Yes happy I felt humbled the good mood is infectious throughout ... No one should die alone ... No one here will. Home time and I hug my son. I can't stop telling him I'm so proud of him

6/6/2015 – Saturday

Spent the day at Wycombe Comic Con, trying to make a living. I went with Alex who helped me run my stall. It was good to be busy and not think of this disgusting thing inside me by interacting with people all day smiling and meeting fans. It was actually fun. We didn't make loads and as things are more than tight at the moment I was grateful that I could buy food for the week at least.

Money has been a struggle and more than a worry since having the terrible HMRC debt hanging over my head. I have had to borrow money from friends and maxed all my cards and overdraft to the limit. I am sure that the stress of all this has contributed to my illness and for that I am extremely angry. Absolutely knackered at the end of the day and my bed is looking like the most beautiful place right now! Night night.

7/6/2015 – Sunday

My garden is a jungle !! Everyone came round to make my garden look nice and make it a good place to sit and relax. Christine brought her Flymo lawnmower and my brother Graeme arrived with his strimmer to sort it out, Alex and Hollie played in the pool. Then nurse Trudie arrived and it was chat, work, cups of teas and coffees, food, more gardening more chats until the garden was complete and the sun was going down – it was nice to be with friends and family. Only Yas is missing. Although people were there I did keep breaking down and having a little cry. Logic says one thing then my heart hurts with sadness it's a weird feeling

8/6/2015 – Monday

Took Alex to his exam and headed into London for a meeting with Emma at Equity, the trade union. I parked my car and on the way walking into the office, I was in a bit of a daydream and I managed to trip on my own sandal and fell smack bang to the ground. My handbag went flying and I grazed my elbow. My dignity was in tatters and I was helped up by a guy walking past. I got up, brushed myself down and started to cry. I felt so stupid and was in a bit of pain but it just felt like "why me... Again?" What have I done to deserve this?

Arriving at Equity offices the lady on reception gave me an antiseptic wipe and I went on to my meeting. Emma entered the room I could tell she was so sympathetic about my recent news about the cancer but after some little chit chat about staying positive etc she helped me fill in all the forms to try to get me some sort of benefit / help with money and living etc trying to make my worries ease just a smidge Driving home I started noticing things I drove past. it was weird, it was like seeing some stuff for the first time. I guess nothing should be taken for granted anymore. Getting home and seeing my son Alex and telling him I loved him felt so poignant. I tell him I love him everyday and I tell him how proud I am of him and his achievements. I hate keeping stuff from him because we usually don't have secrets and are close. I will tell him but he's doing exams right now and he doesn't need to be upset or worry about his mum.

9/6/2015 – Tuesday

I took Alex to his exam and came home and did absolutely nothing. Then I decided to phone up my friend who does beauty to get my toenails sorted and my hairy bloody face de-haired! Couldn't afford it but had to feel a bit normal and anything to make me feel better was good in my book. I then had a terrible Skype time with Yas. I don't know what's going on but I just hope he comes and supports me through this. If not, I have to seriously make some decisions about our future. This is his and my wake up call one way or another. I went to bed in a very bad mood.

10/6/2015 – Wednesday

I got up a little late today and Alex also had a lay-in. He has been working so hard and he only has one more exam left and that's on Friday. We decided as a spontaneous thing we would go to Herne Bay and take the dog. A brisk walk by the sea, some nice food in my friend's restaurant Makcaris and some quality mum and son time was just what the doctor ordered. For me it was a chance to blow the cobwebs away and hopefully get some positive energy from the seaside. The dog loved it, Alex loved it and I have got to admit that I loved it too. We met some old friends made some new acquaintances and had a great time.

On the way home in the car I made the decision to tell Alex about the cancer. It may or may not have been the right thing to do, especially seeing as he still has one more exam to go but Alex and I have no secrets and it felt right to let him know.

Tears were streaming down his face and his lips quivered but I talked and explained everything to him and reassured him that I was going to be fine. I asked if he thought it was wrong telling him and he said "no we have no secrets mum I wish you had told me earlier". He cried a little more asked lots of questions and then after a while we chatted about the day.

I'm so proud of him and I feel better for not lying to him. It feels like a weight off my chest. Also everyone else knew when he didn't and that didn't feel right. He has handled it amazingly. I love him so much.

BEHIND THE SCENES

When we came home, I made dinner while he exercised and showered. Now I'm sitting with my feet up because tomorrow is my scan and x-ray day. I'm not looking forward to either. I am really scared. I am scared they will find something else, somewhere else, and it will be more bad news. But I won't think about it anymore. I will wear myself out catching up on TV stuff then fall into bed until the morning.

11/6/2015 – Thursday

Today I was at the hospital having chest X-rays and an MRI scan. I have been nervous for days. I know I won't get any results today but it's all just a bit surreal. After the X-rays to see if my chest is clear of fluid and ready for op I went along to the waiting area to have the scan.

Trudie was with me. They put a cannula into my hand as they told me they would inject a dye into my body when I was in the scanner. It was so claustrophobic and I kept my eyes shut all the time. I had to stay as still as I could, no movements at all and as it would be noisy they gave me headphones. They gave me instructions to hold my breath then they played music. I remember the first song that played was 'Paradise' by Coldplay and remember thinking this ain't no paradise at all. I am actually in hell. The songs afterwards were love songs and they were quite depressing for me because they reminded me of Yas and the fact he was not here. I wanted to cry at one point but but I stopped myself as knew I would sob uncontrollably and I couldn't let that happen there.

Feeling the cold icy dye running through my veins was the weirdest feeling and one I won't forget quickly. It was a relief after 45 mins that I was allowed to get out of the tunnel but because I had laid for so long on my back, a position I don't normally lay in, and my frozen shoulder meant getting up was not only difficult but complete agony. I soon realised things were gonna be worse than that after the hysterectomy operation. I went home exhausted.

Later that evening I spoke to Yas on Skype and it was not a brilliant chat to say the least. I feel like he is not gonna be here for me but he has so much going on with the family in Morocco and things are different there. Culturally, he is expected to be there by his family to support them. I know he is very torn. I understand that choosing between families is a cruel situation for anyone to be in. At least I have Alex, my son, but he has one [family] over there. In between my sobs and his, it was an unbearable Skype call. I just feel empty inside and I want to be held by him.

12/6/2015 – Friday

Alex's last exam today and last day of school. That's so odd for me to say as his mum, where has the time gone? I can't imagine what he must be feeling. I've been so tired today sleeping lots on the settee maybe it's just the after effects of yesterday kicking in. Trudie popped round to mine and we sat in the garden putting the world to rights. Well, not exactly right. It's currently very wrong. Watched TV in the evening and going to bed now because I have to be up early for hair appointment with Rikki tomorrow. I am also really looking forward to seeing Linda tomorrow night and going to Paul O'Grady 60th birthday bash. Night xx

13/6/2015 – Saturday

I went to Paul's Birthday bash last night and it was lovely to chat to people I have not seen for a while. I told Barbara Windsor and her husband Scott about my upcoming operation and they were so supportive. I also told Julian Clary. He was so lovely and very shocked he made me laugh a lot.

I also chatted to Cilla Black who was lovely, although she seemed to be having trouble because she had lost her hearing aid. Also as Linda and I were leaving we bumped into Anita Dobson and Brian May so had a brief chat down the stairs before we headed off.

Loads of lovely people there and took my mind off stuff for an evening which was good.

Paul looked amazing and he seemed so happy. It was a great night with my Linda.

22/6/2015 – Monday

Went to Barbara Windsor and her partner Scott for tea, cake and chat. They were so lovely and it was such a nice day. We talked about Paul's bash and how wonderful it was. We talked about Enders and our close friends there and of course about my dreaded cancer and the operation. They were so inspiring and encouraging, what an amazing couple they are. I popped to the loo and when I returned Scott had a cheque book out

"How much is your mortgage and bills for a couple of months?" asked Barb, "because Scott and I want to help."
I burst into tears.
I will never forget the look of concern on both their faces and Barb giving me that cheque. The amazing generosity and charity and the much needed relief I needed to help see me and my family through some of this nightmare. I am forever grateful to both of them.

29/6/2015 – Monday

No Yas! Getting ready for my operation tomorrow. I am frightened and scared. I updated my will on my phone.

2/7/2015 – Thursday

Out of hospital today it's painful and I can't move or cough. I feel so low and sore and tearful. Yas could not get here from Morocco to be with me.

19/7/2015 – Sunday

Today will be my first day out. My friends Tony and Colleen Durrant are taking me to the hilltop for lunch. I am definitely going stir crazy indoors. I am still very sore, but I just have to say that Christine, Hollie, Tim, Tony, Colleen, Di Wisdom, my wonderful brother Graeme and his daughter Jade have been amazing. They have visited me and helped me so much. They are all true friends. And of course what would I do without Alex, my son, my pride and joy, my whole life! Mum loves you so much Alex.
I have had lots of calls from Barb and Scott too, as well

as daily calls and texts from Linda and Steve McFadden. Anita Dobson and Juilan Clary have also been showing their love and support. My son has been the most amazing part of this so far. He has gone beyond the call of duty for me, helping me and doing things that only someone who loves you with their heart and soul does.

Yas has not returned. He's called a couple of times and Skyped but hasn't come back to England. It's so hurtful and I feel let down and rejected. This is not good. I think I love too much but I know things are impossible for him too in Morocco. We are both in an impossible situation. It's not easy no matter what people are thinking or saying, they just don't get it! Everything is hard for both of us.

31/7/2015 – Friday

I got a phone call from the hospital to say they have found a small amount of cells after the operation. I will have to go for radiotherapy. I am in shock and total dismay. It will be every day for five weeks, intense blasts, so there is a lot to organise before treatment starts. My brother is taking me away next week, after my doctors appointments, for a few days before the treatment starts, off to a cottage up north with Christine and Hollie, Graeme and Jade and Alex.

So hurt and sad for Yas and I and this whole situation. Hurt by his choices but how do you choose between your wife who is ill and your father who is also ill? I am so very hurt. Everything is too painful to bear. Is this the end of me? Is it the end of Yas's dad?

How is he coping? How am I being strong when I should

just crumble? Yas is not coping with any of this. Although I'm weak, I am the stronger one of the two of us. I know our love is good and strong but I'm hurt by his absence.

6/8/2015 – Thursday

Happy birthday, Barb! Linda has gone away to Greece with her husband Stavros. Steve has gone away to Cornwall. Me? I am going loopy! I feel okayish, I think the scar is healing well. I am still not driving which is causing me so much frustration and boredom in the house. Going a little crazy I think and I am having menopause symptoms. I am so emotional, tearful, angry and very low. I think about Yas and I and how he should be here but he can't. I feel like my body is broken, my heart is broken and my head is completely mashed up. I can't seem to pull myself together but I know I have to, for Alex's sake.

My aim is to get fit for pantomime season. Charities and good friends are helping me keep my finances together. I say together, I'm still completely fucked. My amazing brother Graeme, my beautiful friends, helping me out paying mortgages and bills.

Barbara and Scott, Linda and Stavros, Steve have been so generous to me, as well as the charities. On a benefit called ESA and child tax credit for Alex. I don't quite know how I'm keeping it together because some nights and yes it is the nights, I feel so low and desperate. It is like a black cloud descending and I think of all the things and what has happened to me and I ask God, why me? Why am I ill? Where is Yas and why are my finances so terrible? What did I do that was so wrong for you to choose me to punish this badly.

My agent Howard has been amazing throughout all of this. He has put no pressure on me to take the work offered but I am determined no one will know I've been sick, otherwise they will not want to employ me. So I will carry on from job to job and do everything to the best of my abilities. I need to get fit in order to do my best work and that is my number one aim after this terrible shock and awful disease. I pray that all will be well and that I get through all of this. I pray I live a long life and don't die from this disease that eats you up, consumes and feeds on my body. I pray that my son will have his mum for a long time to come and that Yas and I come through every challenge we face.

I am blessed and I will never take anything, anyone or any situation for granted anymore. This experience has been literally life changing. I know as well I am not the only one who has been through this, who is going through this and or will ever go through this.

Chapter Thirty-Two

"Where are my keys? Alex, can you see them anywhere? Where the bloody hell are they?!" I'm tearing the house apart, rifling through drawers, checking under cushions, and emptying out my handbag. This kind of thing has been happening more and more lately. I keep losing things, forgetting what I came into the room for and getting all muddled. It's like my brain is buffering and permanently stuck on a loading screen.

The next morning, I go to heat up some milk for my coffee, open the microwave door and there they are. My keys are in the bloody microwave. Brilliant, Cheryl. Top marks. Why on earth are they in there? Was I planning to defrost them? What a strange thing to do!

It was because of the menopause, of course, brought on early by my hysterectomy. It turns out that having no womb means hormonal doom. We're talking mood swings, brain fog, hot flushes that make you feel like you're slow-roasting in an oven, night sweats and tears over nothing. Isn't it just marvellous being a woman?

I didn't go on HRT as I was worried about side effects, but the experience rocked me both physically and mentally. It has taken me a long time to recover, and I am not sure if I ever will properly.

But honestly, for all the stress I'd been through over the last few months, I don't know how I'd have coped without my friends. They were a total lifeline to me. People like Barbara and Scott who have always checked in. Steve, with his big bear hugs and cheeky grin, Linda with her never-ending support and long phone calls. As well as Christine, Naomi, my mates Tony and Colleen and both of the Graemes – my best friend and my brother – who are both like a brother and a best mate to me. When the cancer hit, it felt like everything else I'd been juggling finally collapsed around me.

I couldn't work and I had radiotherapy for a few weeks after the hysterectomy. I was utterly exhausted, both physically and mentally, but at least having a health scare like that gives you some perspective. I was now more certain than ever that the most important thing in life is friends and family.

Instead of going bankrupt, I ended up with an Individual Voluntary Arrangement (IVA), which meant I had to stick to a strict repayment plan. I wanted to flog my house to pay off the debt, but I wasn't allowed to sell it while Alex was still a minor. I felt completely stuck under the crushing weight of it all. It was like I was treading water with bricks strapped to my ankles.

One night, I was sitting at the kitchen table with my brother Graeme, going over the numbers with a biro and a notepad like something out of *Only Fools and Horses*.

"I don't know what else to do," I said, burying my face in my hands. "I've got no work, the tax man's breathing down my neck and I can't even sell the house because of Alex. I'm just... I'm drowning, Graeme. I am completely drowning."

He put his arm around me and, calm as anything, said, "Well then, I'll just remortgage my place. Simple."

I paused. "You'll what?"

"I'll remortgage," he repeated, like it was no big deal. "Get the money, cover what you need. We'll sort it. You'd do the same for me."

I just stared at him, speechless. "Graeme, you can't do that! It's your home."

He shrugged. "Yeah and you're my sister."

It was one of the kindest, most selfless things anyone's ever done for me. No drama, no hesitation, just love. With his help, I was able to pay off my debts and if that wasn't enough to win Brother of the Year award, he also helped me to do up my place, patch up the bits that needed fixing and, once Alex was old enough, get it on the market. Six months later, it was sold.

I paid Graeme back every penny and then I used what was left to pay a year's rent up front on a smaller place nearby, so Alex could finish college without any upheaval. He wanted to follow in my footsteps and go into acting and I could already tell the kid had a lot of talent.

The new place wasn't quite as nice as our old house. It was a bit more cramped, a little rougher around the edges, but at least we had a home. It had a nice garden, so I didn't feel like I'd had that much of a fall from grace. Yas was still missing from it though and I was still missing him. He was back and forth a bit during that time, but truthfully... he wasn't really there as much as we both would have liked. He wasn't there when I had cancer, not in the way I needed him to be.

We'd been planning to try for a child and it had been our last chance really, as I was 49 when I got the news. I think losing that hope tipped him over the edge, if I'm being completely honest. Not that it was the main thing that upset him, of course it wasn't, he was also massively worried for my health. He couldn't cope with the harsh reality of my illness, the surgeries and the fear. Yas was never very good with hospitals anyway, but this... it was all a bit too much.

Yas was still so young, only in his late 20s and although now he's like a little old man in his ways, full of wisdom and calm, back then I think he still didn't know how to carry it all. His dad was ill too and that was another weight on his already heavy shoulders. It was overwhelming; the responsibility, the pressure and the pain of it all, and so he stayed away.

There I was, in and out of appointments, exhausted and frightened, trying to keep things together for Alex while missing my husband. I didn't blame him, not really. But it hurt all the same.

Even so, I had no choice but to keep going and things picked up the following year when I landed a role in *Menopause the Musical*. I didn't need to do much research in preparation for the part because, let's be honest, by this point I pretty much was the poster woman for the menopause. I was basically a walking hormone cocktail in comfy shoes. If there had been an audition where they asked for hot flushes on demand, I could've steamed up the casting director's glasses in five seconds flat.

The show itself was great fun, written by the brilliant Jeanie Linders, all about four women who meet in the underwear section of a department store and bond over their shared menopause misery and hormonal mayhem. It was like a support group set to music. Picture four women singing about mood swings, night sweats, hot flushes, brain fog, weight gain and lost libidos in a camp and hilarious way. It was kind of like musical theatre meets *Loose Women* on a prosecco bender.

And the songs were amazing too. Parodies of classic tunes, but with a relatable middle-aged twist. Take Betty Everett's 'The Shoop Shoop Song' for example. The original line, "If you want to know if he loves you so, it's in his kiss," becomes something altogether different when we take to the mic. We belted out: "If you want to know where the fat glands go, it's on my hips. That's where it is." Let's just say it was not quite as romantic, but definitely more real.

Another song we sung was the 'The Lion Sleeps Tonight', a 1961 hit by The Tokens, but rather than do the "a-weema-weh, a-weema-weh, a-weema-weh" part, we sung "she's a witch, she's a bitch, she's a witch, she's a bitch". And, instead of "in the jungle, the mighty jungle, the lion sleeps tonight," it was "in the guest room or on the sofa, my husband sleeps at night".

Every night, we had women in the aisles cackling, fanning themselves with the programme and shouting, "That's me!" And I'd think, I know, love, it's me too. I'm sweating through my costume right now.

The show also starred Linda Nolan of The Nolans fame, *Casualty's* Rebecca Wheatley and *The Al Murray Show's* Ruth Berkley. Three absolute legends and we laughed our way around the UK. I was proud of being part of something that took the stigma away from the silent battle women have to go through. It was not just about laughs, it was about recognition for menopausal women. Audiences left feeling seen and like they weren't alone in losing the plot. I ended up doing that job for four whole years, slotting in pantomimes during the winters. It was joyful, funny and audiences absolutely lapped it up.

But what people didn't see was what happened when the curtain came down. When the lights faded and the theatre emptied and I was alone in some Premier Inn with nothing but the hum of the radiator and my own thoughts, that's when the darkness crept in. Because while I was singing about hot flushes, I was dealing with something much more terrifying. Something that burned far deeper. It was eating me up inside, quite literally.

I'm talking about a private, painful ritual that I carried with me from venue to venue and dressing room to dressing room. After my hysterectomy, one of the doctors had told me, "Cheryl, there are still some cancerous cells present. But don't worry. It's only a few. This is only an issue if they become active again. We'll just keep an eye on it."

I was shocked. Only a few?! That's like saying, "There's only a little fire in the living room." I mean, do you stay in the house or do you run screaming into the garden? I thought about those cells every single day. Morning, noon and night. My brain was obsessed. I didn't want them monitored, I wanted them gone. Out. Banished from my body. I imagined them plotting and multiplying quietly like evil little gremlins in the dark. What if they became active again? What if they were attacking me from the inside out while I was prancing around singing about memory loss and vaginal dryness?

My brain became a broken record. I was terrified that those tiny cells had the power to destroy me and leave my son without a mum and my husband without a wife. I knew the doctors had "washed me out" before the surgery, so I thought, in my foggy, frightened mind, why not wash out the remaining cells myself? It sounds silly and it probably was, but in my head it made perfect sense. I figured: if hot water kills bacteria, maybe it could kill off cancer cells too. I mean, that's what we're told, right? Boil things to sterilise them and burn the germs away. You clean things with hot steam and heat melts things away. Maybe, just maybe, it could work inside me too?

So one day, in a haze of fear and frustration, I stepped into the shower, turned it on and held the nozzle between my legs. I thought, this water needs to be as hot as I can stand it. Maybe hotter. I braced myself and cranked it up high, gritting my teeth.

As the temperature increased, so did the pain. Until it shot through me, sharp and searing. My whole body tensed and I screamed in agony. But in my twisted logic at the time, the pain was the point. If it was hurting me, surely it was hurting the cancer too and I should let it happen. No pain no gain. The pain meant it was working.

So I did it again and again. Short bursts, maybe a minute at a time. Then I'd take a breath, steady myself and repeat the process, making sure not to scream out so that Alex wouldn't hear me. Each time I was convinced I was "flushing" the cancer out of my system and that I was doing something to take control of my body and fight back against this killer disease.

Soon, I was doing it up to three times a day, every day, for ten minutes at a time. The hot water spurting inside me for longer and longer stints as I was building up a higher tolerance. It grew more intense. After two months, I was using the shower on the highest setting and scalding myself. I told myself it was helping. That I was being strong, proactive and fighting back. But really, I was waging war on my own body.

Inside, I was blistered, swollen and raw. I was in constant pain, wincing as I walked. At one of my check-ups, the doctors had to use a smaller speculum to check inside me because of the inflammation. They assumed it was menopausal changes. I didn't correct them, I couldn't. I was too ashamed.

I didn't tell anyone what I was doing, but Yas did start to catch on. When I went to visit him in Morocco, he noticed the way I flinched getting out of the shower and he confronted me about it.

"Yas, I have to do this. I need to do something," I said, voice trembling. "You don't understand. It could be helpful."

"You don't need to hurt yourself, love," he said, arms folded. "This isn't how you cure cancer. Can't you see? Otherwise there wouldn't be cancer in the world if you could just remove it with hot water. Please... don't do this anymore."

"You don't get it Yas, it is better than just doing nothing," I cried. After that he wouldn't let me go and shower alone. He would stand next to me, while I washed to make sure I wasn't hurting myself. But Yas couldn't be with me all of the time and as soon as I was back in England, I started doing it again. I couldn't be stopped, it felt impossible to try.

But while this obsession took its toll on my health, it also affected our relationship too. Mine and Yas's sex life became non-existent, because it hurt too much inside of me to even try. I didn't want him to touch me. I was sore and full of shame. I felt broken. I felt like I'd done this to myself and I didn't know how to undo it.

We moved up to Warton, a village in Lancashire, in October 2017, I used the remainder of the money from the sale of our home in Kent to buy a lovely house. It was built in 1965, the year I was born and had a dormer roof and big bay windows. There was a large conservatory that filled with light in the mornings and a garden that looked like something out of a Sunday supplement. The new home had three bedrooms and the largest kitchen I have ever had and it was just what we needed.

On the outside, everything seemed to be going well. I was still working in panto and touring with *Menopause the Musical* and I was living in a warm, welcoming community close to my brother Graeme.

Yas liked it too and we thought how lovely it was to be by the sea and more peaceful than the hustle and bustle of London. There was, of course, a problem. I still couldn't stop.

The shower, the burning, the belief that I had to finish what the surgeons hadn't. I told myself I was helping, that I was being proactive, that I was doing what the doctors couldn't. Then, two years later, my worst fear seemed to come true. It started with a dull ache in my back.

Then I noticed bleeding. A tiny spot at first, then more. I froze. This is it, I thought. This is how it ends. My stomach knotted with fear as I rang the hospital. I remembered the doctor saying, if you experience any symptoms, go straight in. So I did.

They tried to carry out a smear test, but even the smallest speculum wouldn't go in. The nurse looked puzzled. "I don't know why this is?" she said, her voice full of concern.

And that was the moment I broke. I came clean.

BEHIND THE SCENES

I told her what I had been doing. About the boiling water. The burning. The years of hiding and hurting and trying to cure myself of something I wasn't even sure was still there. She didn't gasp or judge. She just listened, then quietly excused herself to get the doctor.

They then ran tests, scans and bloodwork. They had to track down my old medical notes from the hospital in London. So I went home terrified and shaking, to await the results.

A few days later, I was called back in. I sat in a small hospital room, staring at the floor, trying to steady my breathing. The doctor came in, sat beside me and looked at me with kindness.

"Cheryl," he said gently. "There's no sign of cancer. In fact, there hasn't been since your operation."

"What do you mean?" I asked.

"There are no cancerous cells. Nothing concerning. Your post-op scans have been clear for years."

"But... I was told..."

He nodded slowly. "They may have seen abnormal cells at one point, but they weren't cancerous. You've been cancer-free since 2015."

I just sat there, stunned. Four years. Four years I had lived under a cloud of fear. Four years I had convinced myself I was infected. Four years of burning, of sobbing in the shower, of hiding my body from Yas, of punishing myself for something that didn't even exist.

And the worst part? The damage I'd done wasn't just emotional. It was physical, too. The repeated trauma, the heat, the pressure, had caused a prolapsed bladder. I had injured myself badly.

All that pain. All that shame. All that fear and secrecy. And it had all been for nothing.

But after that conversation, it all changed. It was like someone had finally pulled back the curtain and let the light in. I never hurt myself again. Not once. Finally, I was free.

Chapter Thirty-Three

Life finally got back to something approaching normality and then it hit… the pandemic.

Yas was stuck in Morocco during the coronavirus lockdowns and that was hard, really hard. We were used to long stretches apart, but the uncertainty made it worse. Not knowing when we'd see each other again, not being able to hold hands or share a meal or even just argue over the telly. But at least I had Alex. Thank God for him, he kept me grounded, gave me purpose and reminded me every day what really matters.

Before everything shut down, we'd just started touring *Menopause the Musical 2*. The first show had been such a blast and I was thrilled to be back, but the tour was cut short not long after it began. Curtains down, lights off, everything paused, along with many things across the world. And with that, my income vanished again.

The financial pressure crept back in, like an old unwelcome guest. I was still helping Yas's family in Morocco too, paying for healthcare for his dad and whatever I could manage. They're my family as well now and I wanted to support them, but my mortgage and outgoings stretched me thin and the bills piled up, slowly but steadily. And coming out of lockdown in 2022, blinking back into the world, was harder than I expected. The industry had changed and so had I. Acting is often thought of as a young woman's game and there's truth to that. The roles thin out as you get older, especially if you're not one of the A-listers or permanently on telly. You're no longer the fresh new face, or adventurous lead. You're the "character actor", the "mum", the "cleaner", the "nosy neighbour". If you're lucky, you get a few good lines and a nice costume, but even those roles can be few and far between.

I'd spent my life pouring my heart into this craft, into making people laugh or cry and keeping them entertained, but like many actors it felt like I was back at square one. No steady work, just trying to keep going. I had to convince myself that there is still space for me, still stories I could tell and still value in my voice.

And then one day it happened. I discovered social media. Or more to the point, I realised it had discovered me!

"Mum, do you know you're a meme?" Alex asked one day, peering up from his smartphone. "A what now?" I asked, properly baffled. "A meme? What's a meme?"

He grinned at his digital dinosaur mother. "Look," he said, turning his phone screen towards me. There, in all her glory, was Heather Trott, on all fours, gasping for breath in the middle of Albert Square, mid-way through an asthma attack. Above it, in big bold letters, it said: "When your boss asks you to do something that is totally within your job description."

Another read: "When they don't have garlic bread on the menu."

A third: "Me after writing my name and the title of the essay."

I stared, slack-jawed. "That's me! Well, that's Heather having a panic attack in Albert Square Gardens!"

Alex was loving it, he was laughing so hard he had to clutch the sofa arm. "Mum, you're internet famous now. Heather Trott is a meme queen."

Now, I'll be honest, I didn't quite get it at first, but as Alex explained, a meme is basically an image or video that captures a relatable feeling, turned into a joke and passed around online like a digital whoopee cushion.

Was it my sense of humour? Not exactly. But you know what, I was chuffed that Heather was reaching a younger audience who were probably only young kids when she first bumbled into the Queen Vic. And somehow, I was still culturally relevant, albeit as the poster girl for mild chaos and overdramatic meltdowns. It gave me a kick, it really did.

Heather's image is often the butt of the internet's joke, but in October 2022, I woke up to the most surreal scene. I was Prime Minister. Not even kidding, someone had changed Rishi Sunak's photo on Wikipedia to a snap of me. Yep, the day he was made Prime Minister, there it was: a close-up of Heather Trott looking slightly bewildered, plastered across the internet under the words: "Prime Minister of the United Kingdom."

I can only imagine the confusion. People across the globe, searching "Rishi Sunak" to find out about Britain's new leader and instead being greeted by a chubby white woman in a headband. Not quite who they were expecting for the first PM of Indian heritage. The image didn't stay up long, of course, someone with common sense at Wikipedia caught it and changed it back quicker than Liz Truss managed to last in Number 10.

Still, it gave me a proper giggle. It's a strange kind of fame, being the face that people use for memes, pranks and online chaos.

During the lockdown I had got more and more into social media myself. Instagram and TikTok were my window into the world and my little soapbox to stand on and share my thoughts on life. I was there, posting videos of me chatting, singing, being daft, or just sharing thoughts on life and lipstick. It was like a new stage, one where you didn't need a script or a lighting rig or a director. It could be the Cheryl Fergison show and no one was going to hit me over the head with a photo frame and kill me off.

There is something quite freeing about being able to talk to fans directly. Not through a press officer or a glossy magazine, just me, in my dressing gown, cuppa in hand, telling it like it is. I've done everything from serious chats about cancer and mental health to singing karaoke classics in my kitchen.

But of course, social media isn't all lovely comments and dancing dogs. For every sweet message, there's a troll lobbing nastiness from behind a cartoon profile picture with a username like @SharonSaysUgh456. Honestly, the stuff people come out with, you'd think I'd kicked their nan.

"You look like a boiled ham wrapped in disappointment." Cheers, Kevin from Doncaster.

It used to really get to me. I'd read a horrible comment and feel it in my bones. But over time, I've grown thicker skin. Not rhino-thick, I still cry at episodes of *The Repair Shop*, but enough that I can scroll past the bile and focus on the good stuff.

I do sometimes wish there was a sort of 'Troll Police'. Like, someone who turns up at the troll's house, gently confiscates their Wi-Fi and gives them a cuddle and a colouring book. But that's life, isn't it? You can't control what other people say, you can only control how many filters you put on your selfie.

Alex has told me I'm a gay icon now. When he said it, I nearly spat out my tea.

"A gay icon? Are you sure?" I asked.

He nodded, dead serious. "Absolutely. People love you online and Heather Trott is camp. End of."

I mean, I wouldn't say I am a gay icon, that is probably a bit of a leap. I am not exactly Lady Gaga, am I? But in recent years I have built up a gay following, which I am chuffed about. I am a big supporter of both gay and trans rights and always have been but it's amazing to me that I have been so embraced back.

If I was to put my finger on why, I think it probably started because I was associated with Linda, who had been in *Beautiful Thing*, which is a huge 90s gay cult classic. That film means so much to so many people and rightly so. Then there's the George Michael link, which came through Heather's storyline. She was obsessed with him and he was the icon of all icons. And let's not forget Paul O'Grady, a great friend of mine who was beloved by all. Heather herself, I think, really resonated with LGBTQ+ audiences because she was the underdog and people root for the underdog. She was a bit tragic, bless her heart. Always wearing the wrong outfit, saying the wrong thing and falling for the wrong man. But she wore her heart on her sleeve, usually along with some garish outfit and I think that vulnerability struck a chord.

Let's be honest, she was also a bit clownish. The comedy came naturally with her, the pratfalls, the awkwardness, the way she'd try so hard to be loved and often miss the mark entirely. There was something very over the top and camp about it. That combination of sadness and silliness made her loveable. And queerness has always found a home in the oddballs, the outsiders, the ones who don't quite fit the mould. Then I went into *Celebrity Big Brother* and spent 10 days being my usual daft, singing, overly emotional self, all while sharing a house with Julian Clary, who is not just a comedy icon but a bona fide gay deity. Add to that my performances on *Your Face Sounds Familiar* as Meat Loaf, Madonna, Cher and Adele, well, it's no wonder the gays started to warm up to me. I mean, come on, how many women can say they've worn a pink satin dress and faux diamonds and been carried around by a group of handsome men while belting out 'Material Girl' live on telly?

Whatever the reason, in recent years I have been booked to sing at Prides and in gay bars. I'd started posting little videos of me singing on YouTube and social media, covers of classic songs sung from my home. And somehow, they started to get picked up and shared. Then I got a message asking if I'd come and perform at Mullingar Pride in Ireland in 2022.

At first I thought they'd messaged the wrong Cheryl. Cheryl Cole perhaps? But no, they wanted me to host and sing at their first ever Pride. It was a real honour and I thought about how proud Pete would have been seeing me up there performing Cher at the grand Belvedere House and Gardens, to hundreds of smiling, sparkling faces waving rainbow flags. It was honestly one of the highlights of my career. I stood on that stage thinking, what is my life right now?

I've since sung at Pride in London, on the Hyde Park stage

no less, in collaboration with the Instagram account Hunsnet who throw LGBT+ friendly events and share memes. I was wearing a dress that blew in the breeze like a budget Beyoncé and I had two gorgeous men fanning me like I was Cleopatra.

I've done Lancaster Pride too and other little events across the country and I love every second. There's something magical about a Pride crowd. They get you, they cheer for you just for being you, they don't care if you hit a bum note or forget the lyrics as long as you're there, giving it your all.

And I always do because I'm proud to be an ally of the LGBTQ+ community and a supporter of gay and trans rights. I don't think I am a gay icon, but I am an ally and always will be.

In 2022, I performed at an event at Via in Manchester, right in the heart of Canal Street, in the city's gay district.

I was nervous, I won't lie. It's one thing belting out ballads in a theatre, but standing in a buzzing gay bar with a microphone in one hand and a sea of fabulous faces staring back is a different type of pressure. But then I looked out into the crowd and saw my son, my amazing Alex, singing along, eyes shining. Right next to him was Graeme, my best friend and my rock, doing his very best backing vocals and throwing shapes like he was auditioning for *RuPaul's Drag Race: Dad Edition*. And just like that, the nerves melted away.

It was the kind of moment that makes you stop and go, "Blimey, how did I get here?"

Because honestly, I never imagined my career would take me from the Royal Shakespeare Company to singing Culture Club's 'Karma Chameleon' in a gay bar while being cheered on by a topless man in a sparkly cowboy hat. But I wouldn't

change a single second of my life because in the words of
Gloria Gaynor, an actual gay icon, "I am what I am and what
I am needs no excuses."

Chapter Thirty-Four

My friend TJ Higgs is a wonderful psychic medium. She really does have a gift. None of that vague horoscope nonsense; she is the real deal. We've known each other a long time and shared all kinds of ups and downs, but every now and then, she'll pop up like a sparkly postwoman of the spirit realm with a delivery from destiny.

One evening in November 2021, just as I was about to head out, my phone rang. I glanced down and saw her name flash up on the screen.

"Here we go," I muttered, smiling to myself. I picked it up.

"Hiya Cheryl, it's TJ," she said, all calm and mystical, like she'd just floated in on a cloud of incense.

"Hi TJ, how are you doing?" I replied, instantly curious because I knew something was coming.

She got straight to the point. "I've had a vision, Cheryl. You're going to get a telly job soon, which is great, but and here's the weird part, you're going to be up to your knees in mud."

I paused. "Mud? Like... emotionally? Or literally mud?"

"Literal mud, babes. Proper thick, soggy mud. Wellington boot levels."

I burst out laughing. "Brilliant. Sounds glamorous, TJ. Can't wait. Shall I bring my own spade?"

But of course, because she's always right, TJ's vision came true. Not long after that call, I was cast in *Hansel and Gretel: After Ever After*, the festive TV special created by David Walliams.

It really is a privilege to work with David. We've collaborated so many times throughout my career and he's a total genius, a little bit bonkers, in the best possible way. Ever since we met on Little Britain all those years ago, we've got on brilliantly. He has such a kind heart and he always finds a way to include me in his madcap creations. This time, he gave me a part in the film as the executioner.

It wasn't a glamorous role, I was trussed up in a rough hessian sack, clomping around in big heavy boots, lugging a giant axe over my shoulder like something out of *Game of Thrones*. But you know what, playing an executioner is a fabulous way to shake off any lingering Heather Trott typecasting. Nobody was asking me about cheese or karaoke in this outfit.

We filmed some of it at the Weald and Downland Living Museum in Chichester, which is packed with mock medieval villages, cobbled courtyards and the kind of thatched cottages that make you want to churn butter for a living. It was charming... and absolutely caked in mud.

TJ's prediction was bang on. One day, I was mid-scene, stomping across the set, trying to look menacing, when my boot got completely stuck in the sludge. But here's the thing, it wasn't just the fields of Chichester where I was stuck. I was stuck financially too.

The truth was, I needed more money. The telly work wasn't consistent and although I was always grateful for the jobs that came in, they weren't coming in as often as they used to.

BEHIND THE SCENES

Yes, I did other shows. I appeared in *White Island* and of course *Hard Cell*, a Netflix series written by the brilliant Catherine Tate. That was a total blast. Catherine wrote the role for me, which was so lovely and I got to play myself teaching drama in a women's prison. It was hilarious and weirdly poignant too because it tied in perfectly with the Theatre and Education course I'd done at drama school all those years ago. Life has a funny way of looping back on itself, doesn't it?

But after that, aside from pantomimes, the work dried up a bit. I found myself in a holding pattern; still smiling, still showing up, but underneath it all, I was worried. About money, about relevance, about what came next. It's the side of showbiz that people don't talk about. One minute, you're on chat shows, doing spreads in magazines and on telly every weeknight. Next, you're at home refreshing your emails and wondering if anyone even remembers your name. That's life though, full of ups and downs and I was just in the muddy bit of the journey.

You've just got to keep wading through.

There were some true highlights to keep me going though. It was finally the day of the book launch and I couldn't have been more excited, or more proud.

Writing it had taken so much hard work, skill, talent and determination. Countless hours of editing and re-editing and if I do say so myself it is a fantastic read. No, I am not bragging about my own book. My lovely son, Alex, has written his first book, *Two Lonely Otters* and it is beautiful. I know I could be accused of being biased, but it really is absolutely beautiful. Alex graduated from the Liverpool Institute for Performing

Arts not long ago and now here he is, published, celebrated and shining.

The book is filled with poems about queer love and life and loss, that are raw, lyrical, tender and defiant. It's heartwarming, heartbreaking and uplifting all at once. A reflection of the man he's become and I just want to scream it from the rooftops: My son wrote this.

I stand beside him on stage at a venue in Lytham St Anne on a November evening in 2023, heart pounding with pride, as I host the Q&A. Me! Hosting my son's book launch!

I ask him questions about the inspiration behind the poems, about his process, his hopes. He reads extracts aloud, his voice steady, emotional and full of passion and the room is completely still, hanging on every word. We sing together songs that he listened to when he wrote the book, including the 1970 hit '(They Long to Be) Close to You' by The Carpenters.

Everyone always asks me, "Cheryl, what's your biggest achievement in life?" And I never even hesitate. I always say, "My son." To say I'm a proud mama is an understatement. I'm bursting. Alex has had his fair share of challenges, more than most young people should have to deal with, but through adversity, he's carved out something magical. He's turned pain into poetry, loneliness into connection and now he's offering it to the world.

Of course, he's now officially written a book at 23, many, many years before I ever got round to it! He beats me to everything. He's travelled more than I ever have, graduated from drama college younger than I even started and he does everything with this quiet confidence and creativity that leaves me in awe.

BEHIND THE SCENES

Everything I hoped for him, he's doing it. And not just doing it, he is thriving. If I climbed a hill, he's scaling mountains. If I opened a door, he's built his own house. He takes every opportunity, every dream and he multiplies it. Triple, quadruple, more than I ever achieved in my life and I say that not with envy, but with the deepest, most joyful pride a mum could feel.

But that's who he is: brilliant, driven, thoughtful. He's also smart with money (which, let me tell you, did not come from me), kind to the core and an exceptional actor and writer.

Watching him performing his work in front of all those people, I thought, this is what it's all about, the torch has been passed. I may have played roles on TV, walked red carpets, worn the glitter and glamour, but nothing comes close to this. My son, his words and his light.

I will never stop being proud of him and I'll never stop telling the world what a wonder he is. Alex, thank you from the bottom of my heart for letting me be your mum.

It wasn't the last time we ended up on a stage together either. Alex and I smiled at each other, held hands and took a bow. The audience erupted with applause and we waved at the sea of smiling faces. The lights bright, the music swelling and the energy in the room electric. As I took in the scene, standing next to my son, who looks so handsome in his pale blue waistcoat with matching trousers and crisp white shirt, me beside him in a big, glittering purple dress and sparkly tiara, I felt a rush of emotion so strong it almost knocks the wind out of me. I blinked back tears, careful not to smudge my glittery eyeshadow.

We'd just finished our first pantomime performance of

Cinderella together, at The Cresset Theatre in Peterborough, just a stone's throw from where I grew up. This production was the brainchild of my wonderful and supportive friend Stuart Morrison who knew that casting mother and son in the pantomime in the town I grew up in would set Peterborough on fire. It feels like everything has come full circle.

I'm back performing in my hometown, like I did as a kid, but on a real stage. Not busking on my guitar on a grassy hill on the estate to a group of local elderly people for five pence a show, like I once did. This time, the stage is lit and the seats are filled.

I am playing the role of Fairy Godmother and Alex is Buttons, the loyal house servant who helps Cinderella prepare for the ball. He impressed me so much in rehearsals.

So professional, so prepared. He knew all his lines, he was funny, sharp, instinctive and took direction beautifully. Not that I ever doubted him, but until this moment I'd never actually worked with him before. Seeing him in action, seeing his talent come alive under the stage lights, it's moved me in ways I didn't expect.

There was a special moment in the script where I turn to Alex and say, "Alright, son?" It's just a little line, but then I glance out to the audience with a smile and say, "Oh! Didn't you know this was my son in real life?"

And without missing a beat, Alex grins and says, "Yeah, this is my mum."

The audience loved it and we loved it too, it was a moment of truth nestled inside the make-believe. You could feel the warmth ripple through the room like a wave. Working with my son, who is also an actor and sharing the stage with him is a memory I will have forever. We took another bow, along with the rest of the cast and I was absolutely beaming. My heart feels like it's twice its usual size.

And as I stand there in the spotlight, beside him, I think of Pete too. We starred together in *Cinderella* back in 2012 and he played one of the Ugly Sisters. He passed away not long after that panto run. I wonder what he'd make of this moment, what he'd think, seeing Alex and I up here together, holding hands, taking a bow, filling the theatre with laughter and love. I bet it would make him smile.

I think of my mum, Avril. She never got to meet her grandson. But I like to believe she's watching from somewhere, smiling, clapping, maybe even shouting out a cheeky "He's behind you!" and coming backstage to talk to all the other cast members, the way she would've done in her day.

And I think of my husband, my friends and the ones who've stood by me through the highs and lows. The ones who've believed in me even when I didn't believe in myself. The ones who've cheered me on from the wings and from the stalls and without whom I probably wouldn't still be standing let alone able to make people laugh in a glittery dress. They have made me feel more loved than a thousand cheering audiences.

As the curtains close, I realise something. This is more than a show, because although my life hasn't always been a fairytale, right here on stage with my son, doing the thing I love so much and making people happy – this, right here, is my happily ever after.

Chapter Thirty-Five

It was March 2024, the kind of grey, icy-cold day that seeps into your bones and makes everything feel a bit heavier. The heating had been off for days. I was wearing three jumpers and a pair of old socks with holes in the toes, pacing around the house looking for a fiver I was sure I'd tucked into a coat pocket or under the sofa cushions. I turned out every handbag I owned. I checked the biscuit tin, the bottom drawer, even inside an old birthday card. Nothing. There wasn't a single penny in the house.

I opened the fridge. A half-used tub of margarine, the dregs of a milk bottle and one lonely egg stared back at me like they were waiting for a punchline. The cupboards weren't much better, just a tin of beans, a sad little handful of dried pasta and a dwindling pile of tea bags clinging to each other like survivors.

I leaned against the sink and whispered to myself, "You're completely and utterly broke."

It was one of the hardest things I've ever had to face. I wished Yas was with me, but he has been stuck in Morocco due to caring for family members, so we are stuck on the phone to one another night after night, but at least he was coming back next month to be with me.

I'd always made things work and made do as much as I

could, I'd done my share of juggling in my life, gigs, tours, panto, school runs, press junkets. I wasn't a stranger to struggle, but this? This was different. This was staring into an empty bank account and an emptier cupboard.

And the thing is, I was still trying to pay off debts. Debts from years of trying to hold it all together. When you've had a bit of fame, people assume you're set for life. They don't see the years in between jobs, the freelance gaps, the feast-and-famine rhythm of life as an actor. They don't see the generous heart that says yes to helping others, even when you can't help yourself.

Eventually, I summoned up the courage to go to my local Citizens Advice branch. My stomach was in absolute knots – I hadn't felt that nervous in years, not even before an opening night. I tried to keep my head down, hair tucked into my scarf, hoping no one would recognise me. I'm known in the area and the last thing I wanted was someone clocking me and whispering, "Isn't that her off the telly?"

The woman at the desk was brilliant, soft voice, kind eyes and not a shred of judgment. Just this calming presence, like someone who sees 100 people like you every week but still makes you feel like you matter. She invited me into a small side office and I sat down like a deflated balloon. Every bit of me just sank into the chair.

"Look," I said, my voice cracking. "I don't know. I'm struggling. I'm really struggling here. I can't pay my bills. I can't pay my mortgage. I don't know what to do."

She nodded, handed me a tissue and just listened. No clipboard ticking, no rush, just kindness. Then she got to work. She helped me list out everything I was paying out, direct debits, credit cards, old loans. She made calls for me, helped me speak to the people I'd been avoiding out of fear and shame. She took notes and didn't bat an eyelid, even when I was so flustered I couldn't remember my own sort code.

She could see it, I was broken, and she was wise enough and kind enough, to recognise what I couldn't even bring myself to say: I needed help.

Then she looked down at the figures and then gently back up at me.

"Cheryl," she said softly. "How are you going to do the food shopping this week? Because on paper, you've got no money."

I just stared at her, mouth dry, heart thudding. "I don't know," I said. "We've got a few bits in the cupboard, but... I don't know."

She paused. Then came the question. "Have you ever used a food bank before?" I shook my head quickly. "No. No..." Just as I was about to explain myself, the harsh reality of the situation hit me and I burst into tears. Not polite, single-tear, film-star crying, this was full-blown and messy sobbing.

Shoulders shaking, nose running, mascara smudging. I couldn't stop. The shame poured out of me like a storm breaking and I sat there crying like a child, completely unravelled. How could I have been on *EastEnders*?

How could I have walked red carpets, done magazine covers, laughed on chat shows, and now be here? Asking for food. She reached out and put her hand gently over mine. "It's nothing to be ashamed of," she said quietly. "It's something lots of people use. It's a service that's there for a reason. If you need it, you use it. You don't have to be referred by anybody to go to it." Then she stood up and said, with warmth and certainty, "Come with me."

She walked me down a corridor to a side room where the food bank was. She spoke to the staff there, then told me to sit and wait. I sat on a hard plastic chair, hands shaking, heart pounding in my chest. A few minutes later she returned, holding a mug of tea.

"Drink that, love," she said. "It's going to be okay. We're going to get you sorted. What sort of things do you like to eat? And how many are at home?" I told her it was me and Alex, that he ate meat, but I didn't. She nodded and got to work. She began filling up shopping bags with things for us to eat, pasta, fresh fruit and veg, tins, bread. Bags and bags. Then she paused and looked at me again. "Do you have any pets?" I blinked, startled. "Yes," I said. "I've got a dog."

"Well, you're going to need some dog food, aren't you?" she said, matter-of-factly. I was blown away. They didn't just care about feeding me, they cared about my dog. They cared about the little details that make up a life.

The staff helped carry everything to the car and just as I was about to leave, I popped back in to say thank you, to try and express the depth of my gratitude. And that's when she handed me a small bunch of daffodils. "Here you go," she said with a smile. "Just something to brighten up your home." She also handed me some small bags of chocolates. "Some treats, for you and your boy," she added. "Everyone needs a treat."

And that was it, that was the moment that finished me. I burst into tears all over again.

The kindness and the simplicity of the gesture. The way she'd seen me, not as a former soap star or a celebrity, but as a person. A mum and a woman trying her best. That day is one I'll never forget – and I'll never forget the people. I felt I'd had this amazing, biggest, warmest hug, like a group of angels had come along and said, "We can cope with this for you, Cheryl, we can do this for you."

To anyone who needs to use a food bank, don't be ashamed, please, don't be. I say this from the heart: it could be anyone. One day you're up, the next you're down. Life has a funny way of humbling us. But it also has a way of reminding us there is still goodness in the world.

When I got home later that day and put those daffodils in a vase, everything felt a little brighter. And for the first time in a long while, so did I.

I knew I needed to find other ways to try to bring some money in and I began selling *EastEnders* scripts and memorabilia to try and make ends meet; original call sheets, signed bits and bobs and things I had tucked away in boxes for years. I never thought I'd be parting with them, not really, but needs must. They are only things after all and I'm doing it to survive, to ease the pressure, to pull myself out of the money worries that never seem to let up.

Some days it feels like I'm chasing my own tail, running faster and faster just to stay in the same place. You sell a few things, you breathe a little easier... and then the bills roll in again. It's a constant balancing act and it's totally exhausting.

I get slated online for it, of course. People love to judge. "Why's she flogging her old scripts?" they say. But it's no different to what actors do at Comic Cons, meeting fans, signing autographs and celebrating the work they've done. It's the same principle, just with a less glamorous backdrop and no queue.

BEHIND THE SCENES

Luckily, I do have some fantastic supporters, people who get it and fans who send kind messages and cheer me on from the sidelines. But the trolls, they are just as loud as ever, as well as cruel and relentless. Some days I brush it off and think, they must be so sad to spend their time tearing down strangers. But I'm only human. It gets to me. The nasty comments sting. The assumptions hurt.

I had to sell my house to pay off debts. That was a hard pill to swallow. That home meant everything to me. It had memories built into the walls and all the trappings of a life that, at one point, was starting to look all shiny again.

Now, I live in a small flat in Cleveleys, Lancashire. I'm renting again. It's not much, but it's warm, it's safe and it's mine – for now. A little sanctuary tucked away in a sleepy seaside spot, not too far from Blackpool.

The flat is cosy, full of soft lighting and hand-me-down furniture and stacks of books. Nothing matches, but somehow it all suits me better than the sleek, expensive stuff ever did. It's lived-in and it is home.

It's a two-storey place, which feels like a luxury these days. Alex has his own room upstairs, though he's often off visiting his partner in Liverpool, leaving me pottering around on my own in the evenings with the dog and a hot water bottle. His room stays neat, unlike the hurricane zone it used to be when he was little.

There is a pub across the road that does live music, sometimes brilliant, sometimes tuneless but enthusiastic. Friday nights sound like karaoke through a megaphone. Then there's the traffic, a constant background hum of engines and sirens and right outside my window. There's a set of traffic lights and if a double-decker bus pulls up, the top deck has a perfect view straight into my living room. So I've learned not to sit on the sofa in my pyjamas too often during rush hour unless I want to be part of someone's sightseeing tour.

At weekends, I sing in a nearby Chinese restaurant, which is owned by my friend, called the Dragon Lounge. I host karaoke nights, run themed evenings, get the punters clapping along to Cher and Meatloaf. People laugh at me for it. "Look at her, used to be on the telly and now she's singing at a Chinese buffet." But they don't see what I see. They don't feel the joy I feel when someone in the audience starts dancing, or when someone tells me they haven't laughed that hard in months.

All I'm trying to do is make a living and it is hard, especially when you have a recognisable face. People don't expect you to do "normal" things, they don't expect to see you selling your old possessions, they don't expect you to be queuing in Lidl or singing for your supper. They expect you to stay suspended in the world of red carpets and magazine covers and when you don't, they mock.

At my age, should I be aiming to buy my own house? I don't know anymore. Should I have a pension, a string of invest-ment properties, a walk-in wardrobe full of designer clothes? Maybe. Well, I did have them all. I had the lovely house with an above ground swimming pool in the garden, I had the fancy holidays and the red carpet premieres.

But what I have realised is material things, they come and they go. Status comes and goes. One bad turn, one illness, one financial hit and it can all disappear. Famous or not, getting into debt can happen to anyone. You could lose everything in a fire, get scammed, make one bad investment, or just find yourself, like me, between jobs in a tough and competitive industry.

I have realised that it is memories that make us rich and these are what you have to hold on to. And the best part? You can make more of them every single day, you can collect joy like pennies in a jar. You should be making memories with people around you who mean a lot to you.

So yes, I'm singing in a Chinese restaurant and no, I am not ashamed. I am proud. I'm working. I'm surviving and I'm making people smile.

And the next role? It's just around the corner, I'm sure of it. Life is a roller coaster, it dips, it rattles, it takes your breath away, but it always climbs again.

As for me, I refuse to lose my positive outlook. I refuse to let bitterness win. I'm still here.

Still singing. Still standing.

And I've got stories to tell.

Epilogue

I've just turned sixty! Where did the time go? One minute I was belting out Donny Osmond songs into a hairbrush in my childhood bedroom and now here I am, with a lifetime of stories, lessons, scars and sparkle behind me.

Sixty is a milestone and I don't take a single second of it for granted. It's eight years longer than my lovely mum, Avril Folly, got to live. And it's 16 years longer than poor Heather Trott managed, bless her. So I count my blessings every day, because getting older is a gift, even if the knees creak a bit more than they used to and the mirror sometimes gives you a fright.

Still, if my dear friend June Brown is anything to go by, I've potentially got another 33 years of acting and performing left in me and I really, really hope I do. That woman was unstoppable. She brought sass, grit and class to everything she did, right up to the very end. If I can channel even a smidge of that energy, I'll be laughing.

It's a strange thing, writing a book. Looking back at your life, chapter by chapter. Turning over the pages of your own story and seeing it in a new light. I would be lying if I said that picking over some parts wasn't painful. It was like scratching at old wounds. But if there's one thing I hope you've seen as you've read this, it's that I'm just a normal woman.

BEHIND THE SCENES

A woman who's had her highs and lows. A woman who's fallen down and gotten back up again. Who's made mistakes, learned lessons, worn too many headbands, loved too hard and danced like nobody was watching (even when millions were).

I hope, more than anything, that in sharing my story honestly, I've encouraged people to be a little kinder. To themselves. To others. To strangers on the internet and people in their lives. And to live a little fuller and to sing karaoke on a random Tuesday, because life's too short not to.

I've been through setbacks. I've faced heartbreak and hardship. I've also known joy, love and moments of pure magic. At the end of the day, what really matters isn't fame or money or even how many TikTok followers you've got. It's being happy. It's being healthy. It is laughing until your sides ache and loving the people who make your life brighter.

And now? Well, I can't wait to see where the next chapter of my life takes me. Maybe Heather's long-lost identical twin Ferne Trott will turn up in Albert Square with a dodgy accent and a score to settle. Maybe I'll be handed another role that stretches me, surprises me and lets me work with other actors and directors I admire. Maybe I'll be dancing at Gay Pride, covered in glitter, surrounded by beautiful souls and waving a rainbow flag high in the air until I'm 101 years old.

Whatever happens, I will keep showing up, with heart, with humour and with hope. Because although I have shown you behind the scenes, this isn't the end. This is just the start of the next story. *Duff, Duff, Duff, Duff, Duff...*

Acknowledgements

To Avril and Brian (Mum and Dad), without you two there would be no me and story to tell. Alex, you are my world, my beautiful son. I'm proud of you every single day.

Yas, no one will ever truly know what we have been through, but by "Marchin' On" everyday we both know that love conquers all.

Rosie (this human's best friend), Folly Family and Oldfield family, Brov Graeme, Sis Lesley, Graeme Urlwin (Bestie Boy), Christine Aspell (Bestie Girl), Hollie Danby (Godaughter), Frankie McFadden (Godaughter), Steve "fingers" McFadden (always my big bruv), Barbara (Babs) Windsor (and Scott), Mr George Michael (if I turned a different corner we never would have met), Linda Henry (Shirl to my Hev), June Brown (the soothsayer), Paul O'Grady ("times are hard and friends are few").

Julian Clary, when I think of you I always laugh out loud! The man who put Camp in Campari, I love you and your funny bones. Thank you, friend.

David Walliams, thank you for your kind words and belief in me, friend! Matt Lucas, or should I say "Margerat, Margerat", Yvonne McGuinness, teacher and friend, my inspiration, thank you, Ben Merritt, teacher and friend, my inspiration, thank you. The Durrants (Tony and the Gingers, my favourite band ever!), Naomi Lecko, Gal (This time next year…), Stuart Morrison (Thank you), Richard and David (my boys), TJ Higgs, pure love and light, Angela and family.

Lou Lou (Angel), Scarlett and Jo (your continued support means the world, thank you), River, Rio and Ocean (King, Queen and Prince), Bernard and Eileen (Wigan Mum and Dad), Jean Myles ("Ma!"), Howard Cooke and Sylvia, and a big woof woof to Scarlett (agent of old, you always have my back! Love Bunty x).

Amber Managment, current agents and representation, here's to the future and all the new and exciting ventures we will go on together! Lydia, talented, beautiful and clever, sincere thanks. For all my supporters and those who I've been lucky enough to cross paths with so far. Thank you.

Lastly, to future colleagues, friends I have yet to meet.

In this my 60th year, I raise a glass of fizzy water and look forward to facing all new challenges, projects and adventures with positivity. Love and hope!

Cheryl Fergison, 2025